Dimensions. Journal of Architectural Knowledge
06/2023

Making Sense: Thinking through Making Architecture

Issue Editors
Nicolai Bo Andersen, Victor Boye Julebæk,
Eva Sievert Asmussen

[transcript]

This journal is published bianually (in spring and autumn) and printed editions are available for annual subscription directly from the publisher. The retail price for an annual subscription to the print issue incl. shipment within Germany is 75,00 € and for international purchases 85,00 €. The electronic version is available free of charge (Open Access).

All information regarding notes for contributors, subscriptions, Open Access, back volume and orders is available online at:
https://www.transcript-publishing.com/dak

Additional information on upcoming issues, calls for contributions and the options for partaking as contributors, editors or members of the peer review procedure can be found at the journals website: www.dimensions-journal.eu
If you have any further questions please contact us, addressing Katharina Voigt, at: mail@dimensions-journal.eu

Bibliographic information published by the Deutsche Nationalbibliothek
The Deutsche Nationalbibliothek lists this publication in the Deutsche Nationalbibliografie; detailed bibliographic data are available in the Internet at http://dnb.de

This work is licensed under the Creative Commons Attribution 4.0 (BY) license, which means that the text may be be remixed, transformed and built upon and be copied and redistributed in any medium or format even commercially, provided credit is given to the author. For details go to http://creativecommons.org/licenses/by/4.0/
Creative Commons license terms for re-use do not apply to any content (such as graphs, figures, photos, excerpts, etc.) not original to the Open Access publication and further permission may be required from the rights holder. The obligation to research and clear permission lies solely with the party re-using the material.

Dimensions. Journal of Architectural Knowledge

Lead Editors
Katharina Voigt, Uta Graff, Ferdinand Ludwig

Advisory Board
Isabelle Doucet, Sonja Dümpelmann, Susanne Hauser, Klaske Havik, Wilfried Kühn, Sandra Meireis, Meike Schalk

Editorial Context
BauHow5
The Bartlett School of Architecture, University College London, Great Britain
Chalmers University Gothenburg, Sweden
Delft University of Technology, Netherlands
Swiss Federal Institute of Technology Zurich, Switzerland
Technical University of Munich, Germany

Associated Institutions
Ludwig Maximilian University Munich, Germany
Royal Danish Academy, Copenhagen, Denmark
Royal Technical University of Stockholm, Sweden
Technical University of Vienna, Austria
University of the Arts Berlin, Germany

The initial funding to this journal is provided by the Department of Architecture at the TUM School of Engineering and Design in Munich, Germany.

First published 2024 by transcript Verlag, Bielefeld
© **Nicolai Bo Andersen, Victor Boye Julebæk, Eva Sievert Asmussen (eds.)**

Cover layout: Katharina Voigt (Technical University of Munich)
Copy-editing: Nicolai Bo Andersen, Victor Boye Julebæk
and Filip Ivarsson (Royal Danish Acamemy, Copenhagen)
Proofreading: Lisa Goodrum (London)
Typeset: Filip Ivarsson (Royal Danish Acamemy, Copenhagen)
Printed by Majuskel Medienproduktion GmbH, Wetzlar
ISSN 2747-5085
eISSN 2747-5093
Print-ISBN 978-3-8376-6864-3
PDF-ISBN 978-3-8394-6864-7

Printed on permanent acid-free text paper.

Contents

INTRODUCTION

Making Sense.
Thinking through Making Architecture
Nicolai Bo Andersen, Victor Boye Julebæk and Eva Sievert Asmussen 9

BODY

Motherboard.
Building Conversation
Ida Flarup and Maria Mengel 17

Ephemeral Permanence.
Architects as Change-Makers
Tina Vestermann Olsen, Alessandro Tellini and Mario Rinke 39

Two Bodies
Aileen Iverson-Radtke 53

Good Places.
The Potential of Places of Remembrance
Victoria Schweyer and Jana Wunderlich 73

MATERIAL

Making and Re-Making an Architectural Model
Jonathan Meldgaard Houser 93

Facade Environments.
The Potentials of Large-Scale Adaptive Models
Hisham El-Hitami, Mona Mahall and Asli Serbest 115

Design Build Grow Meghalaya.
Combining Vernacular and Modern Knowledge
Zijing Deng, Ferdinand Ludwig, Elahe Mahdavi and Wilfrid Middleton 127

New Vernacular
Tim Simon-Meyer and João Quintela 151

WORLD

Could This Happen in Nature?
Anne Romme and Jacob Sebastian Bang 169

The Precognitive Perception of Space.
On Primitive Architecture of the 21st Century
Bernhard Leopold Geiger 185

Places of Rural Practice
Niklas Fanelsa 223

Handscapes.
Gestures as Agents of Change and Mimetic Awareness
Otto Paans 243

CONTRIBUTORS

Biographies 265

INTRODUCTION

The focal point of the call for contributions to this issue is on architectural approaches relating to the overall question of *making sense* in architecture, defined as the production of architectural knowledge through the physical act of making. Contributions must investigate architectural sense-making through theoretical, philosophical and/or practicebased perspectives relating to the themes BODY, MATERIAL and WORLD. It is critical that submissions be based on one or more physical artifacts presented as technical drawings and/or photographs in combination with a written text. Rather than thinking on or about architecture, we invite contributors to think through architecture. Perhaps the production of architectural knowledge can be understood not just as a logical exercise, but as an aesthetic practice?

Making Sense
Thinking through Making Architecture

Nicolai Bo Andersen, Victor Boye Julebæk and Eva Sievert Asmussen

In his renowned classic »Experiencing Architecture« Steen Eiler Rasmussen points out that art should not be explained; it must be experienced. Through embodied interaction, each individual gathers a series of experiences throughout life that makes them understand the material world according to weight, solidity, texture, heat-conducting ability, et cetera. According to Rasmussen, it is not the formal properties such as stylistic features, but rather the experienced effects such as hard and soft, light, and heavy, taut and slack that the architect must call into play.

In our modern society, it seems as if value is primarily attributed to things that can be measured and described, leaving aesthetic experience as a purely subjective concern. However, as pointed out by Alexander Gottlieb Baumgarten in 1735, one must distinguish between two mutually complementary ways of acquiring knowledge: »noeta« as the object of logic and »episteme aisthetike« as the science of perception. In this perspective, aesthetics should not simply be understood as a value judgement, but rather as the philosophy of sensitive cognition.

In recent years, renewed attention seems to focus on the whole body and embodied interaction as a genuine way to produce knowledge. For instance, Hanne de Jaeger has developed a theory of participatory sense-making as a way to understand one another and the world. Here, social understanding is not a strictly individual concern, but rather a process of interpersonal interaction. Understanding the process of thinking through the process of making, Tim Ingold describes the relation to the world as a form of call and response. In a process of weaving, thought-processes of practitioners and the materials they use to make things is understood as a continuously emerging process of correspondence and becoming through one another. Criticizing human exceptionalism, Donna Haraway has introduced the concept of

Nicolai Bo Andersen (The Royal Danish Academy, Denmark), nande@kglakademi.dk, https://orcid.org/0000-0002-9301-3024; Victor Boye Julebæk (The Royal Danish Academy, Denmark), victor.julebaek@kglakademi.dk, https://orcid.org/0000-0001-5152-3256; Eva Sievert Asmussen (The Royal Danish Academy,Denmark), easm@kglakademi.dk, https://orcid.org/0000-0002-7311-7571.
Open Access. © 2024 Nicolai Bo Andersen, Victor Boye Julebæk and Eva Sievert Asmussen published by transcript Verlag. This work is licensed under the Creative Commons Attribution 4.0 (BY) license.

nature cultures to describe entangled multispecies' histories. This position advocates an ecology of practices/collective knowing and doing as a way to cultivate response-ability.

Often, distinction is made between the quantitative and the qualitative sciences. Where quantitative approaches are concerned with numbers and measurement, qualitative approaches are concerned with words and meanings. As an often overlooked third approach, Patricia Leavy (2015) advocates arts-based practices that value other representational formats, require a different set of skills, and disrupts disciplinary boundaries. In resonance with Rasmussen, Leavy points at the arts as ways to compel or move by means of aesthetic power rather than to prove or persuade. In consequence, arts-based practices – having a different intention than both quantitative and qualitative approaches – construct knowledge that must be assessed on its own terms.

In this issue of *Dimensions. Journal of Architectural Knowledge*, we assert that architecture is in fact a question of making sense. We understand the production of architectural knowledge through the act of making as involving the interacting body, the material reality, as well as the environmental world. As such, the work of architecture is understood as a language in its own right, communicating meaning from the perceived to the perceiver as aesthetic communication.

Concerned with the production of actual material samples, models, mock-ups and full-scale installations in the fields of architectural teaching, research and practice, we have asked how making architecture may be understood as a way of thinking, defined as bodily interaction with the physical world; how making architecture may inspire and develop the work of teachers, researchers and practitioners and how making architecture may play a role in redefining the praxis of the architect in responses to the accelerating ecological crisis.

Contributors have investigated the question of architectural sensemaking through theoretical, philosophical and/or practice-based perspectives relating to the themes **BODY, MATERIAL**, and **WORLD** in the format of both visual essays and full academic papers. nineteen submissions in total were received through an open call, and twelve were selected for the further process. In the selection and editorial process, the quality of each individual contribution was prioritized. In addition, consideration was given to representing a diversity of voices as well as to securing an overall thematic and aesthetic cohesiveness. Each of the contributions were double blind peer reviewed, proofread and finally developed within the graphic framework of the Dimensions journal.

In chapter one thematizing **BODY**, Ida Flarup Barnett and Maria Mengel argue that collaboration in architecture may in fact be understood as a matter of negotiation in a teaching exercise involving a full-scale model that is both a table and a scale model of a former sea plane hangar. Discussing the results of a 1:1 design-build workshops using reclaimed components, Tina Vestermann Olsen, Alessandro Tellini and Mario Rinke point out the importance of students working with the specific material at the actual building site. Aileen Iverson examines how both the maker and the made are engaged in making. Through the concept of »spatiomateriality« it is proposed that in the act of making, rather than being two separate things space and matter may in fact be understood as a single media. Examining the significance of good memory places, Victoria Schweyer and Jana Wunderlich show how the making of architectural elements and characteristics may create a sense of familiarity and comfort.

In the second chapter thematizing **MATERIAL**, upcycled construction materials are similarly critical in Jonathan Meldgaard Housers investigations of the scale model as both a physical artifact and a digital museum, challenging the common understanding of representation. And in Hisham El-Hitamis, Mona Mahall and Asli Serbest investigation of the potentials of large-scale adaptive models, the installation is not just a tool in the process, but an autonomous performer in its own right. Wilf Middleton, Zijing Deng, Ferdinand Ludwig and Elahe Mahdavi investigates the somewhat unconventional building material of living roots as media to combine vernacular and modern knowledge. Making use of reclaimed materials from a local context as resources in a design-build workshop, Tim Simon and João Quintela present an experimental approach to developing a potential new vernacular architecture.

In the final chapter, **WORLD**, Anne Romme and Jacob Bang create a new, composite landscape model to investigate digital material practices. Bernhard Leopold Geiger gives a captivating tour de force through the historical development of the shift from the physical experience to the cognitive perception of space. Niklas Fanelsa emphasizes place as a key aspect of sustainable practices. Finally, Otto Paans argues that the gestures involved in drawing could create a mimetic awareness that may radically situate knowledge to its context. With a focus on circular use of materials, climate-positive architecture, and regional production,

1.
Friland Reclaimed, 2024
Photo: Victor Boye Julebæk

Rather than just thinking on or about architecture, many contributors have thus been thinking through architecture. In this perspective, the production of architectural knowledge taking place in each visual contribution can be seen not just as a logical exercise, but as an aesthetic practice that must be understood on their own terms. In continuation, it is our hope that this issue of *Dimensions. Journal of Architectural Knowledge* contributes to the appreciation of making architecture as the construction of architectural knowledge, and that aesthetic practices are understood as ways of making sense.

BODY

Motherboard
Building Conversation

Ida Flarup and Maria Mengel

Abstract: This essay explores the topic of collaboration in architecture through making and enrolling buildings, objects, and history as active co-creators. »Motherboard« is simultaneously a table and a scale model of a former seaplane hangar now housing 150 students of architecture. It forms part of an ongoing artistic research project conducted in the workshop and was also an assignment undertaken by a group of first-year students in spring 2023.

Keywords: The Architectural Model; Scale; Tectonics; Teaching; Collaboration; Embodied Thinking; Craft; Aesthetics; Collective Knowledge.

Introduction

The article is based on an ongoing artistic research project conducted by two architects, who are referred to as »we« in the text while exploring collective making through the crafting of, and interaction with, a physical object – a »motherboard«. Our motherboard is simultaneously a table and a scale model of a former seaplane hangar. The term is borrowed from computers and refers to the component that forms the central point for connection and memory, which, in our interpretation, is a place to gather thoughts, knowledge, and people. The first part of the article, »Formation, Action, Reaction« presents the context for our research the table's construction through material and formal experiments, and the table's function as a teaching device, along with the physical actions and methodology used in the table's transformation into an architectural model and, as we argue, a territory for the production of architectural knowledge.

In the second part, »Body, Material, World«, we include Juhani Pallasmaa's thoughts on embodied thinking along with recent research in

---

Corresponding author: Ida Flarup (The Royal Danish Academy, Denmark), ifla@kglakademi.dk
Open Access. © 2024 Ida Flarup and Maria Mengel published by transcript Verlag.
This work is licensed under the Creative Commons Attribution 4.0 (BY) license.

1.
Motherboard – the central point for connections and memory. Model study for tabletop, translating the plan and shape of the seaplane hangar into a pattern of stick-glued pine wood. Photo by the authors.

the social aspects of creativity, especially the term »we-creativity«, as defined by Professor of Psychology and Pedagogy, Lene Tanggaard, to discuss our methodology (of thinking and learning through making) and to reflect on the relationship between embodied thinking, collective knowledge, and the role of the architect, which is based on our experiences around the table.

Formation – Action – Reaction

The Space as Topic. From 2014 to 2023, part of the *Royal Danish Academy* in Copenhagen was situated off-campus in a former seaplane hangar, where 150 students, researchers, and educators worked under one, large roof. The hangar was originally designed by the Danish architect, Christian Olrik and was built in 1921 as part of the naval base in Holmen, Copenhagen. The hangar has a long history of various inhabitants. At first, it housed seaplanes and workshops for trucks, then an artillery school and later, after being transformed by Danish architect Dorte Mandrup, it became newspaper offices and for the past nine years was a school of architecture. The 1,500 square meter rectangular space is covered by a roof constructed from curved, reinforced concrete beams that span the full length of the space

It is our experiences working and teaching in this space over the past nine years that have prompted our interest in the practices of collective making. The physical space and the way we approach teaching are inseparable. The spatial gesture of the hangar – its large, open, flexible space – invites us to experiment with teaching formats and encourage a culture of collaborative practices and methodologies. In our opinion, this has created a unique culture; an open and democratic learning space.

Yet, the hangar is also a place where hierarchies and social interaction become very visible and are directly linked to a bodily experience. Who sits at the top of the platforms? Who sits at the ground level? Who looks at who through the glass offices stacked in the middle of the space? You cannot hide anything and everything is present at the same time. Sketches are pinned up, models collapsed, and discussions, celebrations, and disappointments occur. Our project is a collaboration and dialogue with this space, with the hangar playing a key role as site, topic, and physical language in our research.

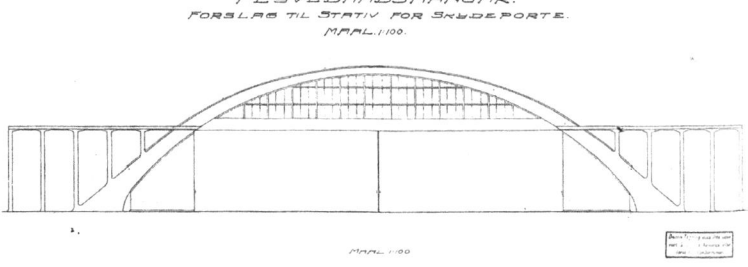

2.
Elevation of the seaplane hangar (1921), with construction for sliding gates.
Drawing: Slots- og Kulturstyrelsens bygningsarkiv.

3.
»Motherboard«.
Photo by the authors.

Making a Territory

Being interested in collaboration as a practice of making meant it seemed fitting to start by building a place to work, a table. Tables are interesting when exploring architecture and collaboration. We all gather around tables, where we share meals, ideas, and disagreements, and play games and make plans. They relate directly to our bodies. They are everyday objects that we hardly notice, as well as powerful tools for civilizing human interaction. A table is an architectural gesture, a construction lifting the ground, establishing a framed territory for social interaction, a miniature version of the world. The architect Sarah Wigglesworth, who famously drew her dining table before, during, and after a meal wrote:

> »The rituals of eating played out on the plane of the dining table are similar to the rituals of domestic life« (Wigglesworth 2002).

Through a series of plan drawings, Wigglesworth maps out the relations between diners and the objects they interact with. She compares it to the interactions between occupants of the home and the last drawing (in the series of four), is an actual plan layout for her combined family home and office.

Tables have a long history of reflecting ideas and ideals. Placed in a household, like the one Wigglesworth describes, the rituals around the table represent hierarchies, traditions, manners, and ideals within the family. Placed in another context, the table can act as a global stage to begin wars and negotiate ceasefires. Consider the images of Putin and Macron negotiating from both ends of a grotesquely long table, or the circular table of King Arthur, which was shaped to avoid hierarchical quarrels between his barons

In addition to exploring the rituals related to tables, we looked at tectonics in traditional workbenches and different kinds of tables, and found an interesting and unexpected convergence between the classic folding table, the shape of the plan, and a section of the hangar, along with the changing hierarchies and power contained in the hangar.

Designing the table occurred solely in the wood workshop. We set up a work schedule that alternated between individual crafting and shared reflection. During the crafting sessions we worked simultaneously, side by side, without talking, with the same references, materials, and dimensions, but we were allowed to explore independently and intuitively within that

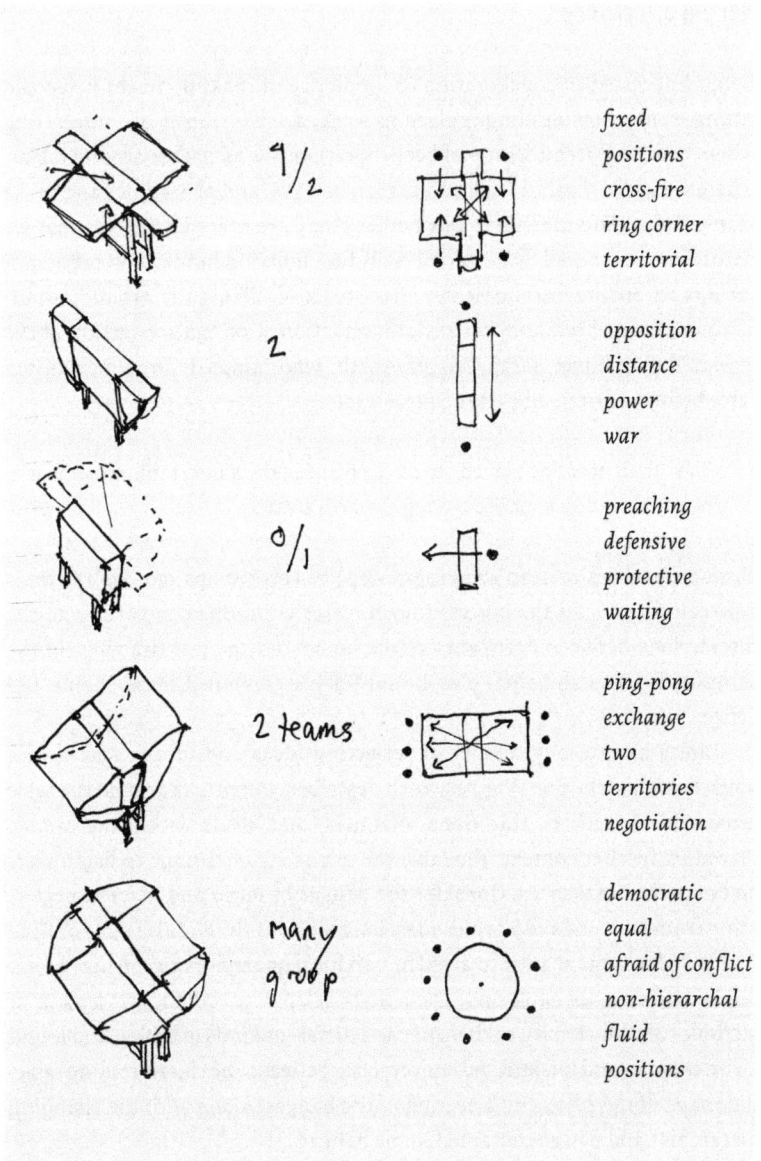

4.
Reflections on the relationship between the shape of the table and the power dynamics around it. Sketch by the authors.

framework. This resulted in a series of 1:3 sketch models: Two table tops and a series of leg systems, »seasoned« differently – which allowed for our individual experiences with the textures and properties of the wood, the happy mistakes, and the crafting process etc. Our shared reflections took place around the models. We would swap models and motifs, sample, extend, overwrite, and enlarge in the next round of crafting. Eventually, the process led to the final set of legs and the tabletop, which we then translated into full-scale mockups, working with the folding system, and experimenting with the material conditions of the pine wood which led to the final table/model.

This »conversation through making« approach had two combined aims: One was to explore a design process led by material conditions and crafting processes. Rather than using the model as a representational tool, we were interested in learning from the material.

The other was to translate questions about authorship within a collective practice into a physical manifestation. The approach intended to make a framework in which both of our architectural voices would be present. We were interested in exploring methods to both embed individual intuition, aesthetic preferences, and a different understanding of the project in the design process and resisted sole authorship by swapping models, ideas, and techniques in the process.

Laying the Table

During the spring semester of 2023, the table was moved from the workshop and placed inside the hangar. Here, it formed the framework for an assignment undertaken by 27 first-year students. The students worked with the hangar as their site and the table as both the site model and meeting place. The overall theme of the semester was »one and many« – focusing on the organization of architecture and the relationship between the collective and the individual.

To establish a shared body of reference in relation to the topic, the students analyzed traditional, historical institutions of power at Slotsholmen[1] in Copenhagen where they investigated both visible and invisible manifestations of power and the role of architecture in structuring behavior. Based

---

1 Slotsholmen, also known as »the Island of Power« is an island in central Copenhagen, which is home to several government buildings, including the Danish Parliament, the Supreme Court, and the National Archives.

Ida Flarup and Maria Mengel

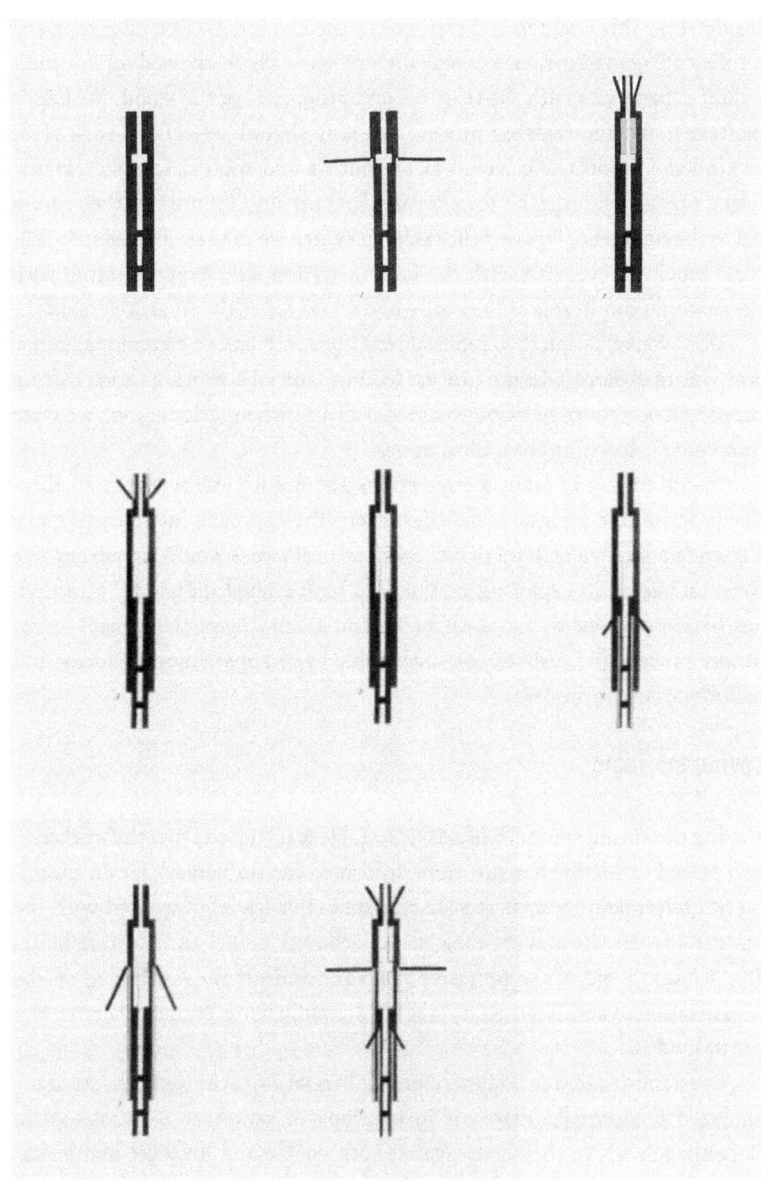

5.
Illustration by the authors.

on their analysis they proposed their own programs and projects for institutions that would inhabit the hangar.

The assignment was structured as a series of changing collaborations between the students, who used model making and collage as their main tools. The assignments were based on physical negotiation between the students, their models, and their collages to shift their focus from the production of an individual proposal to actions relating to one another (by reconfiguring, enlarging, extending, reprogramming, combining etc.) each other's proposals. These methods forced them to react to, and interact with, each other's projects through physical, hands-on actions that used the table as a negotiating board – drawing parallels with a games table and the students' models as playing pieces.

Finally, in groups of seven, the students developed proposals for how the hangar could be repurposed and reprogrammed as a town center for the new development in the surrounding area. The result was three proposals for town centers, which investigated three different organizational principles. These conventions were provided by us, based on what the students proposed in the first round of negotiations. Each of the three town centers consisted of interpretations of classic programs such as the city council, the square, the court of justice, the detention center, the chapel, the library, the museum, the market, and the garden, adding new, imaginary layers of transformation to the hangar's story, as well as addressing the current transformation of the surrounding area from military and industrial territory to a dense housing development.

The architecture school vacated the hangar in autumn 2023 and this assignment was the last one conducted there, leaving the space as an empty vessel that prompted speculation as to what would come next. The assignment inhabited this void – or opportunity – and asked the students to view the space of the hangar as less of a building and more as a framework or world« in which they could organize their institutions.

Like Wigglesworth's dining table, we regarded the actions on and around the table as resembling that of a household. The laying of the table/building of the worlds, like a family dinner, reflected hierarchies, manners, and ideals (both within the groups, between the groups, and in relation to us and the structure of the three worlds). The aim was to create a teaching situation in which the students would be confronted with the physical implications of negotiations to facilitate an authentic experience of co-creation and an embodied experience of architectural production as a collaborative practice.

6.
This resulted in three proposals for town centers for the new development happening in the area, (interpretations of the city council, the square, the courts of justice, the arrest, the chapel, the library, the museum, the market and the garden) adding a new, imaginary layer of transformation to the story of the hangar as well as a comment on the changing nature of the area around it. Photo by the authors.

Body – Material – World

The Flesh of the World. In Juhani Pallasmaa's The Thinking Hand (2009), the architect calls for the reintroduction of embodied thinking to the production of architecture:

> »It is unthinkable that a mind could conceive architecture because of the irreplaceable role of the body in the very constitution of architecture. Buildings are not abstract, meaningless constructions, or aesthetic compositions, they are extensions and shelters of our bodies, memories, identities, and minds« (Pallasmaa 2009: 117).

In our understanding, the term »embodied experience« – or embodied thinking – refers to the idea that cognition, perception, and consciousness are not solely functions of the brain but are deeply intertwined with the body's experiences and interactions with the surrounding world.

Pallasmaa also calls for engagement with »the flesh of the world«[2] and advocates for material and craft-based practices as an antidote to a world obsessed with the visual and virtual and the separation of the mind and body. The limitations of the mind as the primary driver of a creative process and the benefits of a wordless, hands-on approach, based on materiality resonates with our own experiences both as practitioners and teachers and has been key to developing this project's methodology.

Throughout the project we have consciously sought to direct our practice toward the ideas of embodied thinking and we have experienced the benefits on several levels: First in the workshop, where the material properties, the reoccurring time spent on preparing the wood and sharpening the tools etc. initially felt limiting and like it restricted the project's progress, as the mind produces ideas and conclusions much faster than the hand. However, as described earlier, by committing to, and imposing, (strict) rules and a framework for both our individual and collaborative practice, we experienced a reversal of the hand-mind relationship, in which interaction with the materials, the tools, gravity, and the body influenced the project in new and fruitful directions, such as utilizing the textures of the wood, and made

---

2 The term »the flesh of the world« refers to the phenomenology of philosopher Maurice Merleau-Ponty.

7.
Photo by the authors.

the process very productive and much richer than anything we could have deducted from afar.

Second, the teaching space, being the same as the site of the semester project, working – and collaborating – simultaneously with the space as model representation and as a 1:1 physical experience created a situation for the students (and us) where we could not escape »the flesh of the world«.

Living in a culture heavily dominated by the mind and a lust for quick concepts and »brainstorms«, it seems increasingly difficult to practice what Pallasmaa preaches. After being engaged with the topic of embodied thinking for years we still have to trick the mind by establishing frameworks for both ourselves and our students in order not to fall out of the body and into habit – so to speak. One could argue that this tendency is even more reason to keep practicing. Like Pallasmaa, we feel the fundamental urge to shift our focus to a practice of architecture that is reengaged with the direct, bodily experience of material and space as a response to our global, social and ecological challenges. However, Pallasmaa's examples of the successful, creative fusion between mind and body are often conducted by the sole author, whether it is the architect, the writer or the artist creating the (sublime) piece of art. In our experience, words such as collaboration and co-creation seem to be everywhere; in conversations, competition briefs, and council plans outlining how to create a better, more equal and sustainable future. And often architects are expected to participate in, propose, and even lead this discourse.

We argue that a fundamental change to the way we practice is required. Yes, it must be a practice of embodied thinking, but also a practice that fully embraces the fact that »architecture is a collective knowledge produced through the efforts of a multitude« (Ghidoni 2013) and is therefore not afraid to move away from the idea of a sole authorship and into a shared territory.

In the essay »Collective Knowledge«, included in the 2015 book Shared Territory, architect Nicola Louise Markhus builds on Ghidoni's quote by reflecting on a kind of collaboration that expands upon the term to include silent participants such as buildings, objects, materials, and ideas and argues that a collaborative practice is a practice of sharing, recycling, and reusing:

> »I think there is something beautiful about the idea that the things we create separately can have this relationship across time and space, based on similarity in form, technique, material, concepts and theory. I enjoy thinking about art, architecture, objects and ideas as part of a pool of all the things that have ever been created.« (Markhus 2015: 76)

Like Markhus, we argue that through the work of Motherboard, architectural production is always a cocreation with others and what is already there and alters, transforms, and reconfigures it. We are all heavily influenced by the world around us, our embodied knowledge, our shared references and the shapes and materials we encounter, as well as spaces, their atmosphere, and their social dynamics.

We-Creativity

In her paper »Sociomateriality of Creativity in Everyday Life«, Professor Lene Tanggaard defines a type of creativity that includes relational aspects. She describes a shift in the understanding of creativity from focusing primarily on two types of individual, internal creativity, defined as »he-creativity« and »I-creativity« toward a socially oriented »we-creativity«. While »he-creativity« tends to be associated with exceptional individuals like Mozart or Einstein (similarly to the examples provided by Pallasama), »I-creativity« suggests that creativity is inherent within everyone. This concept emphasizes that each individual possesses the capacity for creativity, thus making it a personal responsibility to unlock and nurture this potential (Tanggaard 2010).

Both primary forms of creativity tend to focus on the individual and give limited consideration to the creativity that happens in exchanges between individuals and to the materials, objects, and environments that make creativity possible. In contrast to this, a socio-material perspective on creativity – the »we« that Tanggaard suggests, includes external factors such as interaction and materiality's importance for creativity. To us, the term »we-creativity« is useful when exploring collaborative practices, as it combines the ideas of embodied thinking with the social aspects of creativity and moves away from the idea of a sole author and into shared territory.

We suggest a collective practice which is not mainly focused on consensus (like the kind of group work where every idea is accommodated to include everybody) or erasing autonomy within the architectural practice. It is closer to a polyphonic approach – as seen in music when a series of individual melodies interact without losing their own voice, but still contribute to a perceived whole. In our teaching we have noticed that moving away from the perception of creativity as an »I« (or me) and toward a polyphonic »we« in the way we ask the students to produce projects has been fruitful. We observed that it has the potential to create a freer and more productive process, as the students are less occupied with themselves and therefore more willing to take chances and make mistakes when the focus is shifted toward the collective.

Through »Motherboard« we reflect on the architect's role in this shared territory on several levels. We consider their direct role by proposing a methodology of cocreation and collaborations (between us, and between us and the students) but also in the way we approach the transformation of existing buildings, which we argue – through the collective, speculative transformation of the hangar – is also a shared territory, where architects need to collaborate with what is already there and negotiate with the layers of the past and the ideas of the future. We suggest that a way to really understand – and change – the way we practice architecture is to throw ourselves into the physical, bodily experience of negotiation and the fundamentals of collaboration, which also includes oppositional questions of power, hierarchy, argument and artistic ego in order to – or perhaps – get closer to an actual methodology for cocreation that is not largely concerned with consensus, but instead wants to cultivate and explore the architectural language of a polyphonic approach.

In this project, we want to contribute to the discourse by practicing artistic autonomy in a collective practice ourselves and by engaging the students in hands-on negotiations that we hope can contribute to shaping the attitudes and values of future generations of architects.

Postscript

Folding Time. The students dismantled the world and moved on. We folded the territory to its most compact position and carried it to our new teaching space. For now, it sits in a hallway, partly unfolded in order to fit. It's a table again. People lean against it, put their cups on it, leave their models on it. It is waiting.

The table has been invited to new locations, which calls for reconfiguration and potentially new additions relating to the properties of the spaces it will be situated in. Extracting the table from its origin poses a set of questions about the relationship between objects and memory. It now carries a trace of another place – a memory of a space and a physical manifestation of a set of ideas. In the next phase of the project, we will engage with questions on how the table can carry the memories of the past and what new conversations on/with/in/around it can unfold.

8.
Details of the table in 1:1, play with scale and references.
Photo by the authors.

9.
»Motherboard«.
Photo by the authors.

10.
»Motherboard«.
Photo by the authors.

References

Ghidoni, Matteo (2013): »Editorial«, in: *San Rocco, Collaborations* #6.

Markhus, Nicola Louise (2015): *Shared Territory*, Copenhagen: Another Space.

Pallasmaa, Juhani (2009): »Embodied Thinking«, in: *The Thinking Hand: Existential and Embodied in Architecture*, AD Primers, Chichester: John Wiley & Sons Inc.

Tanggaard, Lene (2013): »The Sociomateriality of Creativity in Everyday Life«, in: *Culture & Psychology* 19/1, 20–32.

Tanggaard, Lene /Warner, Marina/ Franklin, Samuel (2023): »On Creativity«. https://vimeo.com/887180246 (accessed July 24, 2024).

Wigglesworth, Sarah (2022): »The Disorder of the Dining Table«, in: *UOU Scientific Journal* 4, 122–127.

Ephemeral Permanence
Architects as Change-Makers

Tina Vestermann Olsen, Alessandro Tellini and Mario Rinke

Abstract: Architects are crucial to creating a more sustainable building practice. Integrating availability-based design and build workshops with education enables participants to become potential change-makers. A two-week experiment in Denmark showcased circularity through a temporary structure based on reclaimed components and a complex site. The setup allowed deep-learning through personally experienced boundaries and regular reflection for both the interdisciplinary participant and teaching team.

Keywords: Education; Design and Build Workshop; Tactical Urbanism; Interdisciplinarity; Sustainability; Reuse.

Introduction

A Practice in Transition. The building practice is undergoing a massive transformation. Since the construction and operation of buildings causes a large amount of CO_2 emissions and a high global demand for energy, alternative concepts for a more sustainable construction practice and operation of the built environment are needed (UNEP 2021). Architects are essential stakeholdersas they read site potentials, conceptualize the handling of new and existing buildings and landscapes and propose materials and moderate building processes. However, while researchers and practitioners have explored the circular use of materials, components and buildings, architectural education is still primarily based on new buildings. Embracing this complexity, the practice should critically reflect the use of the existing (Rockström et al. 2023). This design approach based on the availability of

---

Corresponding authors: Tina Vestermann Olsen (University of Aalborg, Denmark), tvol@create.aau.dk; Alessandro Tellini (Raplab, Faber Atelier, ETH Zurich, Switzerland), tellini@arch.ethz.ch; Mario Rinke (University of Antwerp, Belgium), mario.rinke@uantwerpen.be.
Open Access. © 2024 Tina Vestermann Olsen, Alessandro Tellini and Mario Rinke published by transcript Verlag. This work is licensed under the Creative Commons Attribution 4.0 (BY) license.

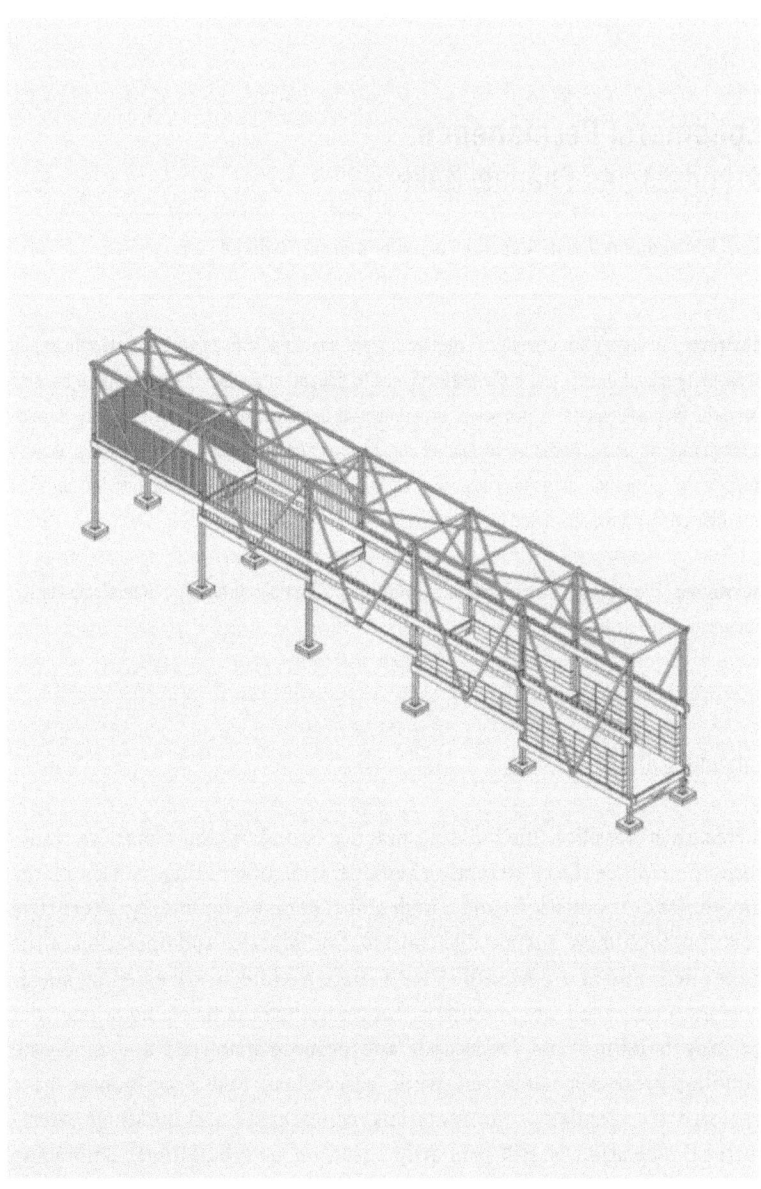

1.
Isometric view of the final project, 2022.
Illustration by the authors.

materials requires teachers and students to familiarize themselves with existing building components, buildings, and urban environments.

Availability-based Design and Build Workshops. Other than conventional studio teaching, design and build workshops allow participants to encounter not only the immediacy of a site's nature and the constructional reality of design, but also the consequences of limited resources, while also collaborating with peers with different skill sets. (Canizaro 2012). This visual contribution discusses a two-week educational experiment at a site in Aalborg, Denmark, which was conducted with eleven participants over ten days in the summer of 2022 and aimed at a multi-level implementation: Reusing building components, working with the site's ephemeral nature and contributing to the local community through the construction of a temporary structure.

Availability-based design inverts the design approach: The participants first look to appreciate the limitations and capacities of the existing and then design and build from there. In addition, the experience of manually building at a particular site connects the approach of design and build workshops (Canizaro 2012; Mohareb 2018) to the method of bodystorming which foregrounds the experiential dimension of architectural teaching practice. The original concept of bodystorming, stemming from interaction design, envisions a product as if it already exists and simulates its usage through improvised tools and physical actions to devise a solution (Schleicher et al. 2010). Similarly, in this case, participants dealt with a threatened site, as well as the limitations of existing construction elements. The participants' actions were intrinsically motivated by their positions as designers, builders, and community members. The teachers, from different disciplines, operated as coaches, listened to the observations and proposals of the group members, and moderated the decision-making processes (Schön 1987). In the following text, the stages of the workshop are described and reflected upon as phases of experience and the participants' growth is the main focus and complemented by the »intentionalities« (Canizaro 2012: 22) of the educators.

The Process of Designing and Building

Cold Open. In the cold open exercise the participants are confronted by material resistance. It spurs them into action to work on a small design challenge which will quickly expose them to the material or construction system used during the workshop. While success in conventional terms is not the primary goal, a gentle learning curve is desired to engage participants and boost their

2. + 3.
Reading the site. On site – Aalborg Harbourfront.
Photos: Mario Rinke, 2022.

confidence. Participants with first-hand experience tend to be more attentive and receptive to explanations about materials and production processes. The learning phase concludes with a guided discussion that focuses on the participants' experience and personal growth by their sharing insights with the group into the hands-on learning necessary to develop embodied consciousness (Pallasmaa 2009: 13).

Reading the Site. As Burns and Kahn powerfully manifest: Site matters as a construct that guides our design focus and as experiential potential that shapes intention (Burns/Kahn 2005). The participants were thus tasked with investigating the specific nature and agency of the site. First, the municipality presented their concerns for the site, whereupon the participants collected impressions of it and translated them through individual sketches and notes. This was followed by calibrations in smaller groups and plenum which were motivated by the question: How can a temporary structure created by reused materials establish a social meeting place here? The group members observed dynamic influences on all site borders: The tidal flooding and its projected rising water levels to one side, a continuous flow of trains and people walking and cycling to the other side, while the gentrifying industrial area and green park created an intricate urban setting.

Reading the Material. Making the construction material the point of departure for the workshop helps to frame and connect the critical concerns of a design and build project. Identifying potentials by collectively reading the material, e.g., origin, type, weight, and workability is part of the inductive process that generates the circular metamorphosis in a craft-driven approach which combines thinking and doing into a continuum (Sennett 2009: 40). Purpose, utilization, design, construction, and fabrication become strongly interwoven due to empirical testing. The material bank not only serves as a source of components, but rather as a world of active materials, that the student joins forces with in anticipation of what might emerge (Ingold 2013: 21).

Design Exploration. With the aim of swiftly translating their impressions, the students began exploring design options in groups while activating knowledge from reading the site and tapping into the bodily material experiences from reading the materials. After a joint discussion on concepts, two ideas were selected to be developed into detailed design proposals via sketches and small-scale models. The design proposals, developed on day three, addressed material compositionand structural principles, including foundations and joints, the desired location on site, and the user experience.

4. + 5.
Material exploration. Skeleton structure.
Photo: Alessandro Tellini, Tina Vestermann Olsen, 2022.

Participants experienced the strain of having to move quickly between open non-binding explorations toward binding, practical decisions.
This necessitated the participant's ability to set aside personal preferences and pursue collective goals instead.

Mockups and Testing. Mockups, minimal viable prototypes, and tests serve as elements that increase confidence in the collective decision-making process after the design phase, which allows the group to manage the building process and capture the design's essence. The moment of rationalizing the construction is crucial to the whole process, where making in terms of architecture becomes construction (Lefebvre et al. 2021: 13). Inevitably, the numerous ideas from the design phase become simplified and problems on a global and local scale are addressed simultaneously. In doing so, recurring elements and modules are developed and get manufactured elegantly, allowing the group to control the building process by strategically repeating specific actions.

Making and Responsibility. The actual size of the group's design, 2 meters wide, 6 meters high and 20 meters long, surprised the group. After organizing groups, the construction, including foundations, rows of steel columns, wooden platforms and wall segments, was carried out in parallel. The group completed the work in six days, during which each participant gained confidence in performing various tasks and assuming routines as they changed groups to increase the number of new experiences they had with materials and processes. The final phase of responsibility was crucial as the weight of the components and the novelty of the process overwhelmed each individual: To ensure construction, they could only be makers as a collective. In addition, the participants also assumed responsibility for the local community's contribution to the public space as they proudly guided the first visitors around the structure and observed how their stairs provided new views of the landscape.

Conclusion

The workshop demonstrated that transferring the studio to the building site is essential to embracing the limitations of design. The contrast between the working atmosphere on-site and the design sessions in the campus studio allowed a productive distance: Field design for specifying and verifying the conceptand studio design for clarifying and rationalizing the project. Bodystorming allowed for a strong immediacy using actual materials on a

6. + 7.
Structural mockup. Preparing the modules. Finalizing the building
Photos: Mario Rinke, Alessandro Tellini, 2022.

real site. The planetary boundaries (Steffen et al. 2015), too abstract to the participants, became personal and communal boundariesthat influenced the project and the personal work stages.

Interdisciplinarity was also important. The participants learned that they could not solve the task alone with only their own skills, but must work together as a team of engineers, architects, and landscape architects. The same applies to the teaching team, who could emphasize and convey the complexity of the problems due to their broad expertise in urbanism, architecture, crafts, and engineering. The periodic reflection-on-action (Webster 2008) allowed for the crucial process of consciously comprehending and framing the boundaries and strategies.

After two weeks embedded on-site and equipped with tools and reclaimed components, the participants reflected deeply on the constraints they faced with locals, experts, and using their own skills. They sought to design and build as if the material was »borrowed« and still meaningfully anchored to its place, thus establishing a full-scale experimental showcase of radical circularity that they generously shared with the local community so they could experience and shape a culture of appropriation and adaptation. A further step to reach an even deeper cognitive process as change-makers could be to participate in evaluating the agency of the structure on site through, e.g. user observation, partaking in the disassembly process upon ending the on-site exhibition, tracing the journey of the used materials and disseminating the acquired knowledge and insight to peers.

Funding Source Declaration. The authors would like to acknowledge the support of the following, who contributed with donations for the workshop: the *Foundation of Realdania*, the *Utzon Center* and the companies: *Stark Gentræ*, *Hustømrerne*, *GreenDozer* and *ErikFalls*.

8.
Photo: Mario Rinke, Alessandro Tellini, 2022.

References

Burns, Carol/Kahn, Andrea, (eds.) (2005): *Site Matters: Design Concepts, Histories and Strategies*, London: Routledge. DOI: https://doi.org/10.4324/9780203997963.

Canizaro, Vincent B. (2012): »Design-build in Architectural Education: Motivations, Practices, Challenges, Successes and Failures«, in: *ArchNet-IJAR: International Journal of Architectural Research* 6/3, 20–36.

Ingold, Tim (2013): *Making: Anthropology, Archaeology, Art and Architecture*, London: Routledge. DOI: https://doi.org/10.4324/9780203559055.

Lefebvre, Pauline/Neuwels, Julie/Possoz, Jean-Philippe, eds (2021): *Penser-Faire: Quand Des Architectes se mêlent de construction*, Brussels: Éditions de l'Université de Bruxelles.

Mohareb, Nabil/Maassarani, Sara (2018): »Design-build: An Effective Approach for Architecture Studio Education«, in: *ArchNet-IJAR: International Journal of Architectural Research* 12/2, 146–161.

Pallasmaa, Juhani (2009): *The Thinking Hand: Existential and Embodied Wisdom in Architecture*, Chichester: John Wiley and Sons.

Rockström, Johan/Gupta, Joyeeta/Qin, Dahe et al. (2023): »Safe and Just Earth System Boundaries«, in: *Nature* 619, 102–111. DOI: https://doi.org/10.1038/s41586-023-06083-8.

Schleicher, Dennis/Jones, Peter/Kachur, Oksana (2010): »Bodystorming as Embodied Designing«, in: *interactions* 17/6, 47–51. DOI: https://doi.org/10.1145/1865245.1865256.

Schön, Donald A. (1987): *Educating the Reflective Practitioner: Toward a New Design for Teaching and Learning in Professions*, San Francisco: Jossey-Bass.

Sennett, Richard (2009): *The Craftsman*, London: Penguin Books.

Steffen, Will/Richardson, Katherine/Rockström, Johan et al. (2015): »Planetary Boundaries: Guiding Human Development on a Changing Planet«, in: *Science*, 347/6223, DOI: https://doi.org/10.1126/science.1259855.

UN Environment Programme (UNEP) (2021): *Global Status Report for Buildings and Construction*, UN Environment Programme.

Webster, Helena (2008): »Architectural Education after Schön: Cracks, Blurs, Boundaries and Beyond«, in: *Journal for Education in the Built Environment* 3/2, 63–74. DOI: https://doi.org/10.11120/jebe.2008.03020063.

Two Bodies

Aileen Iverson-Radtke

Abstract: This article reflects on my doctoral research in architectural modeling. As a long-practicing architect, the findings here are shaped by my years of training and practice. My doctoral research examines analog and digital architectural modeling in their capacity of supporting the critical design process. The doctoral research, as design-driven research, studies the qualities of analogue and digital modeling by developing a composite hybrid analog-digital architectural modeling technique. Connecting analog and digital modeling is achieved using electronics and simple microsensor technology (fig. 1). Sensors connect digital models with manual manipulations and environmental data. This data then animates the digital model, which responds and creates feedback that can be considered by the designer. In this way, model and designer can communicate and make decisions based on the model's reactions to its context and manual manipulations. By animating digital media while providing haptic access, hybrid modeling seeks to establish digital making as non-verbal dialogue between maker and made; designer and model. The dialogue between them is the subject of this paper.

Keywords: Architectural Modeling; Feedback; Making; Hybrid; Microsensors; Animated Media.

Introduction

Making as Collaboration with Design Object. This article introduces the two bodies engaged in making: the maker and the made. The emphasis in my writing is placed on the latter, identifying its embodied intelligence that is ideally suited to making as a form of non-verbal communication. Unlike conceptualization, which is attainable through the efforts of a single mind, making transposes ideas into media. In so doing, making collides with and merges »humanity with the vast domains of life, sentience, and agency that resides outside of it« (Colombino/Childs 2022: 359). Through making we engage media, and therein »the non-humanity that flows around but also through

---

Corresponding author: Aileen Iverson-Radtke (TU Berlin, Germany), aileen@air-architecture.net, https://orcid.org/0000-0003-0671-711X.
Open Access. © 2024 Aileen Iverson-Radtke published by transcript Verlag.
This work is licensed under the Creative Commons Attribution 4.0 (BY) license.

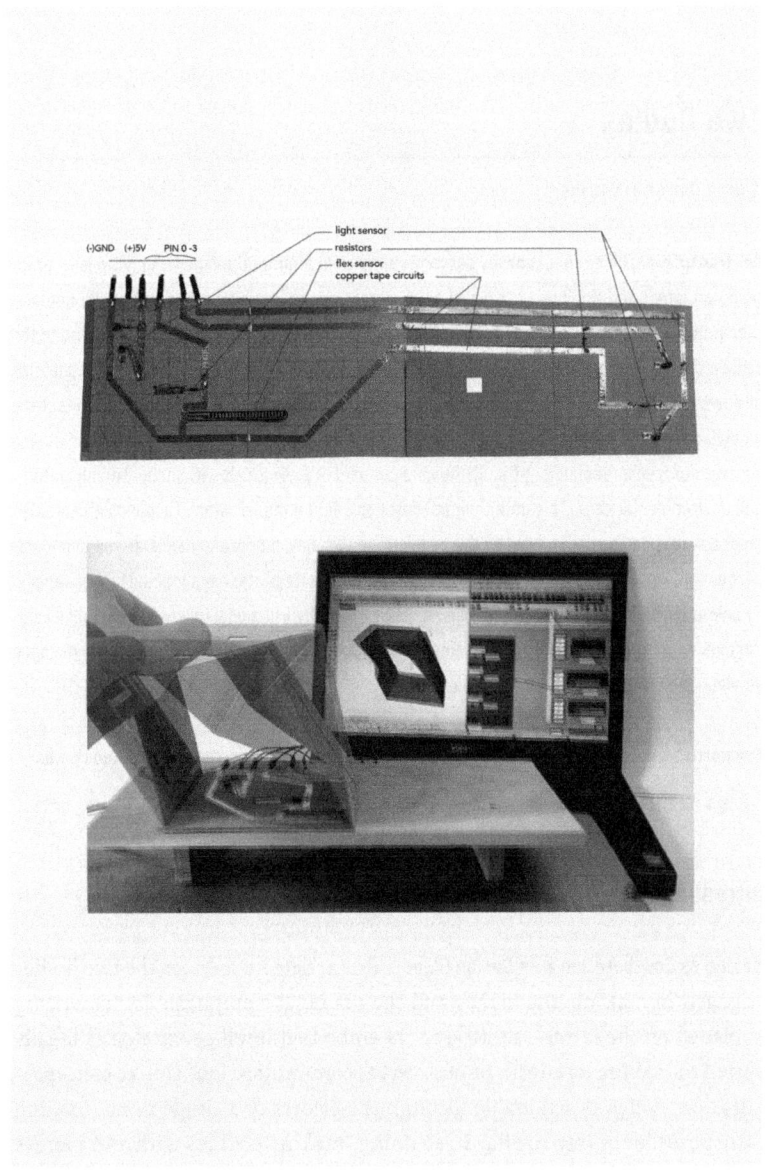

1.
CS02 Hybrid Modeling engagement.
Photo by the author.

humans« (Bennett 2004: 347). This engagement sparks collaboration between maker and made.

In making, the object being made (the design object) functions as one concise unit of the domains engaged. Their media, tools, and rules of engagement guides what is made. For example, the domain of woodworking prescribes a milieu of tools and strategies such as constructing a »jig« or template that is later removed, and cultivates a refined attention to wood grain and species, etc. To make we must inhabit these specific milieus and adopt the logic and rules prescribed by the media. Over time, and making typically requires a significant amount of time, our patterns of behavior and thus our thought processes are gradually altered to align with this material logic. From the outside, the relationship between maker and made is often seen as unequal, i.e., one body is fully formed (maker) and the other body is in a state of becoming (made). However, we should not confuse this initial imbalance as a one-directional exchange. By inhabiting specific milieus of making and thus adopting the logic of the media, meaning is conveyed and insights are revealed – we too are changed.

Context

Literary Sota. Contemporary theory, science, and literature are impacted and influenced by the global climate crisis and its agent, the Anthropocene, is exploding with writings considering the vast systems of which these are only a part. An example of such discourse is object-oriented ontology (OOO) »which proposes a non-anthropogenic concept of »Being« wherein »humans have equal existential status to other »objects«, such as frogs, chairs, or planets.« Furthermore, that »objects« can have agency […] not necessarily bound by relations« (Boulton 2016: 776) to human perception or experience. In related theories such as Jane Bennett's »vital materialism«, »matter is lively and exhibits agency – an ability to act of its own accord« (Boulton 2016: 777). In this context the Anthropocene is just one of many realities being played out which constitute our lived experience. It is one of many occupants of a vast system of imbricated intelligence ecosystems enacted by different bodies – planetary, geological, robotic, digital, etc. – wherein each ecosystem has its own rendition of reality, rules of operation, and systematic logic. In addition, the current literature focusing on climate crisis communication suggests that human ability to reason is largely facilitated by emotions. Here, emotions act as »superordinate programs« encoded in our neural pathways controlling »pre-existing, hardwired ... deep frames« (Boulton 2016: 780) of beliefs structuring our ability to reason and act.

Thesis

Maker-Made Dialogue. This article's thesis is that making acts as an ideal conduit for non-verbal dialogue between imbricated human and non-human intelligence ecosystems. This is because making operates on our »subprograms« of »perception; attention; inference«. Therefore making, a prime characteristic of homo farber, is understood as a superordinate program directing and coordinating human »learning; memory; goal choice; motivational priorities' etc.« (Boulton 2016: 774). The contention here then is that the experience of making, including repetitive actions, prolonged exposure to non-human ecosystems – forms a non-verbal dialogue. Through making, we engage the body of that which is being made, the design object, and the intelligence ecosystems to which it belongs. Making is a collision of our reality with the Pandora's box of external intelligence ecosystems to manifest hidden knowledge otherwise inaccessible.

This article's thesis is therefore examined by reflecting on recently completed doctoral research in hybrid analog-digital architectural modeling. In this assessment the digital made (hybrid models) reveal novel insights into spatial and material characteristics of the digital design space intelligence ecosystem.

Materials and Methods

Hybrid Analogue-Digital Modeling. The hybrid analog-digital modeling developed in the doctoral research sought to integrate analog and digital into one modeling technique using microsensor-embedded analog models. These analog models with embedded microsensors, referred to as »sensor models«, function as an interface to digital modeling replacing the mouse and keyboard (fig. 1). Microsensors can detect both environmental conditions and manual manipulations. Thus, in hybrid modeling, microsensors attach digital models to their site conditions (gravity, light, wind, etc.). Additionally, as hybrids, these models include an microsensors embedded analogue component and thereby attach digital modeling to manual manipulations.

Hybrid Modeling Goal. The goal of this research was to facilitate making as a form of critical analysis in digital modeling. The definition of making-as-critical-analysis is informed by an analysis of modeling (analog and digital) carried out at the beginning of the doctoral research. As design-driven doctoral research (DDDR) this analysis was based on my previous projects, therefore on my experience and training. The research found that the ability of modeling to function as critical analysis is supported by the capacity of design objects to provide feedback during the design process, when such feedback may direct the outcome, and test or critique design intent. Given the above context of imbricated intelligence ecosystems, this feedback from the design object is considered a transfer of knowledge enabled through making.

In traditional physical modeling, feedback is central to making and is experienced as a reaction connected to material properties responding to spatial context (gravity, wind, atmospheric, etc.) and other reactions related to tooling and manipulating form. However, in digital making, digital materials and simulated spatial forces are only intermittently connected, if at all. Therefore, digital materials, and by association the digital design object (the made) are rendered mute and the connection of their properties to spatial forces is severed. Having no ability to react under design manipulations, the digital design object is unable to generate feedback or participate in dialogue in the design process. Therefore, hybrid modeling, linking digital models directly to site conditions (via microsensors), seeks to enable reactions in digital modeling materials (meshes, surfaces, polylines, etc.). The ability of digital materials to react to site forces animates the digital model, thus empowering the digital made to react, providing feedback to the maker.

The Maker

In terms of the maker – making is typically a physical as well as a mental activity, therefore it operates »on different parallel process levels« (Oehlmann 2021: 39) in subprograms of haptic engagement where knowledge exchange occurs at a sensory level of intelligence. This channel of embodied knowledge acquisition operates at the speed of intuition, bypassing conscious thought. In making, therefore, the transmission of knowledge alters our intelligence at a rate that we are largely unaware of. This knowledge is absorbed and performed by our motor skills allowing »the hand ... (to) produce almost independently without cognitive intervention« (Oehlmann 2021: 37). Over

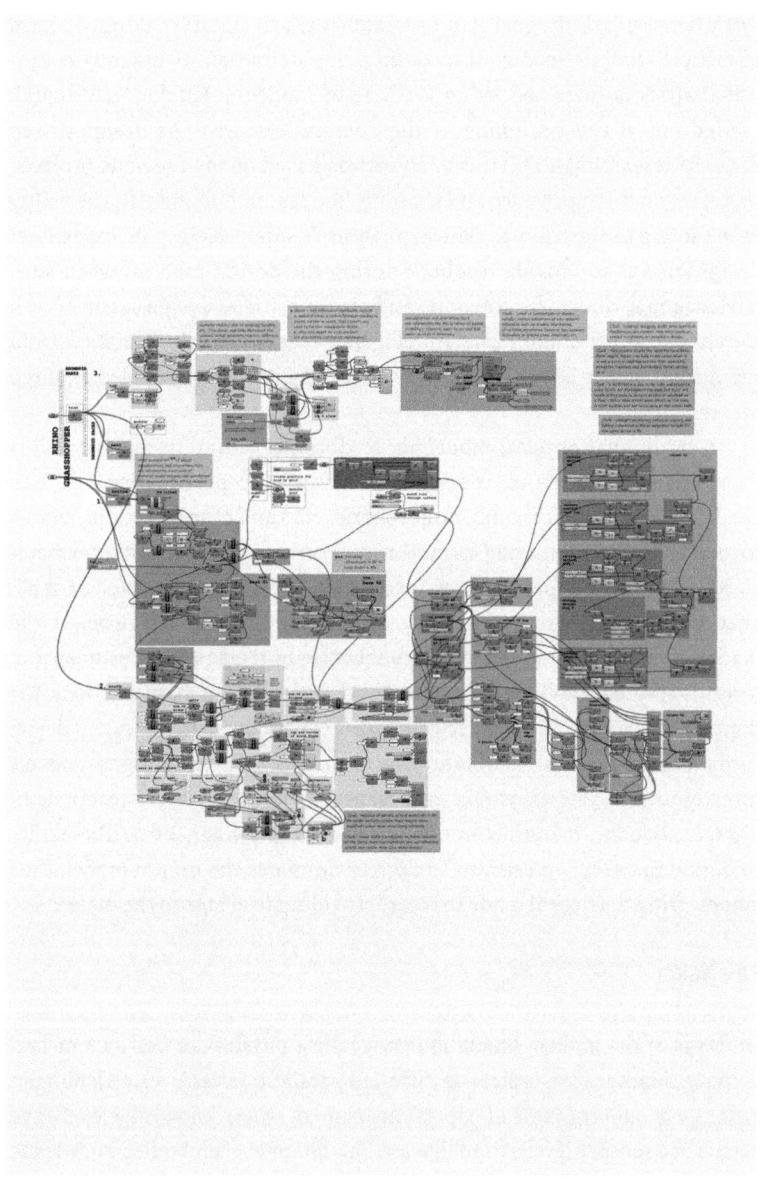

2.
Scripted boxes record non-verbal dialogue during making.
Illustration by the author.

time then, such knowledge becomes embodied habit, technique, skill, and mastery.

The image on the left (fig. 2) shows an example of knowledge transferred on alternative subprograms, such as intuitive and sensory channels during making, i.e. made-to-maker communication. Although there was a conscious effort to record this rapid dialogue in notations (the many scripted boxed notes) only a fraction was captured. In this example, the dialogue concerned adjustments to parametric modeling that are necessary to align the defaults behaviors of digital physical modeling actions. This entailed altering the parametric script of digital surfaces so that rather than stretching infinitely, these surfaces follow the constraints of physical materials and retain the initial dimensions of the surface in bending. By not allowing digital surfaces to stretch infinitely, the digital model must change shape to accommodate the effects of a bending manipulation, just as a physical model would (fig. 3).

Critical Making

Generating Theory. In my doctoral research, the interest in critical architectural making is due to its ability to provide a broad insight outside of the immediate design problem solution, i.e., critical making generates theory. The research describes architectural making as a unique form of analysis conducted through media and thus in material, spatial, and dimensional terms. Given the context of imbricated intelligence ecologies described by theories like OOO and vibrant materiality, the argument put forth in this article is that making can act critically by being a conduit to external intelligence ecosystems. Furthermore, that architectural analytic making, operating on subprograms of haptic, sensory, and intuitive faculties, imparts wisdom through acquired technical skills to effect increased cognitive abilities. The unique power of making as a channel for dialogue and collaboration with systems outside of the anthropomorphic, as experienced in the doctoral research, will be the subject of the remaining text.

Beginning with the prime example of how this research into hybrid analog-digital modeling produced the theory of spatiomateriality (Iverson-Radtke, 2022: xi). Spatiomateriality identifies the true nature of media (analog and digital) to be a composite of bonded spatial and material properties. This means that space and material are not separate entities but rather, continuous, temporal bonded states of both. Spatiomateriality is easily seen in physical media, i.e, materials (wood, metal, etc.) in spatial conditions

 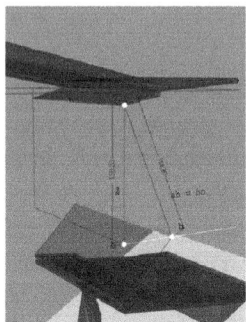 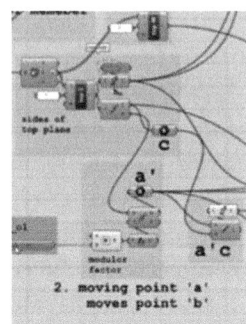

3.
Altering parametric script to hold surface size constant in bending.
Illustration and photos by the author.

(humidity, gravity, etc.) produce a spatiomaterial media of swollen wood or rusted metal. The importance of spatiomaterial media is that it is dynamic and animated by the bonding interaction of spatial and material properties. The inherent reactions in spatiomaterial media enable feedback from the design object during making and enables dialogue between maker and made. The significance of the research is finding the opportunity for digital spatiomateriality, i.e., the ability to connect digital material and spatial properties to provide feedback, thereby facilitating the maker-made exchange between intelligence ecosystems.

Case Studies. As design-driven doctoral research experiments were carried out as a series of hybrid analog-digital models, or makings that were referred to as case studies. These hybrid makings engage, and foster collaboration between, physical, digital, and electronic domains. Reviewed here are the profound findings and influences of these imbricated intelligence ecologies and what they suggest about spatial and material natures.

Dialogue with Digital Ecology. Hybrid modeling requires establishing uniform material behaviors across analog-digital modalities to create an integrated modeling experience. This demanding task requires intense scrutiny to align digital, parametric modeling to physical modeling behaviors. The main task of hybrid modeling therefore was to unpack digital modeling as long-standing habits embedded in the »syntactic structure ... and articulated in a motorized manner ... (thus) incrementally« (Schwarz 2008: 210) absorbed by those who practice in this domain on a daily basis. As such, doctoral research often »discovers« rules that have been »internalized by repetition« (Oehlmann 2021: 39). Although these discoveries will be familiar to some readers, as we will see, the information transmitted through working in digital ecologies over time, i.e., adopting the intelligence of the made, collectively imparts novel implications to our conceptualization of space and matter, such as spatiomateriality.

Three additional space-matter concepts resulting from the research are reviewed here as evidence of dialogue with the made and as a unit representative of analog-digital ecology. These concepts: »materials as containers«, »objects generate space« and »object recognition« lay the groundwork for two larger research findings : »spatiomateriality« and »digital material properties«.

Materials as Containers. In an early hybrid analog-digital modeling experiment that sought to bend a three-cornered rounded plane using pressure sensors (fig. 4), computational materials are observed to act non-uniformly.

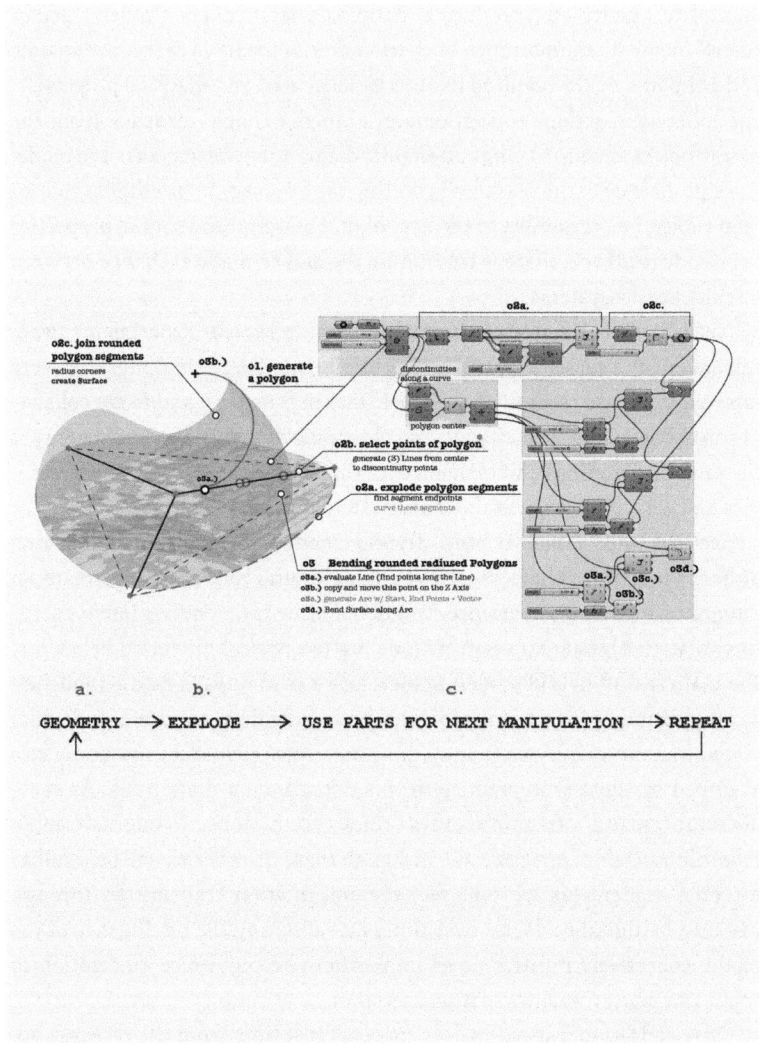

4.
Digital Materials as Containers. Illustration by the author.

5.
Methodology of exploding into component parts. Illustration by the author.

The non-uniform behavior was due to differentiated internal components (perimeter, center, area, etc.) necessary to the construction and definition of digital materials. Therefore, in bending, rather than acting in unison, digital materials act non-uniformly due to their nature as sets of internal components of varying geometric definitions. To create uniform motion such as is found in analog molecular-based materials (rubber, paper, wood, etc.), digital materials must be scripted so that all internal and perimeter parts follow the same uniform bending motion.

Thus, digital ecologies describe materials as containers of components with specific geometric definitions relative to the material in which they are contained or, in digital ecologies, geometric sets manifest as single digital materials (mesh, surface, etc.). In addition, these internal components of digital materials are referenced throughout parametric scripts either to manipulate the material to which they belong or to manipulate other materials of the parametric model. For example, in the image on the left (fig. 4), o3b. is a point generated by coping and moving point o3a. in which both points describe the arc of bending. This is an efficient methodology, reusing the same components with pre-defined associations (with respect to the host material) throughout digital design articulation. Additionally, by referencing these internal components throughout the parametric model, digital objects become mathematically networked. Working in and occupying the milieu of making in digital parametric ecologies over time, the maker adopts the methodology of the made; that is, the logic of continually initiating new digital materials and exploding them into their constituent parts to form the base for the next modeling manipulations (fig. 5).

The lesson of digital ecology experienced in hybrid modeling is that the articulation or manipulation of digital materials must operate through their internal structures or properties. In the research, the manipulations of internal structures of computational matter scrutinized, revealed further idiosyncrasies of digital ecology.

Objects Generate Space. In parametric modeling, geometrically defined internal components of digital materials are often projected or launched into digital space from the parent material, as part of the methodology for further model manipulations. Again in the image on the left (fig. 4) point o3b. is copied and projected in the Z-axis into digital space to define the bending arc. Projecting geometrically defined components that have a specific relationship to their parent object into digital space has three conceptual implications. As mentioned, it networks digital materials that share and

Aileen Iverson-Radtke

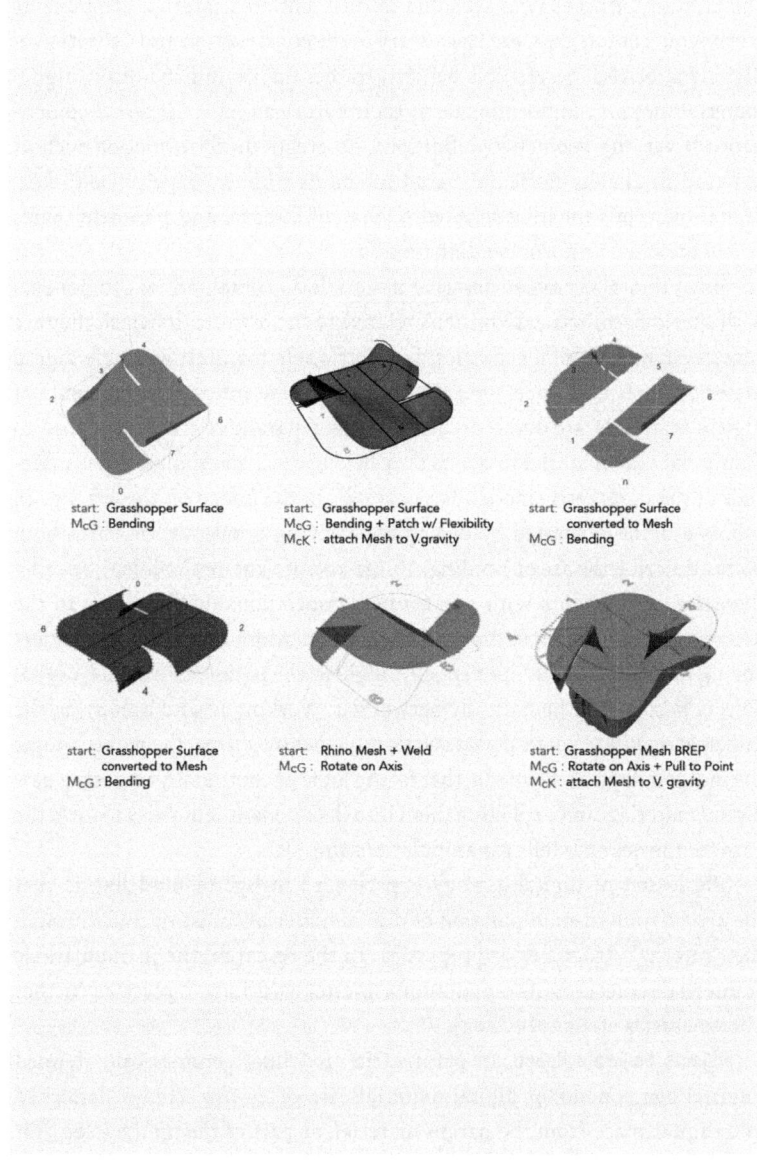

6.
Digital Material Properties.
Illustration by the author.

reference the same components. Furthermore, such projections can be seen to »seed« digital space with networked definitions. In this way, conceptually, digital matter is able to seed the neutrality of Cartesian-grid digital space with inflection and bias. Moreover, each digital material, by projecting its internal components beyond itself, generates an automatic relationship between internal and external space. Over time, working within digital ecologies, wherein the routine exploding of materials seeds space with internal geometric elements as coordinates for further material manipulations – erodes the sense of difference between object and space. Eventually, in what is perhaps an extreme reading, digital ecologies trasmit the idea that objects generate space.

Object Recognition. Using the internal components of host materials as seeds to create other digital objects or points in space also facilitates recognition among digital objects. The mathematically based networking of objects through host and seed elements, suggests that objects in computational space have no inherent relationship or visibility to each other outside of these shared definitions. Instead, in digital ecologies, objects recognize space and other objects only when identified through geometric parentage, i.e., through networked definitions. Thus, despite appearances, digital objects are inherently isolated from each other and thus fundamentally differ from objects of our analog ecology.

Main Research Findings

Spatiomateriality. In terms of the maker, digital ecologies impart the understanding that both space and materials are the same; both are fields containing internal properties that are easily shared. In addition, both are programmable entities, i.e., to digitally bounce a ball or drop a cloth requires scripting both object and space. As demonstrated, hybrid-modeling research uncovers a digital ecology in which objects generate, or at least influence, the composition of space; an ecology in which matter and space are not completely independent or separate but commingle and connect. The erasure of the notion of difference between space and object facilitates the conception of spatiomateriality, a theory founded in this research. Spatiomateriality proposes an entirely new way of understanding space-matter, by viewing it as a single spatiomaterial media rather than as two separate things. Spatiomaterial media is composed of interacting spatial

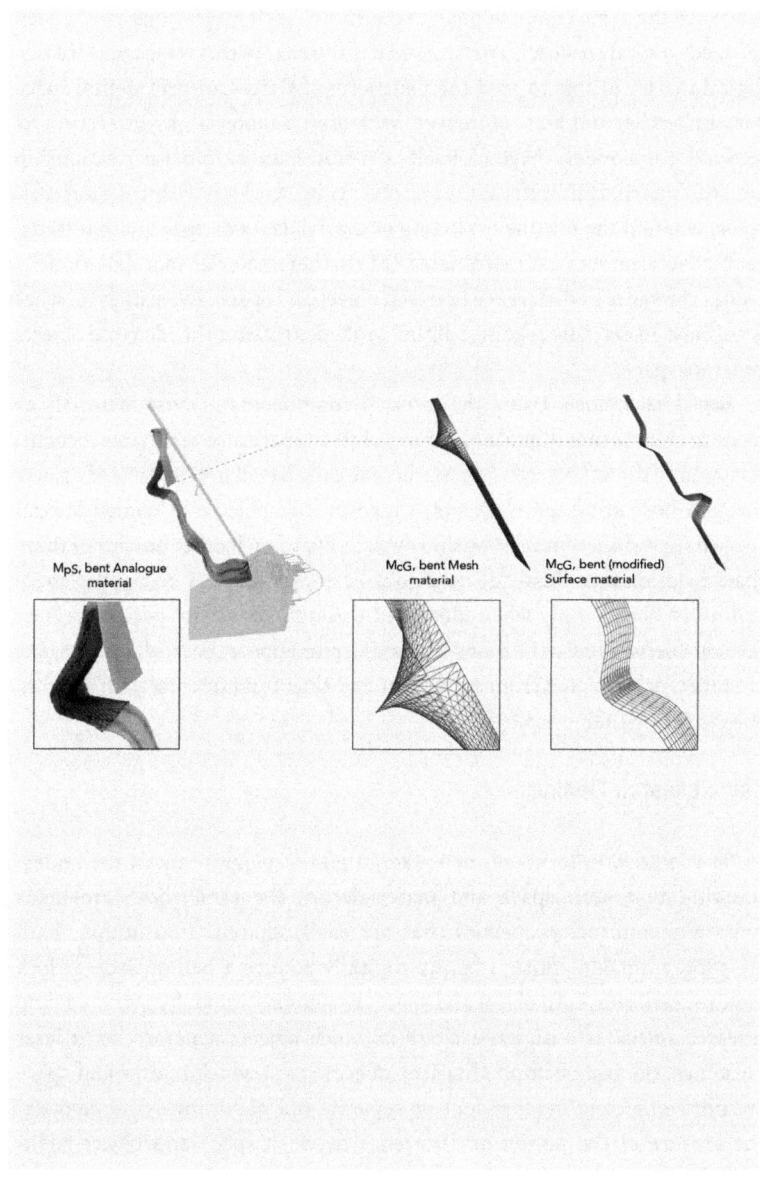

7.
CS04, Digital material behaviors.
Illustration by the author.

and material properties. Their interaction animates design media and allows feedback experienced as material resistance or reactions.

Digital Material Properties. In constructing hybrid analog-digital models, the reality of digital material properties was strenuously encountered and experienced as the »recalcitrance or moment of vitality in things« (Bennett 2004: 348). The existence of digital material properties is illustrated by the variation in the behavior of digital material (meshes, surfaces, etc.) when performing the same action (bending) (fig. 6). The recalcitrance or vitality of digital materials often required adjustments to their internal geometric structure in order to align (thereby create uniform action) across analog-digital modeling.

The tailoring of material behaviors was instrumental to the final experiment, see Case Study 04 (fig. 7 and 8). In this experiment, to align across modeling modalities, a digital material that could match the behavior of the analogue rubber strip material was needed (fig. 7, first frame). Thus, the digital material was to bend in smooth curves as well as be »floppy«, i.e., easily subject to gravitational pull. Digital mesh, which responds well in virtual gravity, and is therefore »floppy«, was initially selected. However, digital mesh defaults to bend in sharp angles, (fig. 7, middle frame) while smooth bending in rounded curves is found in digital surface material. Thus, CS04 required the redefinition of a digital surface material parametrically to significantly increase the number of its internal vertices. The result was a digital surface with mesh-like multiple vertices, which was therefore capable of smooth curves with floppy behavior due to an excess of internal points that were accessible to virtual gravity. This revised digital surface was then used to match the rubber material behavior of floppy and smoothly curved bending (fig. 7, last frame).

Discussion

By acknowledging digital material properties, architects can design digitally from a methodology based on New Materiality, which stipulates that form is generated from the internal properties of active (digital) matter (DeLanda 2015). The doctoral research, influenced by my training and career, is founded on the traditional tropes of architectural design: materiality and site (spatial conditions). Thus, the concept of spatiomateriality – that material and space are connected as dynamically bound instances of animated spatio-material media – is clearly influenced by this training. So too CS04,

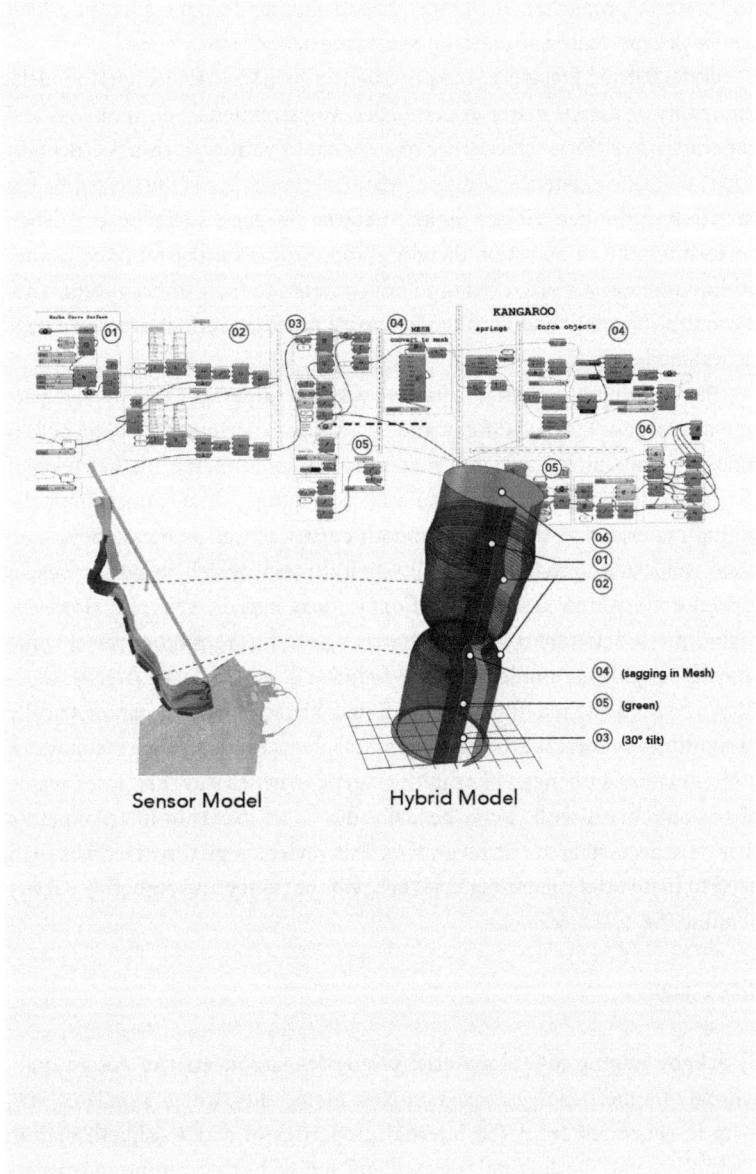

8.
CS04, *Digital spatiomaterial media.*
Illustration by the author.

the final and conclusive experiment of the research in which the formal resolution factors materiality (rubber) and site (gravity unevenly distributed on an inclined figure). In this experiment the rubber strip represents a vertical section rotated in digital space to form a vase, (fig. 8). Influenced by my training, CS04 was considered successful based on the understanding that in architectural practice, form is created as a function of materiality acting under spatial conditions. In terms of pedagogy, hybrid making teaches that design engages animated media as a vital partner in a critical design process. From there practitioners learn to engage spatiomaterial media as »a materialism of lively matter« (Bennett 2004: 347) whose design objects are discrete units representative of ongoing dynamic intelligence ecologies. Thus, making establishes a practice of non-verbal dialogue with design objects as a collaboration with external ecologies of intelligence such as that between maker and made.

Conclusion

This research identifies making as a different kind of science, one that not only observes but converses and collaborates with systems of external intelligence. Furthermore, making-as-analysis is supported by our neural networks which are connected to sensory and emotional inputs, as knowledge-building pathways. Timothy Morton argues »thinking« is redundant. Humans' pre-existing, hardwired, or deep frames are so mismatched to the new era that until they can be upgraded, humans must rely on other ways of knowing, such as sensing and feeling – attuning (Boulton 2016: 780). This research suggests that making provides that »other way of knowing«.

The integration of microsensors into analogue models, »sensor models«, used as an interface to digital modeling, represents a new hybrid design taxonomy and raises the potential for a sea change in how architects digitally make. It is hoped that this research instills in digital architectural making practices a desire to engage with a live media (analog and/or digital), animated by its internal properties, and capable of informing its own becoming as it informs our understanding, thus allowing the act of digital making to be a collaboration between active bodies: maker and made.

References

Bennett, Jane (2004): »The Force of Things, Steps towards an Ecology of Matter«, in: *Political Theory* 32/3 347–372.

Boulton, Elizabeth (2016): »Climate Change as a »Hyperobject«: A Critical Review of Timothy Morton's Reframing Narrative«, in: *WIREs Climate Change* 7/5, 772–785. DOI: https://doi.org/10.1002/wcc.410.

Colombino, Laura/Childs, Peter (2022): »Narrating the (Non)human: Ecologies, Consciousness and Myth«, in: *Textual Practice* 36/3, 355–364. DOI: https://doi.org/10.1080/0950236X.2022.2030097.

DeLanda, Manuel (2015): »The New Materiality«, in: *Architectural Design, Special Issue: Material Synthesis: Fusing the Physical and the Computational*, September/October, 16–21.

Iverson-Radtke, A. (2022): *Rabbithole to Hybrid: Finding Digital Spatiomateriality through Hybrid Modeling*, (Doctoral Dissertation, Technical University of Berlin, Germany).
DOI: https://doi.org/10.14279/depositonce-15983, https://depositonce.tuberlin.de/handle/11303/17204.

MathWorks Videos and Seminars, Overview: *Lidar Processing for Autonomous Systems*, [Video], Recorded: Feb 17, 2021, Mohammed, M., https://ch.mathworks.com/videos/lidar-processing-for-autonomous-systems-1614266031225.html (accessed: June 21, 2023.)

Oehlmann, Nandini (2021): »Embodied Knowledge, Tool, and Sketch: Intuitive Production of Knowledge in Architectural Design«, *Dimensions of Architectural Knowledge*, 1, 37–45. DOI: https://doi.org/10.14361/dak-2021-0105.

Schwarz, Monika (2008): *Einführung in die Kognitive Linquistik*, Stuttgart: UTB.

Good Places
The Potential of Places of Remembrance

Victoria Schweyer and Jana Wunderlich

Abstract: How can we utilize the narration of personal-memory places to create livable and needs-oriented living environments within retirement homes? Through guided workshops, elderly people utilize memory images to collaboratively design spatial interventions and implement them within their immediate surroundings. Architecture serves as a medium to encourage interpersonal connections and facilitate intergenerational exchanges, thereby enabling retirement homes to become places for meaningful interactions between generations.

Keywords: Places of Good Memory; Participatory Sense-Making; Intergenerational Exchange; Communication Architecture; Social Understanding; Needs-Oriented.

Introduction

Germany's changing demographic landscape presents substantial changes, which give rise to profound challenges. The prevalence of dementia diseases is increasing significantly, along with a shortage of caregivers and rapidly rising healthcare costs. Society can play a crucial role as a mediator between individuals with dementia, exhausted family members, and overwhelmed healthcare providers by serving as a central resource to alleviate the caregiving burden on older people. There is a pressing need for more accessible and inclusive gathering spaces that unite different generations, foster interaction and communication, and ultimately combat loneliness while enhancing the overall quality of life. However, what elements should these places incorporate to be appealing? What defines a »Good Place«?

The places of remembrance for older people often portray a pleasant and familiar ambiance, influenced by individuals, situations, spatial qualities, or natural surroundings. These *Good Places* are distinguished not only by their

Corresponding authors: Victoria Schweyer (Technische Universität München), info@pfluecken.net;
Jana Wunderlich (Technische Universität München), info@pfluecken.net.
Open Access. © 2024 Victoria Schweyer and Jana Wunderlich published by transcript Verlag. This work is licensed under the Creative Commons Attribution 4.0 (BY) license.

1.
Workshop, Good Places.
Photo: Valentina Rossa.

physical structures, but also by the personal interactions that have occurred within them. Adopting a nuanced perspective on older people reveals their capabilities and empowers them to have an opinion on shaping their surroundings because they possess valuable experience and can recount significant historical events. Architects assume a social responsibility to design environments that consider the needs of older people, hence, it is reasonable to facilitate their involvement in shaping their living environment. It can be challenging for older people to express their needs as they may not always recognize them or wish not to burden others (Petrich 2011: 52). The potential value of their memories, encompassing both spatial and social qualities, can be utilized to recreate Good Places once more, because »we always sense atmospheres – even if we are not always aware of them« (Uzarewicz 2013:146). In the pursuit of places of good memories, we have developed the Good Places workshop, where we aim to empower the residents of retirement homes to share their treasured memories and draw their Good Places. Through this collaborative process, we access the essence of what constitutes a Good Place by carefully examining and analyzing the unique characteristics of the stories shared by older individuals. These valuable insights serve as the foundation for creating inclusive spaces that appeal to all generations and enhance the residents' overall quality of life.

Methods

When older people recount their stories, they often find solace in reminiscing about their childhood. These memories provide them with a sense of security and, for those with dementia, serve as a connection to their long-term memory (Ehmann/Völkel 2023:115). Most older people, whether mentally healthy or ill, tend to discuss good memories when asked. However, some do take the opportunity to recount their experiences of fear and death during World War II. To avoid burdening other members of the group, we tactfully try to redirect the conversation and explicitly inquire about a place that holds good memories. Engaging in these nostalgic moments helps to momentarily alleviate their physical discomfort and allows them to relive the lightness of their youth (Farías 2023).

Through sharing personal memories within small groups, residents not only receive attention and care from attentive listeners during workshops, but also experience a renewed sense of empowerment when social participation becomes difficult. They discover shared experiences and commonalities

2.
On the Terrace, drawing by Albert Hirschmann, Munich.
»I have always taken great pleasure in inviting friends or hosting parties on my beautiful terrace. During moments of tranquility, I often find myself sitting on the bench in front of my house, viewing into my garden, enjoying the gentle sound of rippling water and the vitalising scent of fresh grass. The narrow plot and low hedges facilitated easy interaction with my neighbors, fostering friendships through conversations.«

with fellow residents, fostering a sense of camaraderie. More importantly, all participants are given ample space to share their stories and an environment is created that values and appreciates their memories and experiences without subjecting them to unsettling interrogations. The significance of good memory places extends beyond personal encounters and pleasant family moments; it encompasses architectural elements and characteristics that create a sense of familiarity and comfort, such as picturesque floral-patterned furniture or a charming semi-circular balcony. These elements form the foundation of an environment that individuals yearn for in their later years. By asking specific questions and encouraging residents to illustrate their memory places through drawing, we are privy to the unique details that define these cherished locations. The act of drawing personal places of remembrance not only strengthens the self-esteem of older people, but also helps to preserve their precious memories, regardless of their artistic abilities (cf. Mocker 2018). Many people with Alzheimer's or dementia lose the ability to communicate verbally, but drawing can provide patients with a new avenue of expression.

Through an extensive collection of these memory places, we have identified recurring patterns that encapsulate their phenomena and characteristics. These patterns supply a generality that can be applied to other places and reveal common motifs such as expansive views, flourishing gardens, inviting balconies, warm wooden interiors, and spaces that support social and communal activities and bring people of different ages together. By categorizing the good memories into themes such as activity or materiality, we gain an overview of the features of the memory that are separate from the actual story. The frequency of the mentioned elements prompts us to apply them when designing a Good Place, taking each attribute of the story seriously and using it as inspiration for architectural design. The various features of the stories are metaphorically connected throughout the design process without directly translating the memory places and characteristics. The listeners' external perspective allows us to assess the essential characteristics of the stories. Once we have analyzed the context of the care home and developed a new Good Place, we engage in discussions with the participants and integrate their suggestions and preferences into the design. Models of the proposed design facilitate a comprehensive exchange of ideas. Together, we explore the reasons behind the appeal of these places to people of all generations and aim to create inclusive spaces that enhance the overall quality of life for residents. These patterns are not only applicable to interventions like

3.
Small Shop, drawing by Jinlong Xu, Qingzhou, Shandong, China.
»*After work, I would always go to a small shop that sold pancakes. The street had a variety of stores selling all kinds of food, which created a lively atmosphere. The shop itself was very small, with only one large table for dough preparation and a big iron oven for baking. Outside the shop, there was a blue awning supported by two iron pipes. Underneath the awning, there was a large wooden table. Customers would stand under the roof and chat with the shop owner.*«

4.
Small Mahjong-Room, drawing by Cuige Jin, Munich.
»After preparing a delightful lunch for my beloved granddaughter, I eagerly make my way to the Mahjong Room, where my friends longingly await. The small Mahjong Room shares a discrete connection with my friend's barbershop through a small door nestled in the corner. The walls, painted in a pristine white, beautifully contrast with the dark tiled floor. A window gracefully opens onto the bustling street, allowing us to observe pedestrians.«

5.
The residents places of remembrance were recorded in drawings and served as inspiration for the design of a new place of communication in the garden of the retirement home.

pavilions or dementia gardens in outdoor areas, but also to renovation projects or the construction of new care facilities.

Results

The architectural interventions, known as communication architectures and gardens in the outdoor areas of the facilities, are collectively built with neighbors, volunteers and skilled craftsmen. By working together in these gardens, a communicative and active community is fostered and promotes meaningful interactions between different generations. Working together leads to knowledge transfer, which incentivizes visits to nursing homes, and allows for long-term relationships to be formed between young and old. Through these workshops, prejudices and stereotypes can also be dismantled, and they help to encourage a deeper understanding and sense of togetherness between generations. Gardens, green spaces, and courtyards are particularly suitable outdoor communal spaces for implementing communication architectures because they extend the living space for residents, guests, and neighbors alike.

In a collaborative workshop held at a retirement home in Munich, we designed a »Room in the Open« with delicate wooden structures, plank flooring, and comfortable wooden benches, as well as a sensory garden containing fragrant plants. An additional requirement was the integration of a tool shed into the garden design. A workshop participant's story about sitting on a bench in front of the house inspired us to create a wooden tool cabinet that also serves as a protective wall in the back. The turned-up small shade roofs along the wooden structure are reminiscent of memories of a grocer´s shop, where the shutters were opened and closed every morning and evening. One of the residents shared her experience of having an allotment garden filled with colorful and scented flowers, which inspired us to include this concept in the design of a dementia garden. This phenomenological approach also absorbs the most frequently mentioned elements of memories into the architecture. The pavilion and garden are now frequently visited by the residents for appointments with their families or to enjoy the view of nature and the chirping of birds. The Room in the Open is also famous for workshops and discussion groups and the nursing staff use the space during their breaks to recharge in the garden.

6.
Together with students, a communictaion architecture for the garden was designed and realized in exchange with residents of the retirement home.
The students prefabricated the wooden construction in a workshop at the Technical University of Munich. Photo by the authors.

7.
The work on site in the garden of the old people's home, which lasted several weeks, stimulated an exchange between the students and the residents and made the students sustainably aware of the topic of living in old age.
Photo by the authors.

84   Victoria Schweyer and Jana Wunderlich

8.
Around an existing pear tree, a new plaza design with a fountain and shade roof has been created, inviting residents to come together, listen to the trickle of water, and observe nature at the same time. The work was built and designed by students in the Master´s Studio Good Places as part of a Lectureship at the Chair of Architectural Design and Conception, Prof. Uta Graff, at the Technical University of Munich. Photo by the authors.

Discussion

When entering a nursing home as a resident, family member or visitor, one becomes aware that a good place is rarely found here. Most people wish to spend their final years in a place whose atmosphere is filled with warmth, security, conviviality, joy and love. This environment is fostered by a dedicated team of caregivers, social workers, housekeepers, and relatives who tirelessly attend to the residents needs and enrich their daily lives with various activities and delights. The architecture of the retirement home also plays a crucial role in creating a setting that promotes the well-being and health of its inhabitants (Brichetti/Franz 2019: 12–15). But what the built environment cannot achieve must be compensated for by the staff. In a society that often avoids confronting the realities of aging, this typology of housing is unfortunately not always viewed as desirable. Moving into a retirement home can be a challenging experience as it involves bidding farewell to one's familiar living environment and adjusting to the institutions established routines (Borgiel 2021: 939). If care is no longer affordable for relatives, they must find alternative care arrangements for their loved ones. Therefore, old people's homes will always exist. What would architecture look like if it were designed according to a variety of needs and fostered a multi-generational living environment? By incorporating diverse facilities such as kindergartens, libraries, housing, bakeries or neighborhood meeting places within a building, it would facilitate an exchange with the local community and society. Homes for the elderly need to meet the residents need for social connection. To achieve this, spaces would have to be designed so invitingly and timelessly that people enjoyed spending time there.

Conclusion

What distinguishes livable places where we want to grow old? With the empirical, participatory and hermeneutic method that we use to explore Good Places and implement them based on patterns, we create a holistic orientation guide for our work. We want to share these findings with architects and project developers to achieve a comprehensive design for a comfortable living environment for older people that promotes health and well-being. Homes for the elderly require sustainable concepts that engage with the people they accommodate and prioritize the potential of needs-oriented care architecture. Due to the forthcoming lack of nursing staff, healthy and supportive

9.
Photo by the authors.

work environments could help to retain caregivers in the profession and make their daily work more attractive and rewarding (Personalmangel in der Pflege verschärft sich weiter n.d.). The previous focus of research mainly relates to the residents' perspective. The memories of older people come from a time when many people grew up in rural areas and digitalization was not yet part of everyday life (United Nations 2016: 7–8). It remains to be discovered whether the Good Places constructed from these memories will change over the next decades.

References

Borgiel, Ursula M., ed. (2021): *Altenpflege Heute: Alle Kompetenzbereiche der generalistischen Pflegeausbildung*, 4th ed, Munich: Elsevier Urban & Fischer Verlag.

Brichetti, Katharina/Mechsner, Franz (2019): *Heilsame Architektur. Raumqualitäten erleben, verstehen und entwerfen*, Bielefeld: Transcript Verlag.

Ehmann, Marlies/Völkel, Ingrid, eds (2023): *Betreeungsassitenz: Lehrbuch für Demenz und Alltagsbegleitung*, 3rd ed, Munich: Elsevier Urban & Fischer Verlag.

Farías, Josémaría (2023): »Warum erzählen alte Menschen immer das Gleiche?«, https://www.apuntateuna.es/all/warum-erzahlen-alte-menschen-immer-das-gleiche.html, (accessed July 10, 2023).

Mocker, Daniela (2018): »Malen hilft dem Gedächtnis auf die Sprünge«, https://www.spektrum.de/news/malen-hilft-dem-gedaechtnis-auf-die-spruenge/1611134, (accessed June 20, 2023).

Pflegenot Deutschland (n/a): »Personalmangel in der Pflege verschärft sich weiter (n.d.)«, https://www.pflegenot-deutschland.de/ct/personalmangel-pflege/pflegekrafte-40798.htm, (accessed July 17, 2023).

Petrich, Dorothea (2011): *Einsamkeit im Alter: Notwendigkeit und (ungenutzte) Möglichkeiten Sozialer Arbeit mit allein lebenden alten Menschen in unserer Gesellschaft, Fachhochschule Jena/Fachbereich Sozialwesen* 6, Jena: Fachhochschule, Fachbereich Sozialwesen.

United Nations, Department of Economic and Social Affairs, Population Division (2015): *World Urbanization Prospects*: The 2014 Revision, 7–8.

Uzarewicz, Charlotte (2013): »Räume zum Lernen – Räume zum Lehren? Über atmosphärische Einflüsse und Gestaltungsmöglichkeiten«, in: Elisabeth Linseisen, Elisabeth/Charlotte Uzarewicz (eds.)*Aktuelle Pflegethemen Lehren: Wissenschaftliche Praxis in der Pflegeausbildung*, Stuttgart: Lucius & Lucius, 146.

MATERIAL

Making and Re-Making an Architectural Model

Jonathan Meldgaard Houser

Abstract: This visual contribution presents artistic research as intersecting projects: a.) Miniatura, a 1:10 scale model museum and b.) the exhibitions within it – one by the author (»Garden of Broken Asphalt«) and one by Spacegirls (»The Ideal Museum«). Miniatura combines model making, photography, and digital exhibitions to catalyze architectural discourse. The modelled exhibitions within the museum explore the potential of material conditions intertwined with text and image-based narratives.

Keywords: Museum; Model Making; Reclaimed Building Materials; Architectural Representation; Aesthetics.

Introduction

This visual contribution explores the 1:10 scale model through the making and remaking of a miniature museum and the exhibits within it. Thus, it centers around two architectural modeling modes conceived within the framework for artistic research at the Danish Royal Academy (Kgl. Akademi 2022). The first, an analog/digital museum named Miniatura, which becomes the framing of the other – the modelled exhibitions. Through text, images, and drawings the intersection of model-museum and exhibitions are examined in relation to the themes: »Material« and »World« outlined in the call: Making Sense through Making Architecture.

First, Miniatura is introduced, its foundational ideas, its making and the results as they are during writing. Miniatura is an ongoing project that bridges artistic research and practice by exploring perspectives and possibilities of model making and co-authorship in a hybridization of 1:1 experimentation, photography, and digital exhibition formats and their combined potential to catalyze architectural discourse through a flexible building system and a hybrid analog/digital gallery space (fig. 1–3, see also

Corresponding author: Jonathan Meldgaard Houser, (The Royal Danish Academy,Denmark), jhou@kglakademi.dk, https://orcid.org/0000-0002-3357-0582.
Open Access. © 2024 Jonathan Meldgaard Houser published by transcript Verlag. This work is licensed under the Creative Commons Attribution 4.0 (BY) license.

1.
Miniatura, building elements made from douglas wood, developed as a collaboratin between Jonathan Houser and Christian Vennerstrøm.
Photo: Christian Vennerstrøm and Jonathan Houser.

www.miniatura.dk). Furthermore, this visual contribution presents and reflects upon the project's intermediary results by focusing on two realised exhibitions: First, the »Garden of Broken Asphalt« (fig. 4–7) by the author and second, »The Ideal Museum« by Spacegirls (fig. 8–10). »Garden of Broken Asphalt« will serve to elaborate upon and discuss the potential of creating an architectural exhibition for Miniatura by making a landscape project engaged with reclaimed building materials that aimed for an aesthetic rather than a technical approach to materials and their interaction with the world. The Ideal Museum exhibition will serve as a tool to unfold the concrete potential of using the model as a meeting space of cocreation made possible by the 1:10 scale museum and its flexible building system.

Making Miniatura: The Model as Reality

The initial 1:10 museum model has been realized as a collaboration between architect Christian Vennerstrøm and the author as a flexible building system of various components which can be taken apart and reassembled (fig. 1). As described in the catalog Practices of Risk Control and Productive Failure (Houser 2022), which accompanied a group exhibition that included Miniatura, it consists of several irregular- shaped tables alongside an array of wooden blocks which can be utilized for walls and ceilings. The table tops act as floors in the museum and can be combined with the wooden blocks to form a variety of spaces (fig. 2–3), thus allowing the museum space to take on many different shapes to suit the specific needs of future exhibitions.

As an experiment to test the idea proposed and argued by Eliasson that a model may be considered real (Eliasson 2007) the project explores the notion that the miniature may be considered an actual place in contrast to the general idea that models are only representations of architecture yet to be built. This consideration has played an important part in the conception and realization of the museum and have so far, resulted in two exhibitions that have appeared online on the museum's website. As a result, the spatial compositions and images have taken on different qualities from the cinematic narrative presented in »Garden of Broken Asphalt« (Author) (fig. 5–7) to the almost scaleless 1:1 experiments in the exhibition »The Ideal Museum« (Spacegirls) (fig. 9–10). Due to the museum not having a fixed form the model must accommodate this foundational condition. Thus, the act of making and remaking in a collaborative effort between curators/initiators, exhibitors, and physical reality and digital presence becomes the fundamental

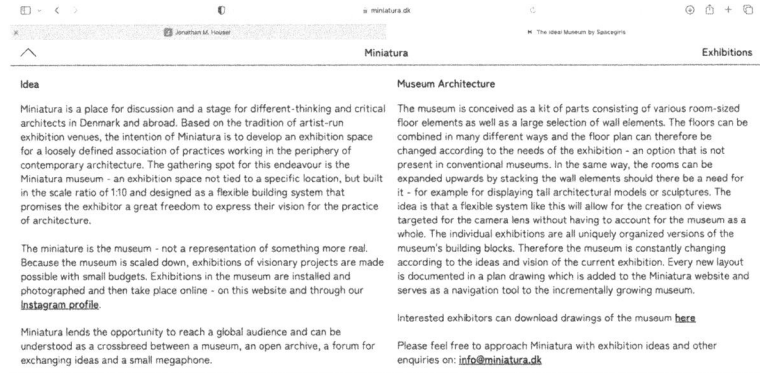

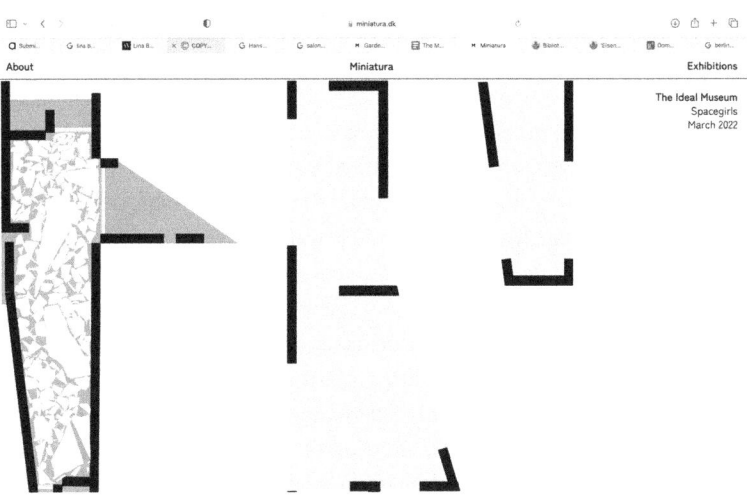

2.

Miniatura: Screenshots of the digital side of the museum showing the »About« page and the floorplan navigational tool, which changes and grows for each exhibition.

characteristic of its architecture. As mentioned earlier, this aspect will be treated at the end of this text in relation to the exhibition »The Ideal Museum«.

The entire museum is constructed from wood cut-offs donated by the Dinesen floor company. Initially, the act of making the museum and the final character of its parts is the result of a negotiation between the inherent material properties of the Douglas wood in conjunction with the vision for the aesthetic outcome. The wood cut-offs, unlike the luxury floor product from which they have been discarded, are characterized by inconsistent vein patterns, knots and holes where knots have fallen out, a roughness, and a 1:1 character which doesn't align with Miniatura´s ambition of being a 1:10 scale museum capable of creating a photographic illusion. The random placement of knots and cracks in the wood and a selection of wooden pieces of various lengths necessitated a refining process. In the Danish language the word for refining a material is »forædling«. This is a word that more directly translates into cultivation rather than the more neutral English word »refining« or »processing« suggested by the Cambridge Dictionary. The Danish term is also used in biology to describe the cultivation and selective breeding of plants in order to strengthen certain properties, including the aesthetic, such as more flowers on a rose bus) and/or functional, such as a higher yield of grain. In the case of Miniatura the cultivation process serves both purposes. Thus, one aim of the initial process of making the museum was to homogenize the wood's aesthetic properties to create building blocks with a similar grain structure on all sides. In this respect, the goal was to achieve a surface character, which could lend the tactile and experiential properties of the wood to future images while at the same time supplying the spaces portrayed with an almost abstract character. Another equally aesthetic and functional aim was to transform a very heterogenous material into precisely proportioned blocks of different sizes which would facilitate the largest possible compositional flexibility for arranging them in the form of a museum model. On a more functional level, the refining process also ensures a more stable product that gave the wooden blocks a formal stability so that they can be stacked and joined precisely. Therefore, to avoid the wood from bending and losing shape over time, along with achieving the intended aesthetic properties, all the cut-offs must be chopped up in a longitudal direction and leveled into sticks with identical measurements in the cross section. Each stick was examined and combined one by two or one by three while the knots and irregularities in the faces were always hidden by gluing them together and making them disappear into the wooden blocks. After this the process of

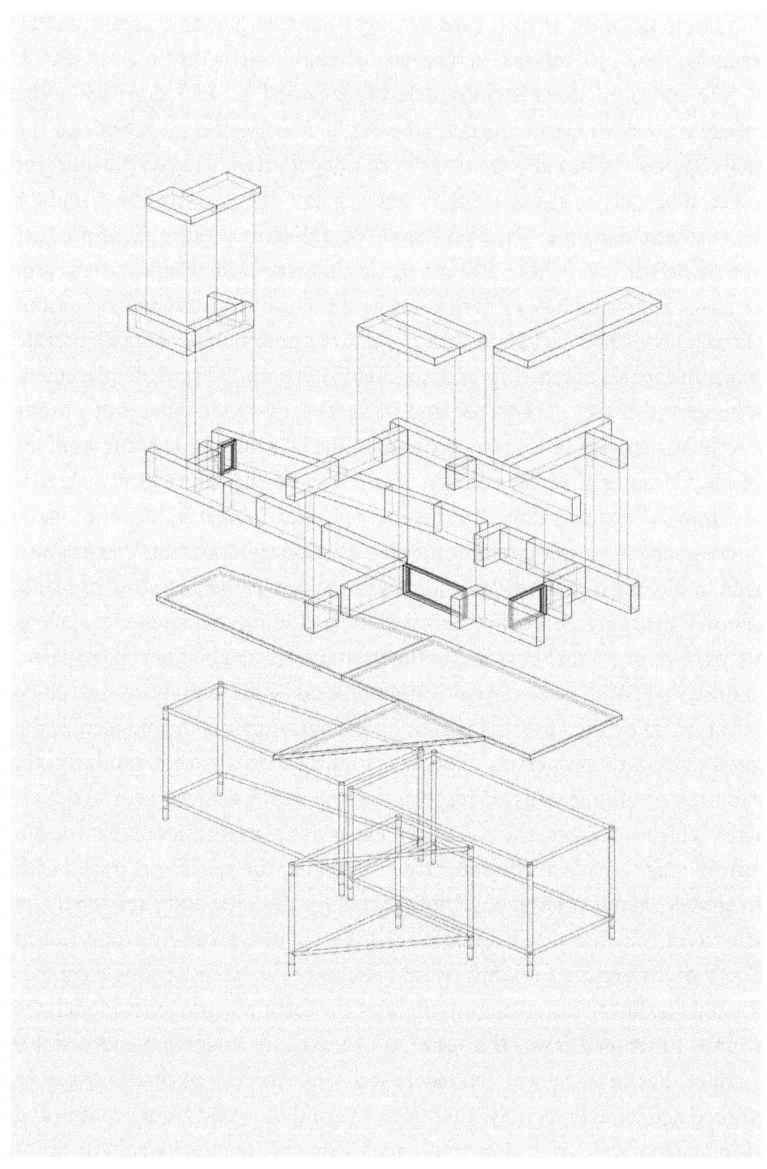

3.
Extruded Axonometry of »the Garden of Broken Asphalt«.
Drawing: Jonathan Houser.

levelling was repeated and the blocks were cut to pre-decided lengths while material waste was minimized. Following the same procedure of cultivation, the floorplates were made from sticks of Douglas wood with square cross-sections that were glued together in sheets, leveled, and afterwards cut and glued together in their specific shapes.

When deciding on a surface treatment, emphasis was placed on finding a solution which allowed the wood grain to be visible but could simultaneously desaturate the inherent contrast between light and dark lines. The treatment conclusively chosen was a handmade mixture of shredded soap diluted in warm water and pigmented with a combination of hydrated lime and coal powder. Due to this treatment, the wooden surfaces become slightly bleached and the process which makes it turn a warm color is partially stopped (hydrated lime) alongside coating the surface (soap) and giving it a grayish hue (hydrated lime and coal). This surface treatment is an important aspect of the final photographic character as shown in the photographic images.

Remaking Miniatura: Garden of Broken Asphalt – Setting the Stage

»Garden of Broken Asphalt« serves a dual purpose of being both a preliminary exploration of the possibilities central to the museum model, its building blocks, photography, and internet presence while also turning it into an exhibition. By letting the museum partner with an experimental exhibition, the museum's potential and limitations are examined in relation to the composition of blocks, the creation of indoor and outdoor spaces, artificial light, image cropping and other factors.

In this experiment the museum is inverted to form an outdoor garden space of which photographs can be taken through windows built for this specific purpose, thus creating the illusion of a context through the making of an image. The museum model is thus arranged to act as a stage set for the camera, which aims to produce photographs that won't show the unfinished character of the museum in the online gallery space. The aim was to discover how the museum could become a framing device, both in concrete physical terms with the museum walls acting as the limiting container, but also in a digital online reality in which the garden exhibition is reframed as part of the museum and its incrementally growing floor plan acts as the website's navigation tool (fig. 2 and 7).

4.
»Garden of Broken Asphalt«, Shown as part of the Exhibition: Practices of Risk Control and Productive Failure, Brønshøj (DK).
Photo: Jonathan Houser.

The 1:10 scale is particularly noticeable in the window frames and through the three-dimensional (3D) printed wild foal which simultaneously appears as both realistic and clearly representational. These elements and the broken asphalt landscape give a sense of scale to the wooden blocks that deliberately oscillate between 1:1 material and scenography backdrop.

> »Only this is I know for sure: a given number of objects is shifted within a given space, at times submerged by a quantity of new objects, at times worn out and not replaced; the rule is to shuffle them each time, then try to assemble them.« (Calvino 1978: 108).

Inspired by the story of the city named Clarice from which the quote above comes, the exhibition investigates a radical vision for the built environment based on the idea of a city defined by one singular rule: No new materials can be added when constructing buildings and landscapes. The founding principle for the modeled garden is hereby the infinite repurposing of building materials, which by extension is the basis of all construction activities in the imaginary context created by the exhibition. Hence, architectural form is explored as an act of transformation in the enclosed garden constructed from repurposed materials and may be considered a kind of dystopian memorial commemorating the 20th century.

Architectural visions based on material processes can be hard to investigate and test in representation. Therefore, the garden was also an attempt to test the potential of the museum's 1:10 scale by experimenting with modeling techniques that resembled how the garden should be constructed, with methods that run parallel to how it was envisioned in 1:1, hereby attempting to mirror the actual process of creation. Therefore, the chosen material is a plaster colored with pigment that has been broken and arranged in the same way as asphalt, which is what the model represents. As a method of investigating the potential of this type of design, the physical model is an important tool, as the computer can only partly be used to imitate principles and character derived from processing and properties of self-organization.

Remaking Miniatura

As the first exhibitors and cocreators of the Miniatura Museum, Spacegirls (Cisse Bomholt (DK) and (Elisabeth Gellein (NO)), were invited to the studio to translate the brief and the building blocks into an exhibition aligned with

Jonathan Meldgaard Houser

5.
»Garden of Broken Asphalt«, View of the museum seen from the garden with a 3Dprinted wild foal.
Photograph and Miniatura Exhibition: Jonathan Houser.

6.
»Garden of Broken Asphalt«, View of the museum seen through a window and into the garden.
Photograph and Miniatura Exhibition: Jonathan Houser.

7.
Miniatura, Screenshots of the digital side of the museum showing the »About« Page and the floorplan navigational tool, which changes and grows for each exhibition.

their own practice. Departing from a low-resolution diagram of the ideal museum as envisioned by Gottfried Semper, their version/exhibition of Miniatura is named after this: »The Ideal Museum«. The brief was very open. They had to make a representation of their practice within the confines of the setup presented to them. As there was no preliminary relationship between us, the invitation was an attempt to begin a dialogue by using the Miniatura model as a space for conversation about architecture; the discipline and the peripheral practice we seemed to have in common but had never discussed.

Having initially imagined a more traditional museum, with smaller scale and curated exhibitions within well-defined spaces, the images from the Spacegirls' exhibition were a welcome surprise. In contrast to »The Garden of Broken Asphalt«, which has an arrangement of the museum examining how it appears from the outside as an object, Spacegirls' strategy of arrangement is completely oblivious to this and uses materials such as tape and plastic on the outside to achieve the desired images on the inside (fig. 8). By inviting someone else to reorder the museum, set the lights and tell the story then, something entirely new was created – regarding both content and compositional strategy. Spacegirls brought a very tactile 1:1 material approach into the museum's orbit. When starting to manipulate and reorganize parts of the museum for the building system to align and accommodate their idea and vision, the separation between museum, architecture, and exhibition became blurred and looking at the final photographic results, the exhibition almost became one with the architecture of the model museum (fig. 9–10). Thus, in a very concrete way, by inviting colleagues to exhibit, the museum can potentially transform itself from exhibition to exhibition. The possibilities intrinsic to this type of museum can, due to its tactile qualities create a starting point for conversation and an unusual meeting space for new ideas and conversations that occur in both words, models, and images that enter a dialogue with an audience through website and social media. As the museum has the potential to grow and take its digital floorplan in many directions though online images and words, it also has the potential to become a concrete meeting place for like-minded practitioners in an evolving professional network, which in this case was centered in Copenhagen but has the potential to broaden the scope to global collaborations.

8.
»The Ideal Museum«, Outside view an arrangement of blocks made to house the exhibition by Spacegirls in the authors studio. Torn Sheets of plastic taped to the model act as projection screens for colored animations.
Photo: Jonathan Houser.

Discussion and Conclusion

Some of the perspectives on the collaborative act of making sense through making architecture, which are put forward by Miniatura, can be elaborated upon by a comparison to »The Open Work« as conceptualized by Umberto Eco. According to Eco (1989) the open work, as famously exemplified through the works of the composer Karlheinz Stockhausen among others, is characterized by the kind of compositions that provide a large degree of freedom for the performer to interpret and execute the musical piece. The compositional framework has such a form so that no two performances of the same piece are identical. In this regard, the museum/model and its other half, the regularly increasing www.miniatura.dk, can be considered an open work in which the physical reality of the wooden building elements, their inherent sizes, proportions, and tectonic logic may be understood as the equivalent to Stockhausen's sheet of music paper. The photographic documentation and presentation online are equivalent to that of a sound recording of a specific performance of a Stockhausen composition. In the Miniatura Museum the exhibitors assume the role of performers and interpreters of the material properties and the given scale of 1:10. Miniatura can then be interpreted as an experiment that has the definition of a work of architecture and the possibilities that arise when considering the model as reality in combination with the characteristics of »The Open Work«.

So, what possibilities do Miniatura and the comparison to properties of »The Open Work« give rise to when considered in relation to the themes of »Material« and »World« as outlined in the call for contributions to this issue of *Dimensions. Journal of Architectural Knowledge*?

Miniatura puts forward a concrete and tangible concept for the engagement, gathering around and discussion of the fundamentals of architecture. The concrete engagement between architectural peers is projected into the world through the museum's online presence and sharing it on social media. In this way the physicality of the wooden model and its flexible building system puts forward a concept for bridging the gap between the physical process of making analog models of concrete materials and the possibility of engaging with the world through digital media (fig. 2, 7, 9–10). As Miniatura is still in an intermediary phase, the results are not yet conclusive. However, when judging the two exhibitions and the photographs of the spatial experiments with different compositional arrangements of the museum elements, it quite clearly appears that the translation of Eco's concept of »The Open

9.
»The Ideal Museum«, Screenshots of the digital presentation.
Dropdown text showing Spacegirls and the curators statement.
Photo: Christian Vennerstrøm.

Work« to an architectural model and building system makes sense. Despite being quite different from each other regarding the relationship to the given 1:10 scale and the atmospheric and sensual qualities they embody, the realized exhibitions have a sense of communality that arises from the underlying presence of the material, its character, and its structural logic.

The idea of a system of building blocks is obviously not new and runs parallel to principles, such as in the proportioning systems developed by Dom Hans van der Laan (Laan 1983) in his teaching at the Bossche School of Architecture. The most important diversion from this parallel is perhaps our contemporary context of digital reality created by diverse architectural modeling and communication tools, which emphasizes the importance of direct engagement with the material world when studying architecture. Given its easy application, transformative setup, and element of photographic documentation, spatial compositions can be tested hands-on without the use of digital modeling which has become the norm. The experimentation with physical reality, made possible by Miniatura, is very valuable as an exercise in understanding both spatial and structural logic. Also, the large scale of the model compared to Van der Laan's building blocks, »The Abacus«, and the freedom from the strict rules of proportioning determined by the plastic number sets Miniatura apart, thus leaving more space for the interpretation by the individual performer seen in relation to the characteristics of the poetics of the open work as Eco defines it.

Considering Miniatura in this context, the prospect of further investigation in the context of architectural practice and education arises. Twice a year, at the end of the semester at most architecture schools, vast amounts of modeling material is discarded. This is also the case in many architectural offices. A position often advocated in response is that we should stop analog modeling entirely and switch to digital techniques of representation. However, Miniatura has a built-in possibility of reuse and may be considered a valuable investigative tool in both teaching and architectural practice. Thus, beside its fundamental properties of investigating spatial compositions, Miniatura can perhaps enter the discussion about design for dis-assembly in architectural practice and education by pointing toward a more sustainable design practice, both in terms of using industrial cut-offs in the fabrication of models but also through its inherent reusability. A further field of inquiry could be to extend the project and its discussion beyond the museum exhibitions and investigate the Miniatura kit-of-parts both as a teaching tool in the form of a discursive platform and an ideal model for the ecology of materials.

10.
»The Ideal Museum«, Screenshots of the digital presentatio, Text Spacegirls.
Photo: Christian Vennerstrøm.

Following this line of thought, the perspectives of Miniatura as not simply a museum, but as an experimental and re-usable system for testing spatial possibilities, may be further extended in correspondence with the ideas underpinning »The Garden of Broken Asphalt«. As outlined above in the Calvino quote, that exhibition deals with the idea of architecture being in a constant state of transformation. To use another phrase borrowed from the field of biology, Miniatura and its components may be interpreted as parts of a metabolism of materials – where the act of modeling becomes a parallel process to a reality based on a radical vision of reuse in architecture. Thus, remaking Miniatura mirrors a hopeful future where buildings and their materials are not torn down and discarded but gently taken apart, shifted, shuffled and assembled again.

Acknowledgments

Christian Vennerstrøm Jensen, collaborator and cocreator in the first phase of making. Rune Secher and Pernille Vincents, workshop assistants in the first phase of making. Spacegirls (Cisse Bomholt (DK) and Elisabeth Gellein (NO), collaborators and creators of »The Ideal Museum« exhibition. Martha Dell'Erba, workshop assistant for the exhibition »Garden of Broken Asphalt«. Orin Bristow and Andreas Vasegaard Nielsen, graphic design and web development for www.miniatura.dk. Miniatura has been generously supported by the Danish Arts Foundation, The Danish Arts Workshops, Dreyers Fond, Dinesen and the Royal Danish Academy.

References

Calvino, Italo (1978): *Invisible Cities*, translated by William Weaver, New York: Mariner Books.

Cambridge Dictionary. https://dictionary.cambridge.org (accessed July 23, 2024).

Eco, Umberto (1989): *The Open Work*, Cambridge, MA: Harvard University Press.

Eliasson, Olafur (2007): »Models are Real«, in: Emily Abruzzo/Eric Ellingsen/Jonathan D. Salomon (eds.) *Models*, New York: 306090, Inc., 19–23.

FKUs formandskab (Chair for Research and Artistic Research), Kgl.Akademi. 2022. https://kglakademi.dk/sites/default/files/imported-file/downloads/article/reviderede_kuv_bilag_2_og_4_til_kvalitetssikringshaandbog_06.04.22.pdf (accessed July 23, 2024).

Houser, Jonathan (2022): A. Romme/P. Bertram/F. Berglund (eds), Practices of Risk, Control and Productive Failure: *Exhibition Catalogue, Brønshøj water tower, May–June 2022*, Copenhagen: Det Kongelige Akademi, 10–11.

Van der Laan, Hans (1983): *Architectonic Space: Fifteen Lessons on the Disposition of the Human Habitat*, Leiden: Brill Publishers.

Miniatura. https://www.miniatura.dk (accessed:July 23, 2023).

Facade Environments
The Potentials of Large-Scale Adaptive Models

Hisham El-Hitami, Mona Mahall and Asli Serbest

Abstract: Facade Environments is a large-scale spatial installation that models an adaptive facade conceived by the authors. This facade is based on research arguing for the negotiability and adaptability of spatial limitations and thus for connections across the architectural facade. The model shows how size and scale create immersive qualities and how the operability of our spatial boundaries encourages relationships between beings and things.

Keywords: Model; Facade; Windows; Environments; Spatial Installation; Inside and Outside

This article is based on the presumption that models exist as their own spatio-material objects, in constant dialogue with planners, architects, clients, and a possible public, as well as a changing political and cultural context. Constructed in part independently of the project design and the plans they represent, they have a material, historical, and symbolical life and affordance of their own. In that, models share qualities with maps, doll houses, or amusement parks.

Thea Brejzek and Lawrence Allen consider models to be »inherently performative and epistemic« (2018: 1). In other words, they intersect with the realms of the »projective design« and the actual lived world. Paying particular attention to large-scale models, Brejzek and Allen argue that it is not so much the scale but the size that can create a sense of immersion in the relationship between the observer and the model. According to them, by being physically accessible and creating a particular atmosphere, such large-scale models can be both an outcome and a reflection of modes of perception. This description applies to the model of a facade case study that we recently realized within the Collaborative Research Center 1244, where we have been developing a comprehensive approach to architectural adaptation as a relational process that involves things and beings.

Corresponding authors: Hisham El-Hitami (Bauhaus-Universität,Germany), hisham.el-hitami@uni-weimar.de; Mona Mahall (Bauhaus-Universität,Germany), mona.mahall@uni-weimar.de; Asli Serbest (University of the Arts in Bremen), asli.serbest@hfk-bremen.de.
Open Access. © 2024 Hisham El-Hitami, Mona Mahall and Asli Serbest published by transcript Verlag. This work is licensed under the Creative Commons Attribution 4.0 (BY) license.

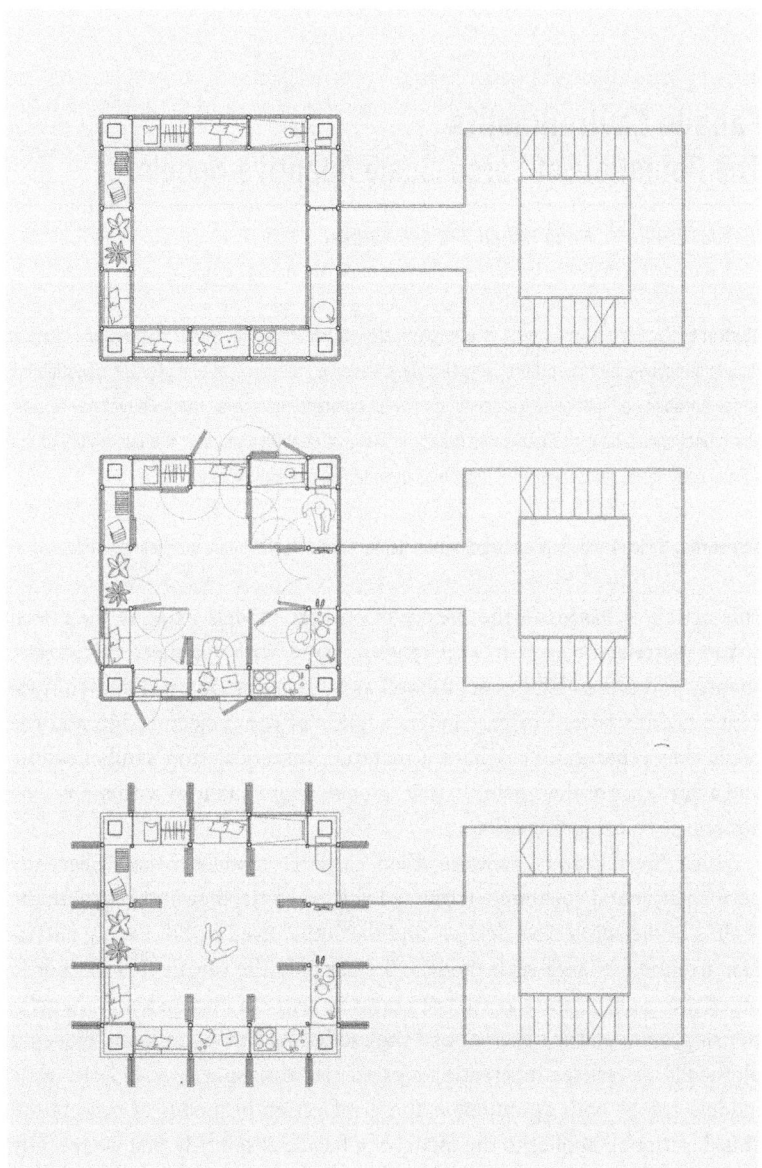

1. – 3.
floorplans of case-study facade, various spatial conditions.
Illustration: Hisham El-Hitami, 2022.

Titled »Facade Environments« and built at a scale of 1:2, the installation models an operable glass facade with a space between the interior and exterior layer, thus creating a variable in-between space (fig. 1–3). While the implementation of the case study is still pending, we have built this large-scale model as a spatial installation that could be visited at the festival of the International Building Exhibition (IBA '27) in Stuttgart (fig. 4–10). The model is large enough to be accessed and experienced spatially, yet small enough to be understood as a concept rather than a concrete inhabitable space. When entering, visitors have an ambiguous sense of being inside and outside the structure: They can overlook it but are simultaneously enclosed by it and can feel the large scale of its interior space. The operable facade elements are almost life-sized, yet they require us to bend over to pass through, reminding us of our physical relationship with the spaces we inhabit. Our perception of the environment is thus reconnected and directly related to the size, position, and activity of our own bodies, even more so as the installation allows visitors to navigate boundaries and inhabit different spatial constellations that require our physical, performative, and playful engagement. Fundamentally an open-ended process, interaction with the installation suggests that space is always in the making, with things and beings equally involved as space-making agents.

Reflecting on the dichotomic conception of interior and exterior spaces (Ulber/Mahall/Serbest 2021), we have moreover been focusing on the design of facades and their potential to allow transboundary connections. Challenging the rigid discrimination between inside and outside (Morton 2010) proves to be a key obstacle in understanding the entangled relations in environments. Previous research shows the potential of two-layered facades to encourage relationships between beings and things on both sides of such spatial boundaries (El-Hitami/Mahall/Serbest 2023). Beyond incorporating the ambiguous space to challenge the dichotomy between inside and outside, the installation allows visitors to negotiate its spatial limits. By moving the facade elements, the boundaries between inside and outside shift and reveal the (often overlapping) spaces as »unstable« and permeable. The fact that the space cannot be stabilized is demonstrated by the enormous variety of spatial situations created by visitors. The elements are moved around in ways beyond prediction during the design phase of both the initial facade and the 1:2 model, using two-dimensional drawings and digital models.

To support the spatial conception, the window panes have different colors depending on their position in the structure: The outer layer is yellow, and

4.
»Facade Environments«, *spatial installation at TOP, Berlin.*

the inner layer is blue. This highlights the double-layered nature of the facade as the visual superposition creates a green color. At the same time, it visualizes the space in between the layers in the fields of vision where the panes do not overlap. In addition, one angle of the installation uses red glass to highlight the spatial extensiveness of the project's corners. Together, the three window pane colors create a variety of different colors and shades, especially when they are moved around and rearranged according to their initial closed position. This encourages active engagement with the installation, which changes spatial boundaries and colors in correspondence with the visitors' interactions. It also challenges the experience of what is regarded as strictly inside versus outside the installation and, more generally, addresses the boundaries between human-made interiors and their surroundings.

Due to its size and scale, as well as material and color, »Facade Environments« anticipates the immersive and participatory experience of an adaptive architecture. Visitors engage with the installation in an enthusiastic manner and create their own spaces and color schemes while exploring and appropriating the ever-changing structure. This realization is of notable importance considering current architectural developments, which require buildings to perform in increasingly adaptive ways to meet the demands of changing societies for mutable spaces. In many cases of modern interiors, air-conditioned spaces surrounded by non-operable glazing, automated sunscreens, and a distant external world make it increasingly difficult to recognize the intimate relationality of beings and things. In contrast, »Facade Environments« might remind us of the mutability of the boundaries we set, the various and shifting relations we maintain with our surroundings, and our own agency as human beings in co-constituting the environment.

5. + 6.
Photo: Hisham El-Hitami, 2023.

7.
Photo: Hisham El-Hitami, 2023.

References

Brejzek, Thea/Allen, Lawrence (2018): *The Model as Performance: Staging Space in Theatre and Architecture*, London: Bloomsbury Publishing.

El-Hitami, Hisham/Mahall, Mona/Serbest, Asli (2023): »An Ecology of Space: Architectural Design for Transboundary Relationships«, in: *AGATHÓN – International Journal of Architecture, Art and Design* 13, 153–164. DOI: https://doi.org/10.19229/2464-9309/13132023.

Morton, Timothy (2010): *Ecology without Nature: Rethinking Environmental Aesthetics*, Cambridge, MA: Harvard University Press.

Ulber, Marie/Mahall, Mona/Serbest, Asli (2021): »Environments: Actions of Adaptation in Architecture«, in: *Loci Communes | International Journal of Studies on Spaces in Arts and Humanities*, Anthropology and Architecture 1/1, 1–17. DOI: https://doi.org/10.31261/LC.2021.01.04.

Design Build Grow Meghalaya
Combining Vernacular and Modern Knowledge

Zijing Deng, Ferdinand Ludwig, Elahe Mahdavi and Wilfrid Middleton

Abstract: With the increasing popularity of regenerative design, vernacular architecture is a growing source of inspiration for architects. This is particularly true in urban settings, where the awareness of interconnected ecological, social, and climatic considerations is growing. In rural Meghalaya, living root bridges play a multi-faceted role in these complex considerations and are present in urban settings such as the state capital, Shillong. This study combines vernacular practices in living root architecture with contemporary design methods to realize a growing pavilion in Shillong, designed and built in the scope of a master's studio, and in collaboration with vernacular architects. Following a research by design framework, this article describes the pre-design collaboration necessary to establish a knowledge base and communication tools, the design development founded on more modern methods, the greater role of vernacular methods in the building, and the post-design reflection. With a firm understanding of vernacular practice, applying modern design tools to living root architecture projects can provide the basis for transferring the rural approach to contemporary urban contexts.

Keywords: Design-build; Research by Design; Vernacular Architecture; Living Architecture; Living Root Bridges; Parametric Design.

Introduction

Vernacular architecture is shaped by a complex network of ecological, climatic, social, economic, and other environmental constraints (Vellinga 2001). As architects turn toward regenerative design and development – buildings that regenerate the social and ecological systems in which they are built (Cole 2012) – we may learn from environmentally embedded vernacular

Corresponding authors: Wilfrid Middleton (Technical University of Munich), wilfrid.middleton@gmail.com; Ferdinand Ludwig (Technical University of Munich), ferdinand.ludwig@tum.de; Elahe Mahdavi (Technical University of Munich), elahe.mahdavi@tum.de; Zijing Deng (Technical University of Munich), zijing.deng@tum.de.
Open Access. © 2024 Wilf Middleton, Zijing Deng, Ferdinand Ludwig and Elahe Mahdavi published by transcript Verlag. This work is licensed under the Creative Commons Attribution 4.0 (BY) license.

1.
A bamboo and rattan short-term bridge over which Ficus elastica aerial roots will grow. Photo by the authors.

architecture. Regenerative design can help architecture see comparisons between similar settings and translate solutions to new contexts (Gabril 2014; Nguyen et al. 2019).

In Meghalaya, the living root bridges are a centuries-old rural transport network formed by the aerial roots of Ficus elastica trees (Ludwig et al. 2019). Many bridges are collaborative social projects, have cultural heritage value, are ecologically significant (as pioneer and climax trees), and are carbon sinks. Most bridge-growers begin with a temporary bamboo bridge that is both a short-term solution and a frame over which to guide the roots as they grow. The timing of the bridge's construction is often informal, fitting around weather changes for example. The bamboos are tied together using a range of materials, most commonly rattan (also referred to as cane). Figure 1 shows one such bridge, a section of a bridge deck interwoven with roots, and a fully grown bridge. In this architecture, the bridges embody the societal conditions under which they are grown: they do not survive without regular maintenance (Middleton et al. 2020). The materials used are specific to the architecture: the bamboos (various Bambusa species are selected for different structural properties), smoked for a week before use and the rattan (various Calamus species) that has been soaked and twisted to tie the bamboos together. Techniques vary across Meghalaya. Some bridge growers have developed specific methods to induce aerial root growth (Middleton 2023). These materials are not only products of the climate-geographic conditions of Meghalaya but also the social conditions: the knowledge of how to grow and treat the materials and their structural limits. Knowledge of these materials fosters versatility. Described as the 'green gold' of northeastern India (Tripathi et al. 2003), bamboo is employed for building houses, furniture, and various everyday objects (Lynser et al. 2015) with many villages developing their own unique weaving patterns. Rattan is often used to create flexible curves in Khasi handcrafts, such as the corners of mats or edges of baskets (Lynser et al. 2015). When utilizing vernacular architecture, designers can draw on this body of knowledge embedded in materials and tools. Examples of vernacular material transferred to modern design can be seen in Anna Heringer's DESI Building (Heringer 2018) or in the standardization of rukarakara adobe bricks, used for construction in Rwanda (LBMTT 2022).

A bamboo and rattan short-term bridge over which Ficus elastica aerial roots will grow (fig. 1); roots woven among a bamboo bridge deck and a fully

2. + 3.
Roots woven among a bamboo bridge deck and a fully formed Ficus bridge in the foreground, a hybrid Ficus and bamboo/rattan bridge in the background.
Photo by the authors.

formed Ficus bridge in the foreground, a hybrid Ficus and bamboo/rattan bridge in the background (fig. 2).

In this project, we focus on the transfer of rural living root architecture to a more urban context. Shillong, the capital city of Meghalaya in northeastern India, is grappling with a range of problems resulting from rapid urbanization (Ryngnga 2018). The key challenges of rapid urbanization in Shillong that have been described include: environmental degradation, in particular the deforestation of large Khasi pine (Pinus kesiya) forests around the city (Hansen et al. 2013); microclimatic problems such as the urban heat island effect (Kachari 2019); water management, particularly in the dry season of October to March (Khadse et al. 2011); and a lack of common cultural reference points that lead to reduced social cohesion (Abbi 2021; Khamrang 2012). Rapid urbanisation often comes with a loss of access – and connection to – nature (Cox et al. 2018), carbon-intensive building practices, (Franco et al. 2017) and degraded ecosystems and insect populations (Czaja et al. 2020). A regenerative assessment of the living root bridges shows that all of these issues are addressed in bridge-growing villages by that practice (Middleton et al. 2020). Based on this, Meghalaya's vernacular living architecture appears to be of potential benefit to Shillong.

This article asks how vernacular and modern knowledge can be combined to transfer living root architecture from remote rainforest valleys to an urban setting, namely a green space at the North-Eastern Hill University (NEHU) in Shillong. Design for an urban setting requires precisely planned interventions with specific timeframes, the flexible use of materials based on complex supply chains, and standardized construction techniques. This is in contrast to the unplanned, growth-responsive interventions of living root architects that use localized materials (of known supply) and diverse techniques (Pelmoine/Mayor 2020). The great diversity of construction techniques used by various practitioners of the Living Bridge Foundation (LBF) is shown in living root bridges (Ludwig et al. 2019). One challenge of constructing in Shillong was standardizing these techniques.

This is explored through the medium of a master's studio, named Design – Build – Grow (DBG) for architecture, landscape architecture, and materials science students from the Technical University of Munich (TUM) and NEHU in Shillong in collaboration with the LBF, a network of living root architecture experts from around Meghalaya.

This article documents and reflects upon the research project. In Section Method, we introduce our methodological framework, the goals for each phase of research, and the tools used to achieve them. In Section Pre-design Outcomes, and Section Design Outcomes, we share the results of our attempts in each phase. Section Post-design Outcomes, focuses on interpreting our findings and includes potential limitations and future directions for research.

Method

Research by Design as Methodological Framework. In examining the DBG studio, this study explores a new design challenge in the research field of living architecture. Research by design, or RbD, is inquiry embedded in the design process (Hauberg 2011; Roggema 2016). In contrast to conventional design, which typically focuses on solving specific problems or creating products based on pre-defined requirements, RbD aims to find creative solutions to open-ended or loosely defined research questions by using a process of trial and error during design (Well and Ludwig 2021; Roggema 2016). The RbD approach is quickly gaining popularity in architectural studies. (Rosa et al. 2014). RbD frames a design project within a research field. In this study, the DBG studio explores the above research question through RbD. In living architecture specifically, research findings feed directly back into the structure through the manipulation of future growth (Shu et al. 2020).

While there is a variety of research methods in RbD (Zimmerman et al. 2007), Roggema (2016) assimilates them into a structure with three main phases: pre-design, design, and post-design. The pre-design phase starts with a broad inquiry into the problem space, which establishes a theoretical base to inform research problems, potential answers, and further design directions. Moving on to the design phase, explicit visions and then solutions are sought out through an iterative and cyclical process. The post-design phase is isolated from design, with the goal of reflecting on the project and communicating new knowledge (Roggema 2016).

This is an intercultural, interdisciplinary study that includes members with varied focuses. Some members are deep but narrow (experts) and the others are shallow but wide (students). Therefore, clear communication is a fundamental requirement throughout the process. In the pre-design phase, the communication is mainly unidirectional: experts teaching students. While in contrast, during the design phase, multidirectional communication is used: students present phased results to the experts from whom they received suggestions and feedback on refining their results.

Pre-Design. In the pre-design phase, the project's foundations are formed. The context of the DBG studio was chosen for the transfer of vernacular architecture to an urban setting, via a park pavilion project. Experts at TUM led students from TUM and NEHU in designing the pavilion, along with input from LBF and NEHU experts. The on-site build was led by the LBF and one member of TUM with input from other students and experts from TUM and LBF. Working across institutions and continents, a mutual level of understanding of particular topics along with flexible communication tools were essential.

These topics were: living architecture design; representation methods; living root architecture, and the Shillong context. Students were introduced to living architecture design by experts at TUM, as was developed in research and practice at TUM and elsewhere (Collet 2018; Ludwig 2012; Middleton et al. 2023; Schuiten 2012). Learning about three-dimensional (3D) representation, students used: photogrammetry to document sites and built models; computer-aided design (CAD) with parametric design using Rhino 6 and Grasshopper (McNeel 2019) to generate built parameters such as material quantities; steel wire physical models; and sketches for representing time. Tuition on living root bridge culture and ecosystems combined with the existing literature (Middleton 2023) and the knowledge of LBF experts. Tuition on other aspects of Khasi architecture and the Shillong setting were provided by lectures from NEHU (Ravishankar and Ji 2021; Sridhar 2020). In addition to structured lectures, students pursued their own research. Through online videos (Chauhan 2020) and botanical literature (Moles et al. 2019) they learned specific methods for aerial root manipulation (details in Section 3. Pre-design Outcomes).

In communicating across continents, the 3D representation tools were useful, particularly during the design phase when moving between physical model-making, online discussion, and prototyping. The software used most frequently, Agisoft Metashape (2019), Cloud Compare and Rhino 6, allow a smooth transition between point clouds and design variations. The other core online communication tools were whiteboards for sharing ideas, sketches, photos and designs, weekly online group meetings, and shared file servers.

Design. Once a common understanding of the context, materials, and tools of design and later construction were established, the design phase began. For this phase, Roggema (2016) proposes three steps: program

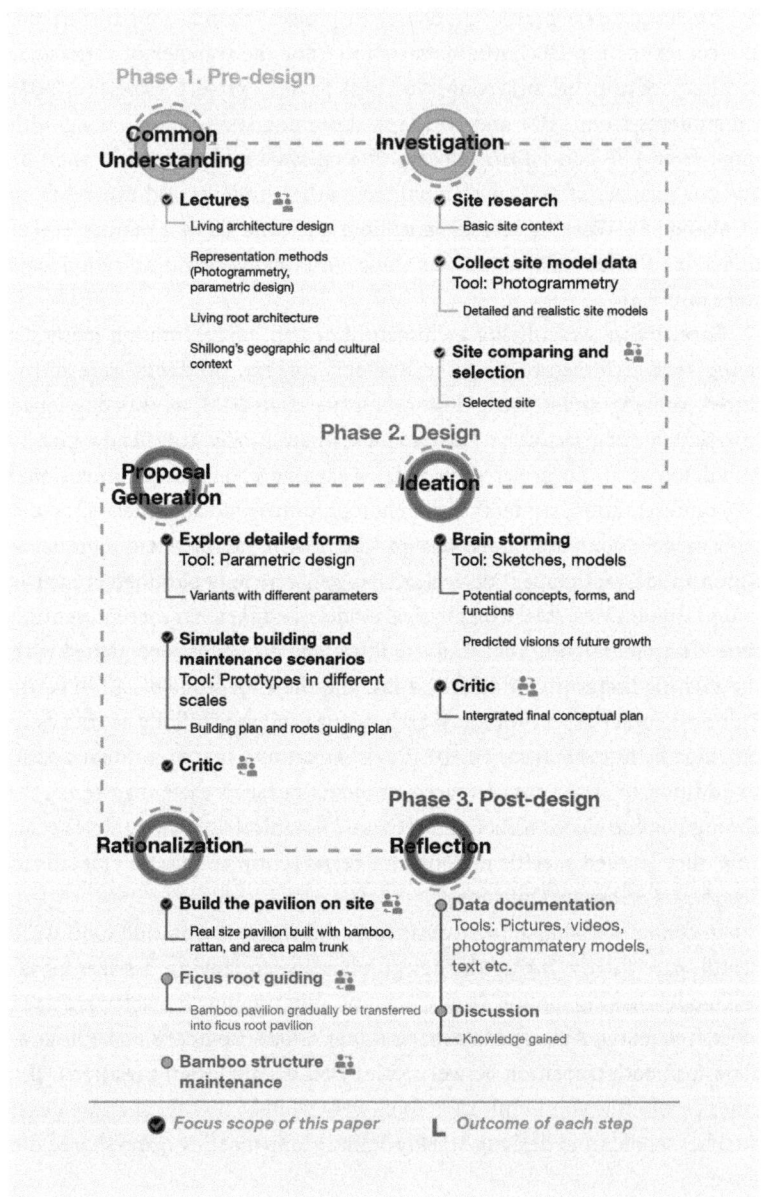

4.
Structure of the design studio, broken down into the phases of the Roggema's research by design framework (Roggema 2016: 175). Illustration by the authors.

(referred to here as »ideation« for specificity, proposal generation, and rationalization.

During the ideation process, brainstorming rounds were held to explore and finalize the assignments and goals of the pavilion based on the knowledge garnered during pre-design. The design team was divided into three groups to develop ideas for the pavilion form, function, and growth. After each round of brainstorming, the ideas were shared, discussed, and selected. This resulted in a conceptual plan of the pavilion that included design intent and function, and predicted visions for the future growth.

With this plan, the design team generated different design proposals, including variants of detailed form (e.g. varied levels and entrances) and structural engineering decisions (section 4.2). When generating variants in form, parametric design played an important role. Using CAD, the designers could quickly modify the form of the pavilion and share the results across continents. The parametric design algorithm used is presented in detail in section 4.2. The core challenge of this proposal generation was to design a short-term buildable functional structure that facilitates the long-term structure's growth.

In the rationalization phase, the team designed details for the foundation, columns, footing, facade, joint, flooring, and sapling planters by studying Meghalaya's traditional architecture and other bamboo projects (Chung et al. 2002; Ravishankar and Ji 2021). Moving from designing on paper to on-site realization involved a change in teams – the build process was led by LBF members while the design process was led by TUM and NEHU members. By experimenting with 1:10 prototypes, the design team proposed a building plan to demonstrate each step of construction in a chronological sequence. These were improved with 1:1 prototypes built by LBF to test and revise particular details, such as the flooring and a planter-column (details in section 4.3). The design team proposed a manipulation plan to guide Ficus elastica growth on the bamboo structure and simulated growth based on certain planting scenarios (shown in section 4.3). The bamboo pavilion was built, and the saplings planted on the NEHU campus in November 2022. Some changes to the design were made due to unforeseen circumstances (detailed in section 4.3.1).

Post-Design. Post-design is a reflection of the project's outcome with respect to research questions, i.e. how a combination of vernacular and modern knowledge can facilitate the transfer of vernacular living root architecture to an urban setting. This then cycles into other RbD projects and

5. + 6.
Point cloud models of the potential sites.
Photos by the authors.

allows future projects to benefit from the findings. The image shows the flow of the three phases, the tools used, and the outcomes achieved in each phase (fig. 2). The illustration visualizes the structure of the design studio, broken down into the phases of Roggema's (2016) research by design framework (fig. 4).

Pre-Design Outcomes

Alongside lectures, students learned about the growth patterns of Ficus elastica by making steel wire models of trees growing on obstacles. Additionally, through a literature review and online research, students found a method to stimulate the Ficus aerial roots to grow in specific places. First, create a wound on the specific spot with a clean knife. Then, cover the wound with moss and a waterproof (e.g. polythene) layer to keep it moist. This method mirrors a technique developed by LBF experts. Extracting the essential parts of this technique by comparing modern scientific literature and vernacular online grey literature and LBF accounts, allowed the students to integrate a dynamic growth process into their design.

The design team investigated the project's location. Shillong has a highly diverse population of around 500,000 which was growing rapidly at around 2.9 percent per year (GoI 2023) and few urban green spaces. Winters (October–March) are cool and dry in Shillong while summers (April–September) are hot with a high level of rainfall (India Meteorological Department 2015). The climate is suitable for Ficus elastica to grow, as shown by multiple trees in the city. Ficus elastica and its aerial roots grow widely in urban settings, including in Hong Kong (Jim 2014), Kathmandu (Rai and Mandal 2020), Singapore, (Harrison et al. 2017) and Sydney (Moles et al. 2019). NEHU students collected photogrammetric data for two sites: Lady Hydari Park and Ward's Lake (fig. 5 and 6). Other sites were documented by photos only: the Lion's Club Park and two sites on the NEHU campus. Both sites have key similarities: open ground with a light gradient and access to a body of water. Within these documentations, designs and site could be brought together in a digital space. One of the NEHU campus sites was chosen for the pavilion.

Design Outcomes

The details of pavilion design presented here include the concept, morphological variants, engineering structure, construction proposals, and root-guiding plans. The building and ongoing guiding processes are also described as part of the realization phase in which the design was revised owing to problems encountered during construction.

Ideation. In the ideation phase, different proposals were explored and certain principles for the transfer of LRBs to an urban pavilion were established. First, the pavilion should fit the community's identity: fitting the campus environment and representing Meghalaya. Second, it should restore connections to nature. Third, it should be multi-functional. Where LRBs are foremost a means of transport, the pavilion should provide different uses for different people. As a result, a combination of the themes of culture, people, and material informed the final design. Culture is the fountainhead of the design concept. The conceptual form of the pavilion comes from mountains and caves – the celebrated landscapes of Meghalaya. Two curved lines compose two different spaces: the higher level represents the mountain, while the ground level creates an enclosed cave space. By integrating Meghalaya's celebrated landscapes, the pavilion draws users from different backgrounds and cultures onto common ground.

Its use by humans turns a pavilion from a giant sculpture into a place of life and culture. Based on the different atmospheres on the ground and higher levels, different functions for people using the pavilion were designed. The enclosed cave is conceived as a shelter from monsoon storms and a maze-like space to explore. The mountainous top has different levels to give the feeling of climbing, and a viewing platform where people can rest and look out over the lake.

For people to gain a sense of material, the design follows a geometric grid of bamboos, tied together using rattan. The Ficus aerial roots are intended to grow between the grid. These three topological roles (grid, knot, and weave) exhibit the three materials from which they are made (bamboo, rattan, and aerial roots). The process of guiding Ficus on the bamboo grid shows the progress from saplings to structural trees and the structure as living in two senses: made from living material and changing with time.

Proposal Generation. The proposed design consisted primarily of a 3D grid of vertical and horizontal bamboos. The nodes at which elements intersect perform two functions: transferring forces across the structural network and creating the form generated from the parametric curves. A grid of multiple intersecting bamboos provides redundancy in the structure. This is beneficial both for ensuring structural stability and for enabling changes over time. Replacing individual bamboos or knots (when decayed or overgrown by structural roots) is relatively easy, allowing the maintenance of the pavilion. These were important considerations given the uncertainties over exactly what bamboo materials would be available. Of the two types of bamboo that are generally used in Meghalaya, »siej« (likely Bambusa vulgaris) has a shorter lifespan than »rñai« (likely Bambusa tulda). This meant that the estimated lifespans of the bamboo elements can vary between two and five years, so a structural system in which individual bamboos can be replaced is essential. Construction is simplified by the regular arrangement of the elements and the repetition of similar knot types.

Once the basic design was decided, it was built using parametric tools in CAD. The core parameters were the diameter of bamboos, the density of the bamboo grid, the site dimensions, and the shapes of the curved surfaces, shown as inputs in. This allowed the feasibility of construction to be considered, such as ensuring the grid had gaps large enough for workers to reach through. Overall, the parametric algorithm follows a three-step process. First, a 3D matrix representing the central axes of the bamboo is created using two parameters: the pavilion dimensions (5 metres in height and a rectangular base of 5 metres x 10 metres) and the grid density. Within this cuboid, several curved surfaces (defined by movable control points) are used to trim the bamboos into the mountain-cave form. Finally, radii are assigned to the bamboos. Designs are then made by changing the variables at each step. The results are conceptual architectural forms with meaningful outputs: amounts and sizes of bamboo and user and construction space.

Rationalization. In addition to the grid, the design included a facade, pillars, flooring, and foundations. A column fitting the grid was designed to be placed at points throughout the pavilion. The column also acted as a sapling planter by rising above the floor level. The planters were designed as a sparsely woven bamboo mat wrapped on to vertical bamboos, to be filled with moss. Almost all connections were made with square lashings (with occasional shear lashings). Prototypes at a scale of 1:10 were made of a section of the pavilion, a planter, and connections (fig. 7). This developed the aesthetic design and viable joint combinations based on string lashings. A 1:1 column prototype was made, developing the design for Ficus planters at the top of each column.

7. + 8.
1:1 prototyping of the grid structure and flooring system in Meghalaya
Photo by the authors.

The flooring was designed from slats of Areca catechu palm trunks, a by-product of the betel nuts farmed in large quantities in Meghalaya that is commonly used in construction. A 1:1 prototype was made (fig. 6 and 7). This helped the design team to understand the time allotted to joint lashing, the stability achieved by hand-tensioned rattan lashings, the space needed to perform this handiwork (and the resulting impact on grid size), and some aesthetic qualities. When designing the foundation, space close to the bamboos is needed for the roots to directly replace them over time. The chosen foundation underpins specific areas of the four walls, with the bamboos sitting on a padstone 60 centimeters below ground. A large stone aggregate concrete was used as infill. Regarding the facade, the outer wall consists of double-density vertical bamboos. These bamboo elements also serve a secondary function and act as handrails at higher levels.

The growth plan for Ficus elastica involved four phases of intervention, as shown in (fig. 7). The saplings are planted on top of the pillars. In the first five years the maintenance focuses on guiding the roots vertically to the ground. When the roots implant, they help to reinforce the pillar. Between the fifth and tenth years, maintenance focuses on weaving roots through the ceiling of the »cave« and gradually guiding them to the ground. In this phase, the roots begin to support the weight of the pavilion. In ten to fifteen years, the roots will be guided through the upper surface (the »hill«) to the ground. In the following years, manipulation involves gradually filling the gaps and reinforcing them as the grower sees fit while maintaining the shape of the pavilion.

Build. The built pavilion (fig. 10) consists mostly of rñai bamboo, including all vertical elements. Around one-third of the less critical elements were made from siej bamboo. All bamboos were smoke-treated in the traditional Khasi method for ten days before use – reducing the starch content on which termites feed (Kaur et al. 2016). A mix-up about who would cut and smoke the bamboo, and transportation issues caused a delay of several days. The rattan was sourced in the village of Laitiam. It was grown on a cliff allowing it to grow into very long pieces. Older rattan pieces were favoured as they are generally more resistant to decay (according to the grower). Connection tying was the most labour-intensive task on site. Sourcing and preparing the relatively small number of Areca palms was simple. Due to the diversity of the LBF's members and their construction methods, some effort went into standardizing key techniques: cutting bamboo sections; lashing with rattan; and attaching the Areca palm flooring.

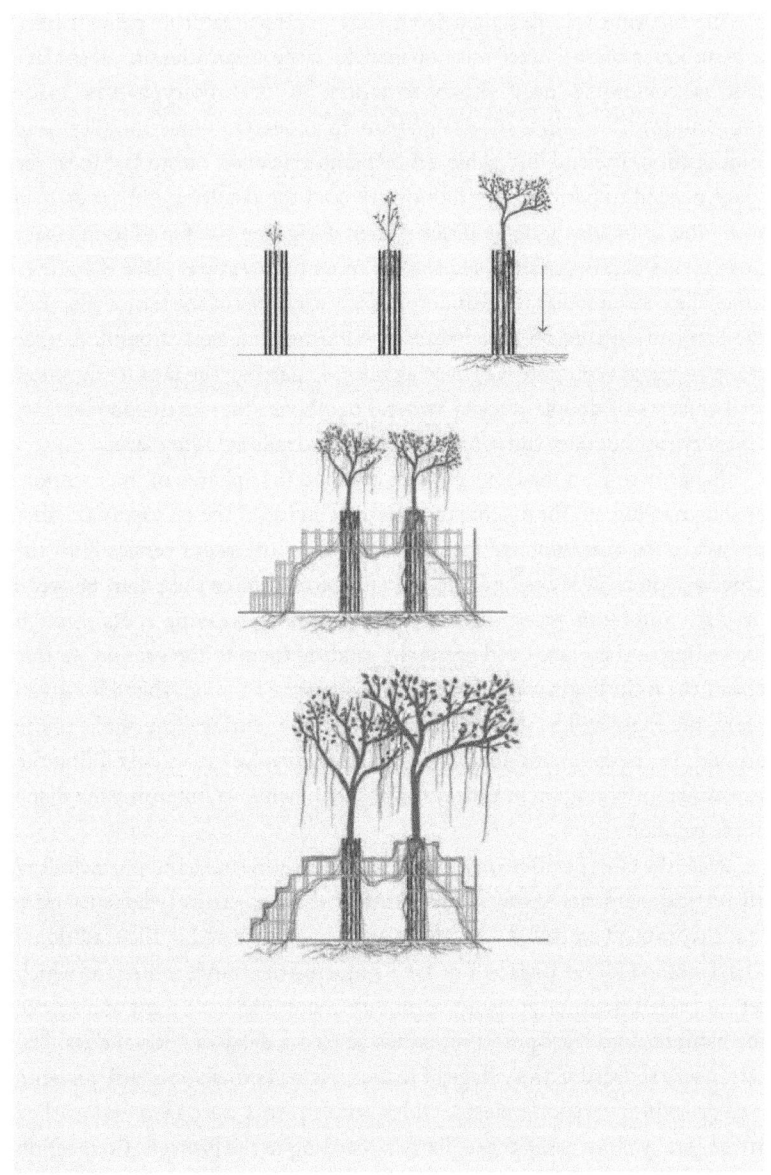

9.
Growth plan for the saplings and aerial roots on columns to show gradual replacement of the bamboo with Ficus trees after 5, 15 and 30 years. Illustration by the authors.

Due to time constraints caused by the delay in sourcing bamboo, two structural changes were made to the design. First, the two separate levels of the structure – the roof of the ›cave‹ and the floor of the ›mountain‹ – were consolidated. To compensate in structural stability, several columns were added. As well as simplifying the build, this changed the growth plan: the separate layers of growth (planned in years five to fifteen) are consolidated, while more roots will need to be guided to the columns. Second, the varied floor levels were simplified. The original design was for stepwise height differences in both horizontal directions with many small levels. The constructed pavilion consists of two halves: a stairway of many wide, short steps rising in one direction to the middle of the pavilion and nine separate levels in a 3x3 grid at different heights in the half of the pavilion facing the lake. This reduced the number of connection tie points from around 4,000 to around 2,000.

Following these simplifications and some small changes in the grid density, the planned construction scaffold was not used. Instead, the four walls were first built precisely and then used as guide points for the rest of the structure. The grown structure will begin to emerge over the coming years. Five saplings were planted in December 2022, with disappointing results after an unexpectedly dry spring in 2023. Just one sapling survived, though it has grown significantly more than expected. In a later planting phase in 2023, the saplings were planted closer to the ground. Annual checks on the state of Ficus growth and bamboo decay were carried out. Photogrammetry will allow this data to be shared with international partners, while assessment by LBF practitioners was essential.

Post-Design Outcomes

This study explores the potential to combine vernacular and modern architectural methods for the transfer of vernacular living root architecture to a modern urban setting. Similar application of vernacular techniques in modern urban design can be found in numerous examples around the world, such as the timber-laced masonry in earthquake-resistant buildings (Langenbach 2007) and courtyards in microclimate regulation (Rojas-Fernández 2017). The studio Design – Build – Grow Meghalaya draws on the local tradition of living root architecture to design a pavilion that integrates living trees to combat the challenges of rapid urbanization as described in the introduction. Through this open-ended RbD project, the benefits and

10.
The built bamboo pavilion in November 2022.
Photo by the authors.

limitations of combining vernacular and modern methods were identified. These are discussed below, as is the role of communication tools in the process.

The group combined desk-based (lectures, research) and practical learning (sketching, modelling, prototypes) to gain a foundational knowledge of the hand-construction properties of bamboo and rattan, the growth properties of Ficus Elastica, and the materials' variables. This led to a parametric design that was adaptable – the structure of the 3D grid and the make-up of bamboo species were changed during construction without having to change the pavilion's form or construction methods. Parametric design allowed for the quick comparison of possible design variants.

While parametric design provides a useful medium for combining modern and vernacular thinking, it has its limits. The scaffolding plan was over-complicated and so not used. This is a potential pitfall of parametric design. It quickly produces complicated structures that don't meet the construction team's needs. More widely, it will be some years before the pavilion's growth and the corresponding design can be assessed in the RbD framework applied to the short-term structure here. Part of the transition from rural-vernacular to modern-urban living architecture is considering the role of community participation in its growth. In this regard, NEHU is a stepping stone: a community of relatively like-minded people – university students and staff – with some institutional structures regarding estate management and rules about use. Periodic photogrammetric surveys that involve NEHU students in the pavilion's development are planned: capturing bamboo decay and root growth, and planning interventions with the LBF. This documentation may inform future growth simulations that could also include manipulations. A further step toward an urban setting would involve a more diverse community.

The pavilion's construction can only be seen as the first step in the transfer of rural forms of living root architecture to an urban context. In fact, the conditions of the realization within the municipal area of Shillong can be described as urban in terms of the legal framework and users. Nevertheless, the project is located in a green area and not in a dense urban context. To realize living root architecture that combines vernacular and modern knowledge in such a context is the research project's long-term goal. This endeavour comes with a number of additional challenges, including growth conditions. Examples such as the Ficus Walls in Hong Kong (Jim 2014) show that banyan trees such as Ficus Elastica can grow very well under such conditions, thus illustrating the project's feasibility.

The ongoing communication between groups at TUM, NEHU and LBF was key at several points in the project, with different communication tools being used at different points. In particular, pre-design teaching by experts in several countries was enabled by video meetings; site understanding was allowed by photogrammetry; and prototyping, the subsequent feedback, and design changes during construction were allowed by 3D digital models. As the pavilion and its associated body of knowledge grows, photogrammetry, derivative 3D models, and online meetings will remain useful.

Conclusion

The potential interactions of vernacular and modern architectural methods are diverse. This study shows the use of modern design methods (e.g. CAD and photogrammetry) that integrate vernacular knowledge (e.g. Ficus growth) and techniques (e.g. bamboo construction and rattan lashing) to deal with the challenges of an urban setting (e.g. complex supply chains and limited construction time). This urban design approach must be informed by, and adapt to, the body of vernacular technological, material, and botanical knowledge. This is facilitated by various types of communication: spoken lectures, questions, and conversations; sketched and built ideas; and precise digital models of sites and designs. This combination can both broaden the potential uses of vernacular architecture and give modern designers access to new areas of knowledge.

Acknowledgments

We would like to thank several parties for their help in the completion of the master's studio Design – Build – Grow, the construction of the pavilion, and the associated study. The project was partially funded by The Ove Arup Foundation, a UK-registered charity. The LBF and their members, particularly Shiningstar Khongthaw, were essential to the project. Several people at NEHU, especially Ibynta Tiewsoh, helped to complete the project.

Various people at TUM helped to bring the project about, including Jasmin Raudensky. We thank the peer-reviewers for their valuable input. The students involved in the studio were particularly essential to the project's completion.

References

Abbi, Anvita (2021): »Social Cohesion and Emerging Standards of Hindi in a Multilingual Context«, in: Wendy Ayres Bennett/John Bellamy (eds.), *The Cambridge Handbook of Language Standardization*, Cambridge: Cambridge University Press, 115–138.

Chauhan, V. S. (2020): *Top 3 Ways to Create Aerial Roots on Banyan Bonsai*, https://www.youtube.com/watch?v=NQ-iPIdQYXA (accessed July 23, 2024).

Chung, K. F./Chan, S. L/Yu, W. (2002): »Recent Developments on Bamboo Scaffolding in Building Construction«, in: *Advances in Building Technology 1*, 629–636.

Cole, Raymond J. (2012): *Regenerative Design and Development: Current Theory and Practice*, London: Taylor & Francis.

Collet, Valérie (2018): *Les fabuleuses cités végétales de Luc Schuiten*, www.hortus-focus.fr, https://magazine.hortus-focus.fr/blog/2018/09/17/les-fabuleuses-cites-vegetales-de-luc-schuiten-1/, accessed: April 7, 2024.

Cox, Daniel T./Shanahan, Danielle F. /Hudson, Hannah L./Fuller, Richard A./Gaston, Kevin J. (2018): »The Impact of Urbanisation on Nature Dose and the Implications for Human Health«, in: *Landscape and Urban Planning 179*, 72–80.

Czaja, Monika Agata/Kołton, Anna/Muras, Piotr (2020): »The Complex Issue of Urban Trees – Stress Factor Accumulation and Ecological Service Possibilities«, in: *Forests, 11/9*, 932.

Franco, Sainu/Mandla, Venkata Ravibabu/Rao, Ram Mohan (2017): »Urbanization, Energy Consumption and Emissions in the Indian Context: A Review«, in: *Renewable and Sustainable Energy Review, 71*, 898–907.

Gabril, Nadya (2014): »Thermal Comfort and Building Design Strategies for Low-energy Houses in Libya« in: *Lessons from the Vernacular Architecture, Conference: Next Genereation Research*, University of Westminster, London, UK.

GoI, G. o. I. (2023): Shillong Urban Region Population 2011–2023, https://www.census2011.co.in/census/metropolitan/176-shillong.html (accessed: July 5, 2023).

Hansen, M. C./Potapov, P. V./Moore, R./Hancher, M./Turubanova, S. A/Tyukavina, A./Thau, D./Stehman, S. V./Goetz, S. J./Loveland, T. R. (2013): »High-resolution Global Maps of 21st-century Forest Cover Change«, in: *Science, 342/6160*, 850–853.

Harrison, Rhett D./Chong, Kwek Yan/Pham, Nguyet Minh/Yee, Alex Thiam/Yeo, C. K./Tan, Hugh T./Rasplus, Jean-Yves (2017): »Pollination of Ficus elastica: India Rubber Re-establishes Sexual Reproduction in Singapore« ,in: *Scientific Reports 7*, 11616.

Hauberg, Jørgen (2011): »Research by Design: A Research Strategy«, in: *Architecture & Education Journal 5*, 46–56.

Heringer, Anna (2018): »DESI Training Center: Self-sufficiency and Appropriateness«, https://urbannext.net/desi-trainingcenter/, accessed: April 7, 2024.

India Meteorological Department (2015): »Station: Shillong (C.S.O) Climatological Table 1981–2010«, in: DEPARTMENT, I. M. (ed.).

Jim, C. Y. (2014): »Ecology and Conservation of Strangler Figs in Urban Wall Habitats« ,in: *Urban Ecosystems 17*, 405–426.

Kachari, R. (2019): »Swelter in the City: Population Distribution, Land Use Change and the Urban Heat Island Effect in Shillong, India«, in: Anup Saikia/Pankaj Thapa (eds.), *Environmental Change in the Himalayan Region: Twelve Case Studies*, 173–187.

Kaur, Perminder Jit/Satya, Santosh/Pant, K./Naik, Satya/Kardam, Vikas (2016): »Chemical Characterization and Decay Resistance Analysis of Smoke-treated Bamboo Species«, in: *European Journal of Wood and Wood Products 74*, 625– 628.

Khadse, Gajanan/Kalita, Morami/Pimpalkar, S./Labhasetwar, Pawan (2011): »Surveillance of Drinking Water Quality for Safe Water Supply: A Case Study from Shillong, India«, in: *Water Resources Management 25*, 3321–3342.

Khamrang, Leishimpem (2012): »Perceived Quality of Life in the Cities of Northeast India: A Welfare Geographical Perspective«, in: *International Journal of Social Science Tomorrow*, 1/3, 1–10.

Langenbach, Randolph (2007): »From ›Opus Craticium‹ to the ›Chicago Frame‹: Earthquake-Resistant Traditional Construction«, in: *International Journal of Architectural Heritage 1*/1, 29–59.

LBMTT (2022): »Best Practices in Adobe Block (Rukarakara) Construction in Rwanda«. https://massdesigngroup.org/work/research/adobe-block-rukarakara-standards (accessed April 7, 2024).

Ludwig, Ferdinand (2012): *Botanische Grundlagen der Baubotanik und deren Anwendung im Entwurf* (PhD thesis), Technical University of Munich, Germany.

Ludwig, Ferdinand/Middleton, Wilf/Gallenmüller, Friederike/Rogers, Patrick/Speck, Thomas (2019): »Living Bridges Using Aerial Roots of Ficus elastica : An interdisciplinary Perspective«, in: *Scientific Reports 9*/12226, 1–11.

Lynser, M./Tiwari, B./Nongbri, B./Kharlyngdoh, E. (2015): »Bamboo Mat Making and Its Contribution to the Rural Livelihood of Women in South Meghalaya, India«, in: *J Am Bamboo Soc 28*, 23–31.

Middleton, Wilf/Habibi, Amin/Shankar, Sanjeev/Ludwig, Ferdinand (2020): »Characterizing Regenerative Aspects of Living Root Bridges«, in: *Sustainability 12*/8, 3267.

Middleton, Wilf/Erdal, Halil Ibrahim/Detter, Andreas /D'Acunto, Pierluigi/Ludwig, Ferdinand (2023): »Comparing Structural Models of Linear Elastic Responses to Bending in Inosculated Joints«, in: *Trees 37*, 891–903.

Middleton, Wilf (2023): »Methods and Workflows for Design and Engineering, in: Living Architecture:«, in: *Learning from Living Root Bridges*, Munich: Technical University of Munich.

Moles, A. T./Jagdish, A./Wu, Y./Gooley, S./Dalrymple, R. L./Feng, P./Auld, J./Badgery, G./Balding, M./Bell, A. (2019): »From Dangerous Branches to Urban Banyan: Facilitating Aerial Root Growth of Ficus rubiginosa«, in: *PLOSOne*, 14/12, e0226845.

Nguyen, Anh Tuan/ Truong, Nguyen Song Ha/Rockwood, David/Le, Anh Dung Tran (2019): »Studies on Sustainable Features of Vernacular Architecture in Different Regions Across the World: A Comprehensive Synthesis and Evaluation«, in: *Frontiers of Architectural Research 8*/4, 535–548.

Pelmoine, Thomas/Mayor, Anne (2020): »Vernacular Architecture in Eastern Senegal: Chaînes opératoires and Technical Choices«, in: *Journal of Material Culture 25*/3, 348–378.

Rai, Asmita/Mandal, Ram Asheshwar (2020): »Performance of Cinnamomum camphora, Ficus benjamina, Ficus elastica, Prunus cerasoides and Syzygium cumini against Air Pollution in Kathmandu Valley Nepal«, in: *Biomedical Journal of Scientific & Technical Research* 25/3, 19118–19125.

Ravishankar, Srinidhi/Ji, Shiva (2021): »Influence of Culture and Tradition in the Tribal Architecture of Meghalaya«, in: A. Chakrabarti/R. Poovaiah/P. Bokil/ V. Kant (eds.), *Design for Tomorrow—Volume 3: Smart Innovation, Systems and Technologies* 223, 775–782.

Roggema, Rob (2016): »Research by Design: Proposition for a Methodological Approach«, in: *Urban Science* 1/1, 2.

Rojas-Fernández, Juan/Galán-Marín, Carmen/Roa-Fernández, Jorge/Rivera-Gómez, Carlos (2017): »Correlations between GIS-Based Urban Building Densification Analysis and Climate Guidelines for Mediterranean Courtyards«, in: *Sustainability* 9/12, 2255.

Ryngnga, Phibankhamti (2018): »Characteristics & Consequences of Urbanization in India's North East: A Case of Shillong«, in: *International Journal for Scientific Research & Development* 6/8, 581–585.

Schuiten, L. (2012): La Cité Végétale d'Arte Sella en Italie, http://www.vegetalcity.net/en/arte-sella-2012/, accessed July 5, 2023.

Shu, Qiguan/Middleton, Wilf/Dörstelmann, Moritz /Santucci, Daniele/Ludwig, Ferdinand (2020): »Urban Microclimate Canopy: Design, Manufacture, Installation, and Growth Simulation of a Living Architecture Prototype«, in: *Sustainability* 12/15, 6004.

Sridhar, Harsha (2020): »Building Disaster Resilience through Sustainable Housing: An Initiative in Meghalaya«, in: Janki Andharia (eds.), *Disaster Studies: Exploring Intersectionalities in Disaster Discourse*, 221–253.

Tripathi, Yogesh Chandra/Singh, Sushma/Hazarika, Prosanta (2003): »Bamboo – The Green Gold of Northeastern India«, in: G.Tripathi/A. Kumar (eds.), *Potentials of Living Resources*, 378.

Vellinga, Marcel (2024): *Encyclopedia of Vernacular Architecture of the World*, London: Bloomsbury Publishing.

Well, Friederike/Ludwig, Ferdinand (2021): »Development of an Integrated Design Strategy for Blue-Green Architecture«, in: *Sustainability* 13/14, 7944.

Zimmerman, John/Forlizzi, Jodi/Evenson, Shelley (2007): »Research through Design as a Method for Interaction Design Research in HCI, Human–Computer Interaction Institute«, in: *Paper 41*, http://repository.cmu.edu/hcii/4, accessed July 5, 2023.

New Vernacular

Tim Simon-Meyer and João Quintela

Abstract: The aim of this article is to explore an experimental approach to the topic of a new vernacular architecture by presenting and reflecting on a design-build project done with reused materials from a local context and developed and realized with a group of students and people from diverse contexts. We will take a look to the process of creation and its specific conditions. Followed by a reflection on shifting perspectives within the design process and a conclusion on the relevance of such projects.

Keywords: Tectonics; Design-Build; Vernacular Architecture; Reuse; Teaching.

Introduction

In the past, it was natural to build houses from the materials available in the immediate surrounding area. Architecture was not primarily the result of a design process that culminated in the realization of an idea. Rather, it was the result of an examination of the available materials and their potential for building a house. The common knowledge of how to process these materials was part of a local community's cultural heritage and embodied knowledge. Vernacular architecture was not seen as an individual achievement, but rather as the outcome of community actions(Rudofsky 1964). Its self-evident beauty evolved out of, and with, the place and all its social, physical, climatic characteristics and it naturally had a sustainable character as it unfolds its strength in the close relationship with resources and people.

Today, the building materials are being transported around the globe. They are universally available, along with the knowledge and possibilities of their processing. As Anne Holtrop points out: »if you construct something you always have at least two sites, you have the site where you get the material from and you have the site where you construct on«.

Corresponding authors: Tim Simon-Meyer (Bauhaus-Universität Weimar, Germany), timsimonmeyer@gmail.com; João Quintela (Atelier JQTS).
Open Access. © 2024 Tim Simon-Meyer and João Quintela published by transcript Verlag. This work is licensed under the Creative Commons Attribution 4.0 (BY) license.

152   Tim Simon-Meyer and João Quintela

1.
Demolition Hamburg Wilhelmsburg.
Photo: Tim Simon-Meyer.

This means that choosing a material that is geographically distant from the site you construct on, not only has an economic and environmental impact, but also affects the distant landscape and territory in a very profound way. With the advancing climate crisis and the increasing awareness of the responsibility of the building industry (as architects we are part of it), the critical scrutiny of this situation has become a necessity, because striving for climate change means striving for a change in building. This change does not only entail building without having negative impacts on the planet but creating positive implications, such as that envisioned by Bauhaus Earth:

> »A future where our buildings, cities, and landscapes proactively contribute to climate restoration and have a positive impact on the planet and its inhabitants.« (Bauhaus Earth 2023).

In order to engender change in building culture, architects and the building industry must become more aware, but must also rethink the idea of society as users – without yet discussing the political responsibility to define rational parameters for a sustainable way of building.

Expectations and claims surrounding the »new«, the »universally available« and the »always better« must be interrogated both ethically and aesthetically. Instead, considering the »regional available«, giving value to a »beauty of the used« and creating an attitude of sufficiency can support forward-looking approaches to our material world. In their research project Under Construction: A Real World Fiction, Daniell Norell and Einar Rodhe imagine »a city that is constantly being rebuilt using the same stock of materials (Norell/Rodhe 2021: 189).

Understanding the built environment as a »stock of materials« means being confronted with demolition simultaneously, a practice which is still being carried out on a large scale (fig. 1). If we consider the demolition material as raw material for future buildings we enter into a new relation with our built environment and the materials currently stored within existing structures. This could be the way to a new kind of vernacular thinking.

However, due to globalization, an architecture that emerges from the available materials of any globalized place will by no means be as site-specific as the vernacular architecture described earlier. The »same« materials have been used in different cities, countries, and continents.

In this particular context, we as designers are asked to be inventive in order to turn the universal into something specific that can

2.
Zinnergie.
Photo: Tim Simon-Meyer.

establish a relationship to place and people, as well as to culture and nature. And as Dirk Hebel points out:

> »This architecture must have its own aesthetic, a breathtakingbeauty, otherwise it will not be loved and cared for and therefore willnot last.« (Hebel 2020: 166)

Experiment, Methods, Material

As mentioned previously, a genuine change in building culture requires the willingness and proactive participation of numerous players and institutions related to building.

In the case presented here we focus on the academic context as it offers space for speculation that enables us to ignore certain criteria like economic efficiency and focus on very specific ones like material flows. As such, they should be seen as laboratories for experimentation that explore new paths and develop different strategies to be implemented in public life as a reaction to current societal problems.

In this way, our design-build project ZINNERGIE is an attempt to create the architecture for a small urban biogas plant from locally collected and reused materials in a collaborative design and construction process. Integrated into a social context and framed as a collective experiment, students and teachers from different disciplines and institutions, such as HCU Hamburg, UAL Lisboa or TU Hamburg, worked together with local schoolchildren, experts, and residents. Individual knowledge and collective experience was shared to inform the project on different levels.

In doing so, we intended to make reusing building materials accessible on a physical and sensory level, translating it into an aesthetic experience through the potential of tectonics, i.e. »the poetics of construction«. (Frampton 1995) (fig. 1). On the one hand, this happened during the process of designing and building through direct manual and physical work with the available materials to investigate their constructive and creative potential.

On the other hand, it happened in the experience and »use« of the architecture by highlighting the sensual qualities of the materials and an architectural expression that seeks a dialogue with the user. As all of the constructive joints were designed as reversible solutions they expressed the way they are thought of and made. As such, the entire project could be easily dismantled in the future so that the materials could be given a new lease of life.

156 Tim Simon-Meyer and João Quintela

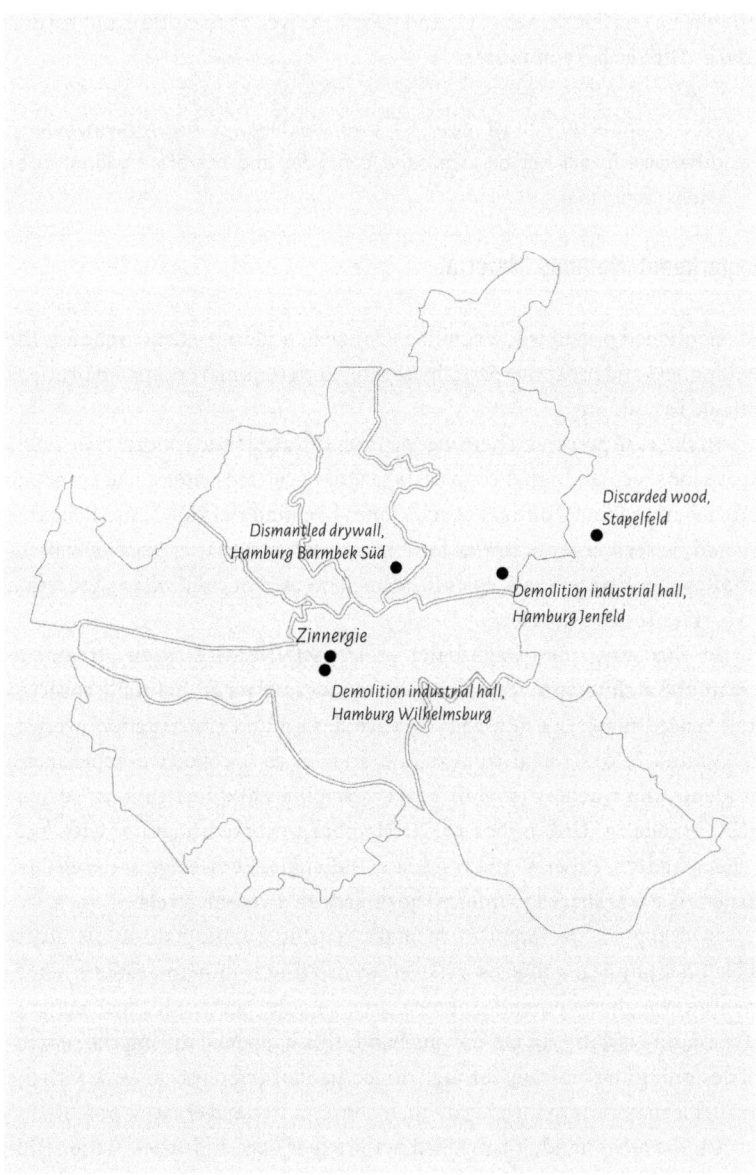

3.
Collecting, Map of Hamburg.
Illustration: Johanna Schmeifer.

Result

Following the demand to only use existing materials and to avoid the use of »new« materials, a change inevitably occurred in the design process. The following steps marked the design work:

Collecting: Before starting any process of actively designing, we searched for building materials available in the immediate area – be they found materials, building materials reclaimed from demolition, or discarded low-grade materials.We contacted demolition companies, located demolition sites, and asked vendors for useless and discarded materials. This was followed by the collective deconstruction of potential building materials on demolition sites (fig. 2–3). It is important to stress that materials from demolition do not mean that they don't have an associated value. On the contrary, they have their own value, and this should be seen as a way of supporting a local and circular economy and a paradigm shift in consumer society.

Sifting: After collecting a stock of materials we were cataloging them through photographing, measuring, and drawing and determining the specific number of items. This also helped to form an initial assessment of the quality of the materials and a categorization that organized them by their properties (fig. 4–5). One might think that the existence of a catalog containing available discarded materials related to a certain geography would encourage this new approach and lead to its expansion.

Testing: Through physical interaction with the materials we experienced their properties bodily. Through the act of making, constructive and creative ideas arose and through critical observation the concept was clarified. Different joining tests revealed the materials' tectonic potential. This helped to determine and formulate design requirements in addition to construction specifications (fig. 6–7). The final solutions became inevitable due to the material properties themselves. In a similar way to Louis Kahn asking the brick what it wants to be, we searched for the materials' inherent qualities and capacities through a physical dialogue with them (Kahn 1971).

Configuring: Detached findings were brought together to form a coherent whole. Using tectonic solutions, we tried to acknowledge structural necessities and at the same time, to respond to creative claims (fig. 8–9). According to Renzo Piano, construction details can confer civic dignity upon a buildin (Piano 2018). The same is true in this case. Constructive details and joints not only provide the building with civic dignity, but they also reveal a direct response to the problems we face today.

4. + 5.
Collecting and Sifting.
Photo: Maischa Souaga, Tim Simon-Meyer.

Discussion

Rethinking how we build starts with questioning how we currently think, develop, and teach architecture. Reflection on the presented design process revealed a shift in emphasis. For example, steps 3 and 4, which mark the actual design work, occurred during a two-week summer school, while the search for materials took several months, due to issues of localizing potential materials, evaluating their constitution, excavating and transporting them. It was only personal motivation and the investment in this project that made it possible to act in this way, as there is currently no market for used or unexcavated materials. Organizations and platforms such as the German Concular or the Belgian Rotor Deconstruction mark a significant shift in creating a framework for trading materials that have already been used.

To resort to what is already available also means to deal out decisions, like the precise choice of materials to build with. In turn, this often means being confronted with the heterogeneity of materials and with materials that do not initially complement each other.

Working under these conditions resembles the work of the bricoleur who »makes do with what is at hand« (Lévi-Strauss 1962). The challenge is to combine these heterogenous materials to make something coherent and meaningful, aiming for a tectonics that celebrates »being different«. This approach is unavoidable and also questions aesthetic standards in architecture, such as the requirement for materials to be perfectly clean and not show any marks of processing or of a previous life. On the other hand, if we consider demolition as a natural phase in the life of a building, we begin to think of an architectural project in a radically different way. It will begin with a set of previously existing demolition materials, but will be thought of in a constructive way as a reversible structure. The tectonic solutions that emerge from this way of thinking open up new possibilities for the discipline and immediately introduce an ethical and aesthetic perspective at the same time.

6.
Testing.
Photo: Maischa Souaga.

Conclusion

As architects we have the responsibility to force a change in building culture and as academics we must incorporate its meaning into the teaching of architecture. Universities can be understood as laboratories that provide the answers to questions about our society's future.

To convey not only an intellectual awareness, but to make it a physical experience and ›embody‹ it in the truest sense of the word, we believe physical interaction with the world of materials and resources to be extremely valuable. The format of the design-build project allows designing and building to occur simultaneously while including numerous actors.

It moves from a theoretical confrontation with the climate crisis to a physical one and furthermore, it conceptualizes it as an issue of design and aesthetics.

Although projects like this are unable to resolve contemporary problems, they allow us to test forward-thinking approaches on a smaller scale and integrate them into society. In this way, experiences and knowledge can develop in a specific context, which can in turn be shared with a wider community. Cause confronting architecture with climate issues is a global agency, translating it into new design strategies remains a question of individual and local investment, the merging of both could then lead to a new vernacular approach of universal authority.

7.
Testing.
Photo: Tim Simon-Meyer.

New Vernacular 163

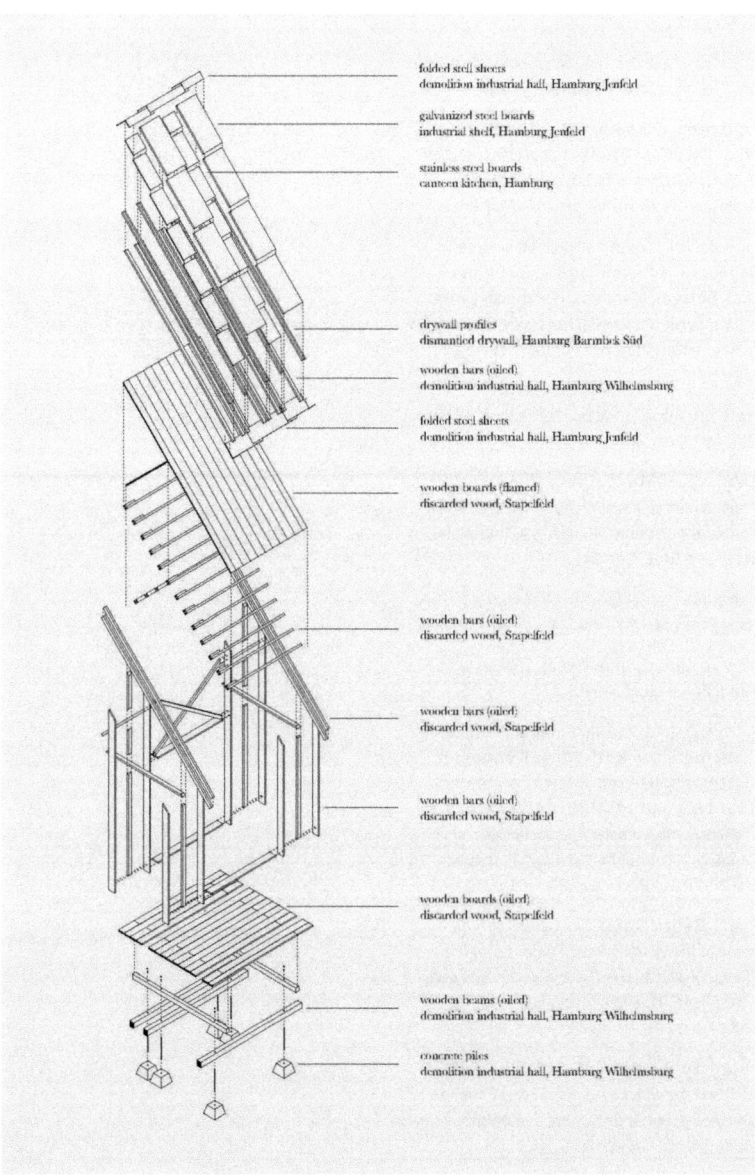

8.
Configuring
Illustration: The authors.

References

Bauhaus Earth: https://www.bauhauserde.org/vision, accessed June 6, 2024.

Frampton, Kenneth (1995): *Studies in: Tectonic Culture: The Poetics of Construction in Nineteenth- and Twentieth-Century Architecture*, Cambridge, MA: MIT Press.

Hebel, Dirk (2020): »100% Ressource: Bauten als Rohstofflager«, in: Bahner, Olaf/Böttger, Matthias/Holzberg, Laura (eds.), *Sorge um den Bestand: Zehn Strategien für die Architektur*, Berlin: Jovis Verlag, 165–177.

Holtrop, Anne (2022): *Interview with João Quintela*, Lisbon.

Kahn, Louis, Master Class, University of Pennsylvania, April 14, 1971, https://www.youtube.com/watch?v=UA95GlwZWUw, accessed June 6, 2024.

Kahn, Nathaniel (2003): *My Architect*, USA: New Yorker Films.

Lévi-Strauss, Claude (1962): *The Savage Mind*, Paris: Librairie Plon.

Norell, Daniel/Rodhe, Einar (2021): »Under Construction: A Real-World Fiction«, in: Matthias Ballestrem/Marta Fernandez Guardado (eds.), *CA²RE / CA²RE+ Hamburg. Conference for Artistic and Architectural Research – Book of Proceedings*, Hamburg: Hafen City University, 189.

Piano, Renzo (2018): *The Genius Behind Some of the World's Most Famous Buildings / Renzo Piano*, https://www.youtube.com/watch?v=GRfudKFLAmI, accessed June 6, 2024.

Rudofsky, Bernard (1964): *Architecture Without Architects: A Short Introduction to Non-Pedigreed Architecture*, New York: The Museum of Modern Art.

WORLD

Could This Happen in Nature?

Anne Romme and Jacob Sebastian Bang

Abstract: This article presents a physical artefact, a wooden relief of the condition between wet and dry. Following a description of the methodological aspects of the artefact, the essay uses the notion of a »material practice« (Allen 1999) to discuss the making of the relief, and to qualify our observations about the finished work. Finally, the essay suggests that material practices have the potential to addressing the accelerating ecological crisis.

Keywords: Material Practice; Relief; Digital Fabrication; Artistic Research; Theory and Practice.

Introduction

This visual contribution presents and discusses a physical artifact, a wooden relief titled »Could This Happen in Nature«. The relief consists of four squares, which altogether measures 2 x 2 meters. It is made of CNC-routed plywood, 40 millimeters thick at its thickest point.

The relief is the culmination of a series of reliefs, which were all made using the same technique but have varyied subject matters and scales. The entire series has been used to experiment with the topology and subject matter »island« and zoom in from a relief of an entire archipelago to details of parts of an island (fig. 1).

»Could This Happen in Nature« zooms all the way into the shoreline, the line along which a large body of water meets the land. It is a stretch of land that is interchangeably wet and dry and is in constant flux as the waves roll in and objects shift around. The precise position of the shoreline can change depending on the tides, floods, and shifting water levels and although the capacity of the physical components (sand, seaweed, larger drifting objects, rocks, the quality of the water, temperature, degree of pollution, etc.) vary, the amphibious condition can be found on any shore. The site is entirely universal (fig. 2). Following a description of the methodological aspects of the

Corresponding authors: Anne Romme (The Royal Danish Academy, Denmark), anne.romme@kglakademi.dk; Jacob Sebastian Bang (The Royal Danish Academy, Denmark); jbang@kglakademi.dk.
 Open Access. ©2024 Anne Romme and Jacob Sebastian Bang published by transcript Verlag. This work is licensed under the Creative Commons Attribution 4.0 (BY) license.

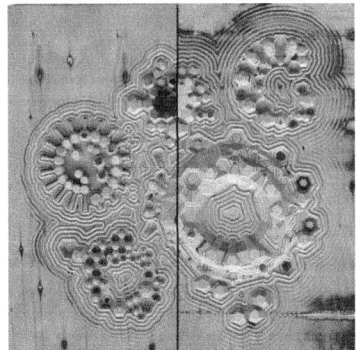
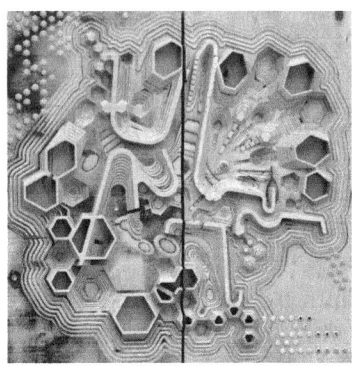

1.
Earlier reliefs, zooming in from an entire archipelago (top), to an island (top-left), to part of an island (right) CNC-milled plywood, all 90 x 90 cm. Photo: The authors.

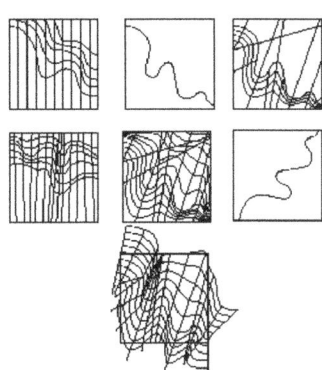

2.
The site where land meets the ocean is universal. These drawings are our first attempts at drawing that site using only curves. Illustration: The authors.

relief, this article reflects upon possible readings of it and our observations about the finished work.

Method

The relief is the result of a collaboration between two architects. As such, it is a collage of two design positions and two bodies of existing work. Making a new relief begins with a conversation (fig. 3). Having decided on the subject matter, the interaction between the wet ocean and the dry land, we search existing work for drawings which contain, for example, geometries which mimic natural growth, marine phenomena, piers, and jetties. Some of the existing drawings might have had relationships to the theme, whereas others are chosen based on their formal or organizational similarity to the amphibious condition. In short: Anything which inspires the process of form-making and contributes to the entanglement of previous work goes (fig. 4).

With deliberate disregard to the scale of the original two-dimensional drawings, a digital three-dimensional file is made. Structures are overlapped, merged, and entangled as the previously flat drawings are made three-dimensional. To achieve a level of complexity, yet still establish forms which are technically suited to CNC-routing, the process requires many stages of sampling, overlaying, and weaving together. Not only the drawings from previous work, but elements like seaweed, waves, a spiral and clusters of bacteria-like forms are also sampled.

With the specific parameters of the production method in mind, the three-dimensional-file is calibrated in tune with both material and technique. For example, the smallest details are sized to match the smallest tool bit in our toolbox, and the thickness of the material never goes below what is needed to maintain the plywood's structural integrity. Knowledge of the thickness of a single ply within the composite plywood determines the changes in depth needed for a change in nuance in the finished relief. The scope of the machine bed determines that the relief needs to be cut into four parts.

At last, the three-dimensional file is cut into plywood using CNC technology and the transformation from existing analog drawings, via digital tools, to a tactile plywood relief is complete.

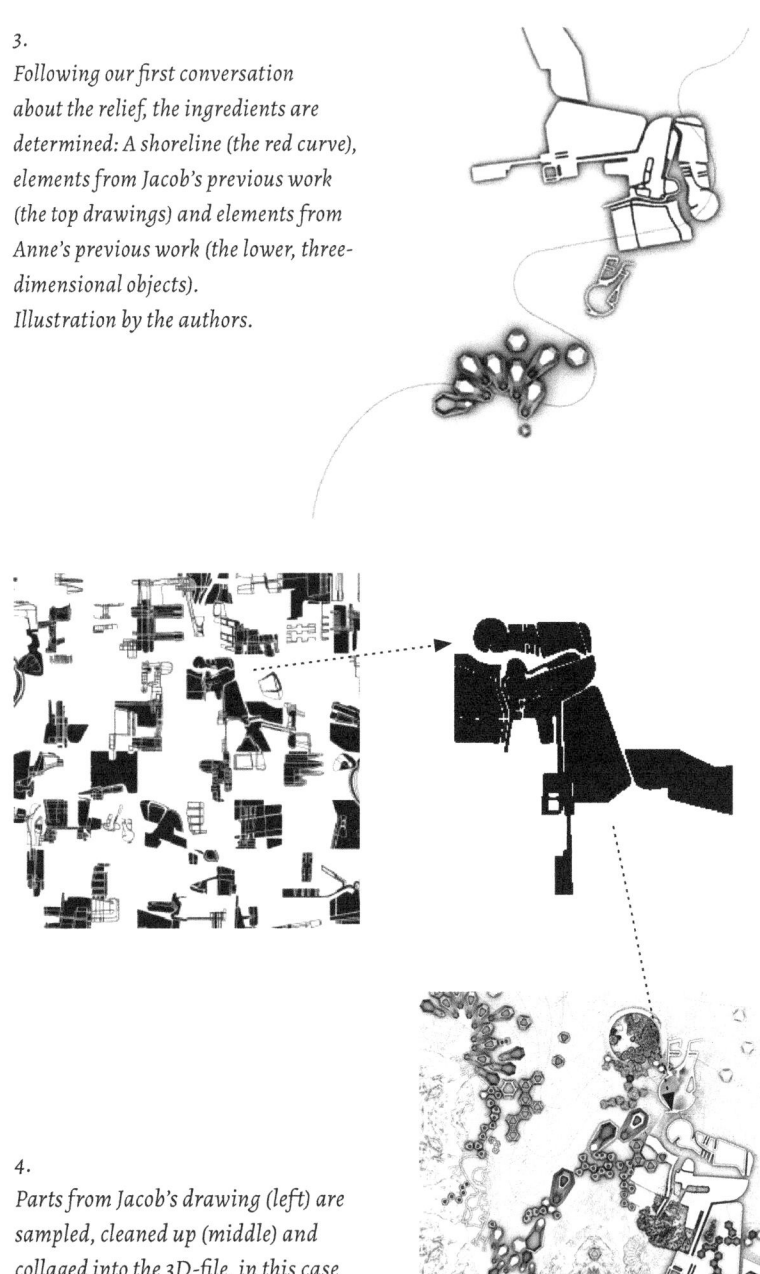

3.
Following our first conversation about the relief, the ingredients are determined: A shoreline (the red curve), elements from Jacob's previous work (the top drawings) and elements from Anne's previous work (the lower, three-dimensional objects).
Illustration by the authors.

4.
Parts from Jacob's drawing (left) are sampled, cleaned up (middle) and collaged into the 3D-file, in this case mirrored (right).
Illustration by the authors.

The Result

Predicting the physical result based on the three-dimensionalfile is tricky, not to say impossible. The drawing program offers an abstract, homogeneous view, which have not yet been confronted with the materiality of the plywood. Only when the code for the CNCrouter has been generated and the machine begins to draw in the plywood will the multi-toned, tangible relief appear. The complex amalgamation of a digital, three-dimensional form (in itself a conglomeration of other drawings), the CNC-routing method, and the material condition of plywood appears as a new, composite landscape (fig. 5).

It is an inevitable condition of reliefs in general that they contain more dimensions than a flat drawing, thus allowing lighting conditions and side views to inform and alter the perception of its motifs. In this specific case, the material presence offers several further readings. As plywood is a common material, well known to architects and non-architects alike, the surprises, anomalies, and additions to the intended design gives the viewer the opportunity to reflect upon the relationship between fabrication, material, form, and intent. In other words, it comes as no surprise that knots of the organic material, as well as shifts in nuances of the thin ply appear, but the way they intermingle with the design offers a reading in several scales: the one-to-one plywood scale as well as the designed scale. Reflections upon how the relief is made, degrees of intentionality, and the relationship between material and design effects seem unavoidable.

A closer look at the relief will reveal many instances in which readings in several scales are possible. Fig. 6–9 account for how – when translated into the striated plywood condition – sampled objects and ideas can be read in different capacities and scales. Figure 10 gives a sense of how the entire relief also fluctuates between different readings, none of them naturalistic. Depending on focus, the viewer might see human-made structures on an urban scale, or a close-up of some natural phenomena, or anything in between.

Anne Romme and Jacob Sebastian Bang

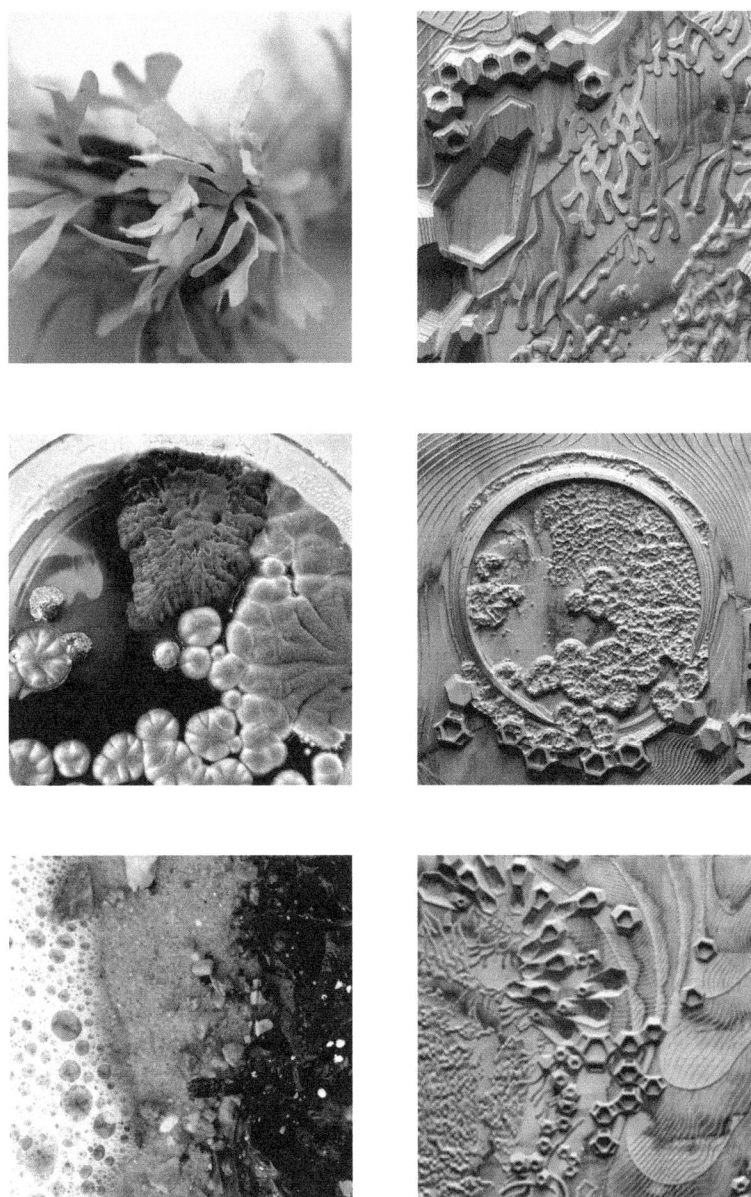

5.
A close study of dried seaweed (left), compared to the abstracted seaweed-like figures in the relief.
Photo by the authors.

6.
A circular form in the relief can be read as a petri dish in 1:1 scale, or as a large landscape feature – perhaps a tank for future energy harvesting.
Photo by the authors.

7.
A typical shoreline with pebbles, seaweed, shells, organic foam, sand, etc. As we all know from our intimate interaction with this site (making sand castles in our childhood, searching for gems and treasures), the complexity exists in many sizes. Sea shells can be found almost infinitely small, the bubbles of the foam is part of a much larger body, etc. The relief has a similar capacity. It can be read in the scale of a microscopic view, or as an urban plan.
Photo by the authors.

Reflection

We both teach young architects.[1] We teach our students to collaborate and not to rely on the idea of the individual genius. To qualify these didactic principles, we practice them ourselves. That is our main motivation for merging our two existing design practices. The results are more complex than those we could have achieved separately. The degree to which one design practice and approach alters, erases, or contrasts with the other is an ongoing conversation. In the case of »Could This Happen in Nature«, our individual elements are accumulated and juxtaposed with each other more than merged.

We were inspired by Stan Allen's argument for a reciprocal relationship between theory and practice, defined by action and agency, in which the architect lets tactical improvisation accumulate over time.[2] Our assessment of that is to let the relief emerge as a series of iterations, in which the entanglement of thought, form and scale are increased at each step. Rather than using analytical deduction, the relief appears as a result of juxtapositions and coincidences, a »promiscuous mixture of the real and the abstract« – of thought, references, conversations, forms and operations within a three-dimensional drawing program, and of material effects and machine parameters. As such, the relief does not offer one coherent reading, neither in scale nor in subject matter. It demands of its viewer that they speculate and decide for themselves which scale to read it in. There is not one given reading of the forms.

On the other hand, because our forms are generated entirely by us without any automation in a traditional form-giving manner, every singular form is detectable. Two forms might collide and overlap, but they never disrupt each other or mutate. No algorithms or scripts take control of our forms and intentions. The striated character of CNC-milled plywood, acting as contour lines in a landscape, is predictable. Even the scattered knots and other irregularities of the previously hidden layers can be expected, although not planned.

---

1 Jacob is the head of program of the B.Arch. teaching program Helhed og Del, and Anne is the head of program of the B.Arch teaching program Finder Sted, both at The Royal Danish Academy.
2 »PRACTICE vs PROJECT«, in: PRAXIS: Journal of Writing + Building 1, 112–25. http://www.jstor.org/stable/24328803 (accessed: June 18, 2024)

178   Anne Romme and Jacob Sebastian Bang

9.
The relief as a whole, exhibited at the Royal Danish Academy.

The decision to not let algorithms create a landscape beyond the direct influence of our hands and mindshas to do with our understanding of purpose. The relief shares some characteristics with typical CNC- milled work – textures and the smooth transition between forms, for example – but its distinctive forms suggest a more traditional approach to collaboration and design. As custodians of an exhibition of the relief (among other works),[3] it is our experience that the combination of recognizable figures within a surprising field sparks the imagination of viewers. Provoked by the title of the relief, they question nature and our role within it. They see and discuss a future, a nature-culture in which humans have interfered with every aspect of our planet, and in which the distinction between the natural and the human-made has been blurred.[4] The relief becomes an object of speculation and imagination – not just ours, but more importantly, everyone else's.

Conclusion

Acknowledging that our result is a decadent use of a high-tech machine to create a non-functional relief, we do not claim to provide answers to our accelerating ecological crisis. Instead, we propose to view our work as a catalyst for conversations. By making an open-ended prototype, we invite viewers to speculate and discuss. Microscopic, architectural, geological, territorial: The relief can be read in various scales simultaneously. It does not generalize but takes advantage of using known forms – such as an architectural maritime structure, seaweed, and a petri dish – to link the viewer's observations with reality. We like to think of the relief as an entanglement of technology, thinking, and making, an attempt to develop a pre-form for the complex and unpredictable future that awaits us.

The ecological crisis extends beyond singular problems and is as intricately connected to our cultural, aesthetical realm as it is to the economic and political. While the future needs verifiable results, it also needs methods for handling the arbitrary and inconsistent. We need to operate in the world, not at a safe distance from it. The relief may be a prototype for something that will happen in nature, but that is not the point. The point is, that it provokes us to think about a radically redefined nature, in which architects need to reinvent our patterns of inhabitation and use the entanglement between scales, growth principles, structures, and species as a necessary and desirable tool.

---

3   At Block Architecture Gallery in Stockholm, Block32.se, September–October 2023.
4   As described by Cecilie Rubow in: Rubow, Cecilie, Indendørsmenneskets Natur, Aarhus Universitetsforlag, 2022.

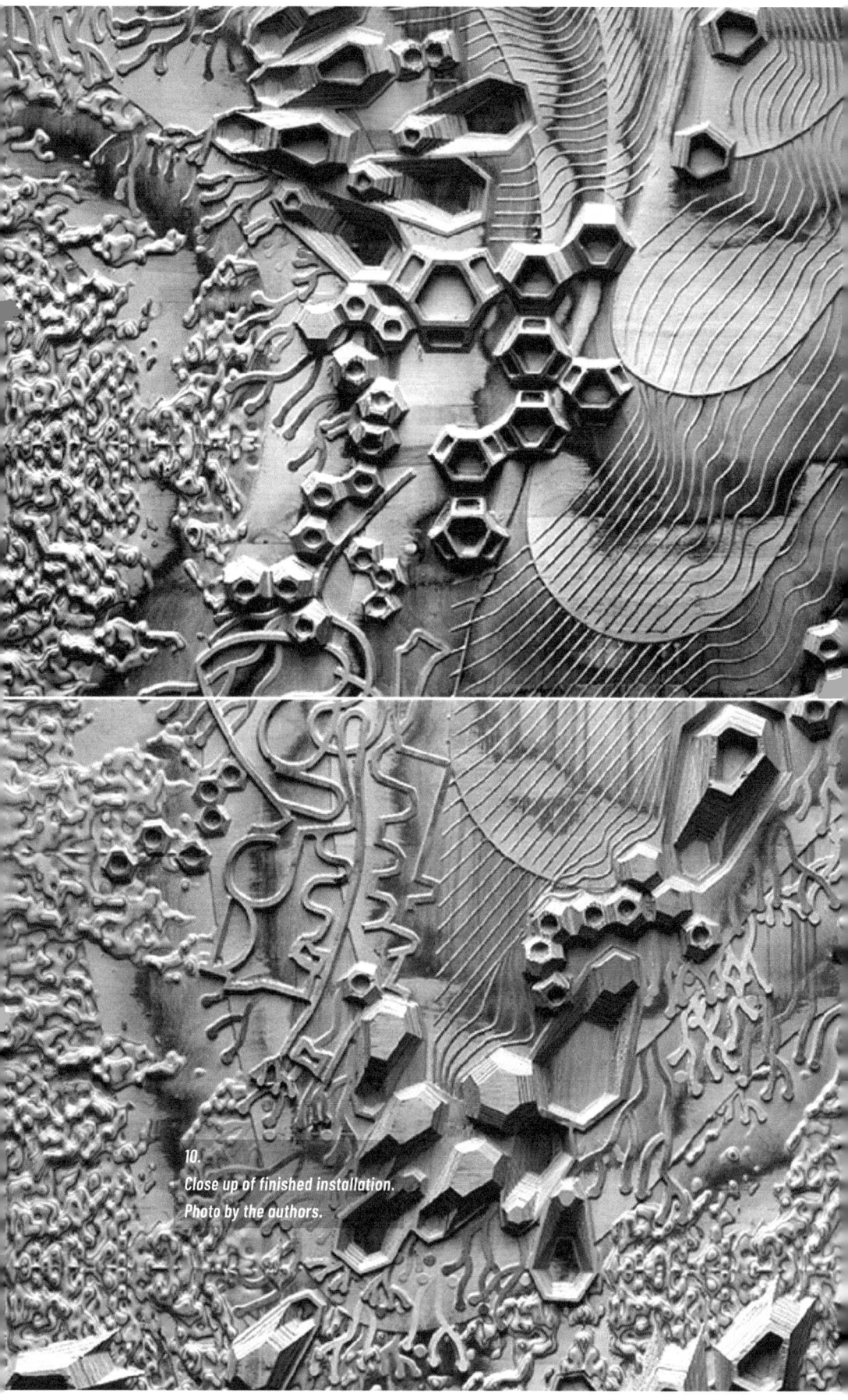

10.
Close up of finished installation.
Photo by the authors.

References

Allen, Stan (1999): »PRACTICE vs PROJECT«, in: *PRAXIS: Journal of Writing + Building* 1, 112–25.

At Block Architecture Gallery in Stockholm, Block32.se, September–October 2023, https://www.block32.se/blank, accessed June 6, 2024.

Rubow, Cecilie (2022): *Indendørsmenneskets Natur*, Aarhus: Aarhus University Press.

The Precognitive Perception of Space
On Primitive Architecture of the 21st Century

Bernhard Leopold Geiger

Abstract: In analogy to the double meaning of the word sense – rational coherency and the means of bodily perception – the experience of space can be informed both by an intellectual reading and a tacit, somatic feeling. Starting from the question of how these two antagonistic modes of perception can be described on a phenomenological level, this article reflects upon the role that pre-cognitive, bodily experience might play in the production of architecture in today's digitalized environment, it attempts to identify interrelations between technical progress and the contemporary appearance of primitive spaces (or the primitive appearance of contemporary spaces). Rather than being understood as a completed work of research, it aims to raise questions and propose hypotheses for further investigation: Delineating our subjective desire for immersion in an irrational physical reality (a condition in which we perceive ourselves as indistinct from a pre-temporal, comprehensive world) as the counter-moment to a fundamental historical tendency to objectivating, rationalising and fragmenting space, a link may be traced from the dawn of artificial intelligence and virtual realities to an ontological and very analog – process of making architecture, that draws from intuition, focuses on the site, material, and atmosphere, and eventually contributes to the recent (re-)emergence of buildings that appear to be raw and non-architectural in classical terms.

Keywords: Gestures; Drawing; Phenomenology; Embodiment; Design Cognition; Perception; Fragments; Material; Presence.

Introduction

Sense as Rational Meaning, Sense as Bodily Feeling: Making sense can be understood in two different ways. The word sense refers both to the rational meaning of something – like the symbolic content of a sentence, the result of human understanding – and someone's subjective feeling – intuition and the bodily means to perception. Sense is the link between the reason and the body, between abstract meaning and the physical world. Bodily perception through the classical five senses, that is to say: the act of feeling is the inevitable basis of knowledge. It is through feeling that we create knowledge and meaning, and this creation of knowledge is what we call science. The word science derives from the Latin »scire«, to know (Allen 1990: 1081) and while knowledge is linked to our primal sense, seeing, in so far as the gothic word »saihvan«, to see, relates back to the Latin »scire« (Grimm 1848), too, the Latin word for seeing, »vedere«, in return led to the German word for knowing, »wissen«, from the gothic »vitan«, to know (ibid.). Now, lat. »scire«, just as the English word sign, from the Latin »signum«, derive from the Ancient Greek σχείω, which means to divide and split (Lewis 1879). The creation of rational knowledge is an act of division. It is the splitting off of an abstract meaning from its physical body and the division into signifier and signified. *Making Sense* means creating rational knowledge through sensitive perception, means dividing what we sense into meaning and body, and thus divides our conscious mind from the material world. And yet, *Making Sense* simultaneously anchors our concious mind back to the material world, for it is an act that involves the use of our senses which are the physical link between thought and body.

It is this ambivalent nature of the word sense – the moment of division between our rational consciousness and the physical reality of things versus the moment of their direct connection and unification – which leads to the question of what bodily perception means and implies as opposed to rational perception. How can these two antagonistic moments be described on a phenomenological level? What is the role that precognitive, bodily experience plays in the production of architecture in today's postindustrial, digitalized environment, at the dawn of an age governed by artificial intelligence and virtual realities? Rather than being understood as a completed work of research, this article aims to bring together a broad range of voices to propose hypotheses for further investigation.

After outlining a fundamental historical shift from the primordial bodily experience of being one with the world to the dominance of a cognitive, fragmented perception of space – this fragmented perception both informing the production of architecture and being enhanced by architecture, as described by Jameson (I) – something like a subjective aesthetic need for immersion in a comprehensive and pre-temporal physical reality can be delineated as a reaction or countermoment to this objectifying and rationalizing historical tendency. Thereafter, parallels are drawn between the pre-cognitive perception of space – a Heideggerian experience of being-in-the-world – and Frampton's conception of »Critical Regionalism« in architecture (II), leading to the suggestion of regarding the design process as analagous to Merleau-Ponty's phenomenlogical description of the emergence of a painting. Here, a model or drawing would have to be understood as a realization of the project in itself (rather than just a re-presentation), implying the primacy of sensory experience over form and meaning – with a fundamental impact on the process of making. Architecture may thus be described as an aesthetic mediator, where the desire for pre-cognitive perception of space can find expression in an ontological – and very much analog – approach to design, which draws from intuition, focuses on atmosphere and the sensation for material realities and eventually results in the recent emergence of raw and archaic, by classical standards rather non-architectonical spatial structures (III).

The World as an Object

One might imagine the world of prehistoric man as a comprehensive and indivisible unity. Nature constitutes nearly everything for him: his food, his tools, his home and building material, eventually, even his law and his beliefs. He is also ruled by nature, which enacts violence upon him. Nature cannot be left. The prehistoric concept of space is free of directionality or spatial boundaries (Giedion 1965: 358), does not distinguish between dwelling and environment (cf. Descola 2013: 63–98), nor between human and animal (cf. ibid.: 60–61). The prehistoric man probably has little feeling for the passing of time (cf. Descola 2011: 78–81). He has little abstract knowledge, but lives in a world full of magic and myths.

About twelve thousand years ago people began to settle and to inscribe their own worlds into nature. In archaic Greece, (the gods were on Mount Olympus already halfway to the beyond) time, formerly holistic and static, started to pass with the concept of »generations« (Schuller 2002:28) and turned into chronology. An dualistic view of the world was developed, distinguishing between »being« and »non-being« and thus discovering the »principle« as an alternative to the mere existence of substance. Nature turned into an accumulation of objects whose outer form was differentiated from their subjective appearance (Gehrke 2003: 100), that is: from the reality of the beholder, as man, declared to be the »measure of all things« (Schuller 2002: 43–44), was not anymore dispersed among them but was now standing

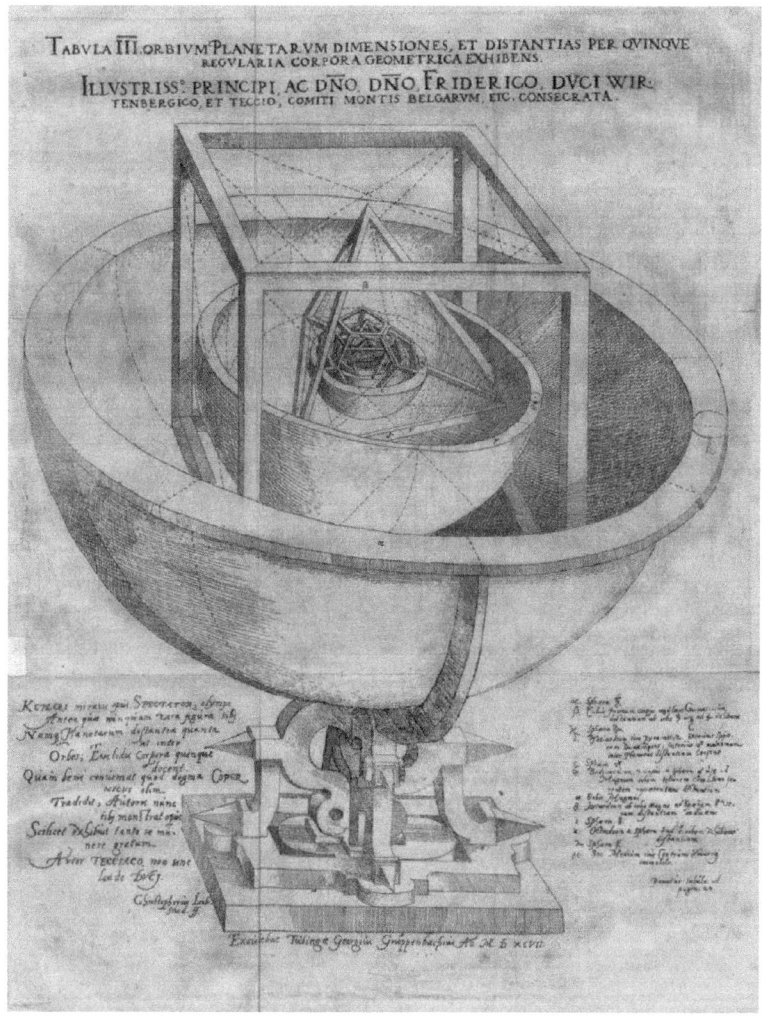

1.

Johannes Kepler's 1596 model of the universe. Orbium planetarum dimensiones, et distantias per quinque regularia corpora geometrica exhibens. In Johannes Kepler, Prodromus dissertationum cosmographicarum, continens mysterium cosmographicum, de admirabili proportione orbium coelestium, deque causis coelorum numeri, […], 24 Tubingæ: Excudebat Georgius Gruppenbachius, 1596. ETH-Bibliothek Zürich. , Rar 1367: 1 https://doi.org/10.3931/e-rara-445 / Public Domain Mark.

apart. Soon, the logos was discovered – a participation of the individual in universal reason (ibid.: 87–88) – and while the reason still appeared as something global in character, the understanding of individual participation in the same formed is a first step toward intellectual individualism (cf. ibid.: 59). It was this very reason that allowed man to emancipate himself from the cosmic forces of action, for which Epikur, around 300 BCE, declared the world's events to not be driven by destiny anymore, but by chance instead (Gehrke 2003: 88–89). The superordinate causal connection of things had turned into chaos while the concept of science had evolved.

Due to this new approach to knowledge, ancient Greek thinkers developed their mathematical skills and managed to envisage the heavenly bodies. In accordance with their newly gained self-consciousness, they constructed the Ptolemaic view of the world, with Earth at the very center. This concept remained unquestioned until the Copernican Revolution began in the 16th century, when, maybe for the first time in history, man not only stepped outside nature, but also outside himself and made his world the object of observation from an imaginary point of view – a precondition for the imagination of a heliocentric »universe«. In this heliocentric world, man could scarcely be called the »measure of all things«, as he himself became a thing. While for Copernicus (and for many generations to follow) there was empiric probability, but no direct scientific proof that the sun was orbited by the planets, instead, Copernicus argued for his new theory on an aesthetic level, following his sense for harmony and symmetrical order (Miller 2010: 69). And still, despite his attempt to describe the world as a unity »In the middle of all sits the Sun enthroned. In his beautiful temple could we place this luminary in any better position than from which he can illuminate the whole at once?« (ibid.: 131), Copernicus made Earth just one planet among many by removing it from the center – a mere object fragment of the solar system. It is as if reason would dissect the world from independently the human intention.

About half a century later, Johannes Kepler exemplified the conceptual ambiguity that this scientific change brought. He was struck by Copernicus's notion of a supreme order, believing in a reality beyond appearance and in the eternal universe being an indivisible whole: »Although Center, Surface, and Distance are manifestly Three, yet are they One (ibid.: 70). On the one hand, he was an alchemist, regarding the Earth as a living organism, and yet, on the other, he had to treat it as dead matter when making it the subject of calculation. His 1596 model of the universe (fig. 1) illustrates this contradiction: It is both an object – a rational scientific tool – and an aesthetically driven attempt to depict the world as a unified system. Kepler was caught between two worlds. He was a mystic, guided by intuition, and a rigorous scientist, who would only accept mathematical evidence as proof of a theory (ibid.: 75pp). Numbers and data were about to replace the mythical thought.

Only a few years after Kepler's death, the separation between aesthetic experience and logical thought found its ultimate expression when Descartes, mistrustful of his own physical existence, formulated his »cogito ergo sum«. The legacy of this reasoning was a disembodied subject facing the now objective world and to whom things present themselves as a purely geometric surface (Gumbrecht 2012: 193–194). It reflected the increased modern doubt about the physical base of cognition, while the logical gained more and more authority. When, in the early 19th century, it was recognized that the production of knowledge on the basis of bodily perception was dependent on the location, the body became completely divorced from intellectual experience (ibid.: 197pp). To be scientifically accepted, experience based on the senses hasd to be abstracted from location-specific factors, an act through which it lost its place in physical reality. According to that approach, knowledge would not lie in nature anymore, but have to be created by the mind (ibid.: 196).

It seemes like man, in a fundamental historical shift, has lost his sentient body and now faces the world as an isolated consciousness, as if reason, in order to liberate man from the violence of nature, would dissolve their primordial unity and displace him in irreconcilable opposition, from where the world can only appear as an accumulation of fragmented objects. The development of the rational mind may be described as the dissection of our perception of the world. At the end of the 18th century, Schiller believed that human freedom was indispensably bound to the loss of the unity between man and the world (Ritter 1974: 161):

> »Whilst man, in his first physical condition, is only passively affected by the world of sense, he is still entirely identified with it; and for this reason the external world, as yet, has no objective existence for him. [...] As long as man derives sensations from a contact with Nature, he is her slave; but as soon as he begins to reflect upon her objects and laws he becomes her lawgiver. Nature, which previously ruled him as a power, now expands before him as an object. What is objective to him can have no power over him, for in order to become objective it has to experience his own power.« (Schiller 2023)

During Schiller's lifetime, an unprecedented change in the human environment occurred. With the onset of the Industrial Revolution, human-built infrastructure caused nature to decompose more and more and dissolved the dichotomy between city and landscape. The temporary and ugly became part of the latter, turning it into a non-hierarchical conglomerate (Fischer 2010), while nature, in the classical sense, seemingly disappeared from our living world. City borders began to diffuse and also the cities inner structure – formerly the closed perimeter block – started to dissolve into an aggregation of fragments. In the modern open-plan city, buildings no longer formed a uniform system of space but rather, as described by Rowe and Koetter, a »congeries of conspicuously disparate objects« (Rowe 1979: 58). As such, they stood in opposition to (meaning outside of) space (ibid.: 62). This rift between the object-like building and space is analogous to the rift that had occured between the individual and its environment.

Firstly, the built environment of modern times is rationalized and objectivated. Through economy, tax policy, construction law, technical aspects of the building process and so on (in short: through numbers and codes rather than subjective criteria).

Secondly, the individual perception of space becomes increasingly fragmented. With shorter journey times, spatial relations become harder to grasp – commuting to work in a city like London might take just as long as traveling from London to Paris by plane. On both the Underground and the airplane, there is hardly any understandable relationship between the transport space and the »outside« space. If there is any, it is largely visual, via the window, and from distant movement. The generic appearance of transport spaces themselves, which can, as such, barely be called places (cf. Augé 1992), does the rest: Different places are not perceived as interconnected anymore, but as a series of independent fragments.

And just as the spatial connections within modern and postmodern landscapes are becoming more difficult to read due to the temporal confusion caused by different travel speeds, Koselleck describes how the experience of the temporal present is also becoming corroded. Predicting the future becomes more difficult with the ever- increasing complexity of our world and formerly linear time turns into a chaotic structure. The present can no longer be experienced as a whole (cf. Koselleck 1979).

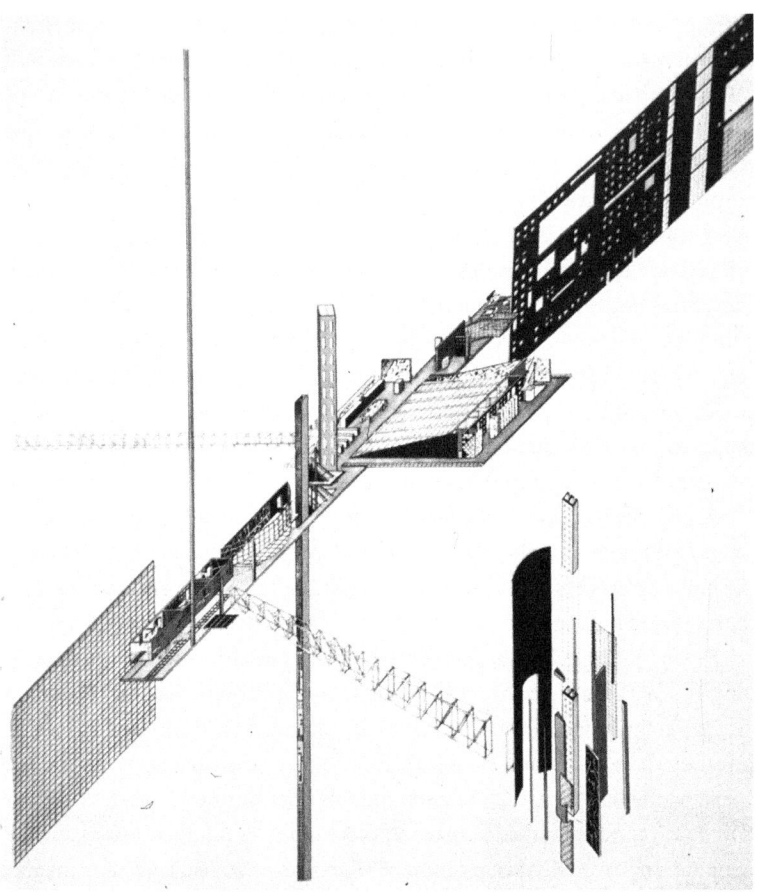

2.
Axonometry, Dutch Parliament Extension. The Hague, Netherlands, 1978.
Illustration: OMA.

In his 1984 essay, Fredric Jameson provides a striking analysis of the psychological effects of this fragmented postmodern space. Diagnosing a »schizophrenic« experience caused by the »breakdown of the signifying chain« (Jameson 1991: 27). He describes how Portmans technophile Bonaventure Hotel not only attempts to achieve a quasi-complete spatial separation from the city (ibid.: 40), but also compromises the integrality of our spatial experience as our self-localization is hindered by its hypercomplexity:

> »Postmodern hyperspace has finally succeeded in transcending the capacities of the individual human body to locate itself, to organize its immediate surroundings perceptually, and cognitively, to map its position in a mappable external world. It may now be suggested that this alarming disjunction point between the body and its built environment [...] can itself stand as the symbol and analogon of that even sharper dilemma which is the incapacity of our minds, at least at present, to map the great global multinational and decentered communicational network in which we find ourselves caught as individual subjects.« (ibid.: 44)

It must be emphasized that, by choosing an authorship architecture as an example, Jameson implies an intentional analogy that goes beyond the non-intentional parallel between economic and technical circumstances and built space, a concrete affirmation of the fragmentary. And indeed, Jameson portrays the style of an entire generation of artists and architects. Rowe and Koetter propose the »Collage City« as an alternative to the emotionally discarded modern city, which, as an accumulation of micro-organisms, itself remains a composition of fragments, at least on the urban level (cf. Rowe 1979: 149). In doing so, they seamlessly integrate their urban ideal into the postmodern world, where the symptoms of modernity are superficially combated, while structural development continues to progress in the same direction.

In analogy to these descriptions, Leupen identifies the late 20th-century city as a »topologically« experienced structure, that is, as a space without spatial connections. In his view, a whole range of deconstructivist architects, among them OMA, deliberately work with chaos and the assembly of fragments on an urban level (Leupen 1990: 27–30) and indeed one might also argue that some of OMA's buildings are conceived as an accumulation of fragments. This becomes visible, for instance, in the drawings of the Dutch Parliament Extension, in which the project (very much in the spirit

3.
OMA. Universal Headquarters. Los Angeles, USA, 1996.
Photo: OMA.

of the Biennale di Venezia, curated by Koolhaas in 2014 and dedicated to »Elements«) is broken down into its very diverse individual components (fig. 2).

Rem Koolhaas himself, commonly known as the »intellectual genius« of architecture today, has precisely analysed both the decoupling of a building's interior and exterior, which only leaves behind a multi-functional collection of surfaces (keyword: »Bigness«), as well as the overvaluation of the economic, which forces architecture into permanent chaos (keywords: »junk space«) (Burgdorff 2008). He openly admits to being driven by the market (ibid.) and doubts whether 21st-century planners can still have any real influence on the city's appearance, as it is so overwhelmingly dictated by capitalism (Michaelsen 2018). And yet, Koolhaas also attempted to counter the atomizing momentum of economic constraints within his architecture: For example, he explained that the Universal Studios Headquarters were conceived as a »machine« that would reunite components of the company scattered around the site (Burgdorff 2008). However, a look at the project's publication on OMA's homepage casts doubt on the realization of this narrative (fig. 3). Not only does the building itself appear as a composition of different individual parts, but it is also clearly understood as an object – the choice of a model image with people in the foreground repeatedly confronts the viewer with the fact that he stands opposite the building.

It is undoubtedly due to the development of reason that man has emancipated himself from the violence of nature. The legacy of this progress is the dissolution of the primordial unity of man and the environment, which has instead become an objective, disembodied juxtaposition. Today, the world is no longer perceived as a whole, but as irreconcilable chaos, in which the built space alsoappears to have become fragmented and detached itself from our bodies. In this way, architecture not only reflects the global condition, but also contributes to our self-perception as isolated minds. Koolhaas speaks about an attempt to counteract this spatial fragmentation. The following chapter attempts to examine the possible foundations of such an endeavor and the architectural means to make us experience space as an indistinct part of our physical reality.

4.
Gustave Courbet: »Les Casseurs de pierres. C.«, 1849.
Oil on canvas, 56 cm x 65 cm.
Photo: Collection Oskar Reinhart, »Am Römerholz«, Winterthur, inv. no. 1923.15.

The Mergence of Subject and Space

In his early magnum opus »Being and Time« (Heidegger 1927), Heidegger subjects the Cartesian theory to harsh criticism. He points out that human existence cannot be reduced to reason, but is first and foremost a »being-in-the-world«.[1] By distinguishing between what is practically »ready-to-hand« and what is merely objectively »present-at-hand«, he illustrates that in the use of tools, for instance a pre-cognitive bodily exchange with the world takes place – an unconscious, thoughtless impacting, a merging into the world. Courbets Stonebreakers emphasize what Heidegger describes: The figures lean into the ground, their posture is informed by physical labor and gravity. They work the stone with their hands and tools and they are almost blur with the space (fig. 4). Our existence expresses itself here as familiarity with the material world and not as isolated consciousness. To grasp and to judge what we perceive rationally is therefore only one possible form of interaction with the world, but the very essence of being [German: ›Dasein‹] is not only thinking, but existence itself, which includes both the rational and corporeal perception (Thomä 2013: 48–49).

The first chapter outlines a fundamental historic shift in the predominance of these two principles of being, the physical and the intellectual. It is now elementary to stress that drawing a typology of such antithetical character does not suggest that cultures, or individuals, should be located at one of the two poles listed therein, but rather somewhere in the field of tension lying in between, the forces of which only the antagonists can illustrate. Both forces coexist and are inherent to the human condition (hence the shift appears to be initiated by the development of human culture, not by a change of the external condition). And hence it would be premature to conclude that contemporay man has to perceive the world as a detached and fragmented surface.

How must Heidegger's advocacy for the affirmation of our bodily existence be understood? Schiller's demonstration of the foundation of human freedom on the development of the intellect cannot be doubted. What does the physical experience entail? Perhaps the discrepancy between the

---

[1] World derives from Old High German »weralt«, meaning »age of man«. *The Concise Oxford Dictionary of Current English*, 1413, s.v. »world«. The concept of »being man« therefore is directly contained in the term »world«, or in other words: the concept of being human is directly connected with the experience of »being-in-the-world«.

5.
Ferdinand Bellermann: »Waldpartie bei San Esteban (Südamerikanische Urwaldlandschaft mit Ureinwohnern am Lagerfeuer)«, 1862.
Oil on canvas, 44.5 cm x 55.5 cm.
Photo: Stiftung PreußischeSchlösser und Gärten Berlin-Brandenburg / Roland Handrick, 2000, inv. no. GK I 51037, https://brandenburg.museum-digital.de/object/73379.

scientific attitude and the work of Copernicus and Kepler and their mystic, pre-modern ideas can be interpreted not as a delay of the aesthetic imagination compared to the intellectual development, but rather as the result of a coexisting physical counter-tendency.

Since antiquity, scientists have tried to describe the universe as a comprehensive whole. Pythagoras claimed that numbers would describe the cosmos as a whole[2] – his followers believed his construct of the »tetraktys« to be the »original source and root of eternal Nature (Miller 2010: 72). On the one hand this is an absurdly rational and abstract idea and on the other hand a clear expression of the search for supreme order. Similarily, Kepler tried to find »the« single number that would describe the world (ibid.: 85pp) and until today physicists, who in the meantime discovered condensed formulas and fundamental constants to describe large parts of the universe, are searching for the grand unified theory »that explains the large and the small, the universe and the atom – a theory of everyting (ibid.: 276). These attempts seem to reflect the opposite impulse of the fragmentary tendency of the intellect within the realm of science. In 1844, Humboldt expressed the concern »that the mind could succumb to the »mass of details with the rapid spread of physical research« (Ritter 1974: 152) and thus no longer perceive nature – in its multiplicity – as one. Pleasure, should be added to the objectivity of science , which dissects the world, as a »stimulus« for sensing the eternal laws and to convey »harmony in the cosmos« by means of poetry and pictorial representations (ibid.: 151pp).

About 500 years before that, Petrarch described his ascent of Mont Ventoux, which was motivated solely by aesthetic curiosity, supplied what is perhaps the first record of how man, alienated from nature at the beginning of modern times, conceived of the same as a landscape in order to visualize its greatness in »enjoying contemplation«. When Petrarch noticed himself sinking into earthly self-forgetfulness, he abruptly renounced his actions and immediately left the mountain – but his ascent was of epochal significance. On the »ground of modern times,« writes Ritter, an »organ« is required to experience nature as a holistic unity, that is, to replace what does not exist anymore as a concept with aesthetic feeling (ibid.: 141pp). Though, whereas seemingly for Petrarch it was sufficient to simply step into the landscape in order to experience the world as an enitity, the development of industry in

---

2 The word Cosmos itself, from Gk. κόσμος (kosmos), means order. The Concise Oxford Dictionary of Current English, 260, s.v. »cosmos«.

Humboldt's time initiated the eviction of the natural from the landscape. Humboldt thus refers to art as a necessary mediator for the world's experience as an entity (ibid.: 158pp) and consequently supports painters to make what he studies on his scientific journeys aesthetically accessible (fig. 5) (cf. Achenbach 2009). Similarly, Schiller regards landscape painting as the means with which to obtain the required reunion of man with nature, now occurring in freedom (Ritter 1974: 158pp) and as per Baumgarten's definition of art, according to which it has a character of physical language for its »truth« (expressed in the imitation of nature) can only be perceived by the senses (ibid.: 155–156), Schiller considers the truth of landscape painting to be nothing other than earth life itself (ibid.: 158pp).

Humboldt and Schiller suggest a subjective need to compensate for the divorce of man and nature with aesthetic experience. Their theories are congruent with Heidegger insofar as »being-in-the-world« is expressed here in bodily perception – and they differ insofar as the physical exchange with material reality does not constitute a »real« active impact, but instead, it is reduced to the passive contemplation of landscape painting. In line with these observations, Böhme writes:

> »We somehow become ill and don't know what is happening in our world. We notice that something is entering our state of being but we don't know where it is coming from. Hence my thesis that art has the task of returning this sensuousness to people.« (Böhme 2013: 17)

The difference with Humboldt is that art as a whole takes the place of landscape painting. Accordingly, this text proposes to read the early modern theories in a more open way. The connection to nature can also be interpreted as rootedness in material reality – perhaps, the subjective need described above is first and foremost a desire of the rationally driven man to be assured of his physical existence. This desire would not only be fulfilled through the experience with nature, but by any kind of sensory perception. The experience of physically inhabiting space would be decisive.

Ultimately, Böhme also interprets the beautiful as »phenomena that assure us of our existence« (ibid.: 300). And indeed, looking at diverse definitions of »beauty« throughout history, one can find descriptions of a spatial relationship between the beautiful and the beholder: Plato's conception of the beautiful is everything that lets its idea shine out (ibid.: 290–291). The Platonic idea might be interpreted as the supra-temporal nature of a thing, that is its participation in the universal existence as opposed to what exists in a specific form. Furthermore, Plato relates the beautiful to Eros and speaks of the desire to »have« it (ibid.: 300) – which we could call incorporate. Also, Vitruvian proportion theory, which chooses the human body as a measure of reference (ibid.: 292), implies a spatial relationship between the observer and the »beautiful« thing. Kant then transferred beauty from the object to the mind, yet he distanced himself from the beauty of pure thought and referred instead to an emotional participation in the object, which appears beautiful when it prompts an »activity of the mind« (ibid.: 293) for him, too, the search for the nature of things plays a decisive role (cf. ibid.). Finally, Böhme himself, also states that the beautiful presupposes a »participation of the perceiving subject« (ibid.: 288). He goes on to note that underwater photographs convey the »feeling of presence [German: ›Anwesenheit‹]³ in a way that would never be possible in an object-determined world« (ibid.: 297). All these descriptions have the concept of a mergence of self and space in common.

It is now quite evident that our material affiliation with the world cannot only be conveyed through pictorial representations. On the contrary, just as architectonic space can reflect the objectification and fragmentation of our world, as described for instance by Jameson, it must also be able to express and fulfill a subjective need for irrational, physical experience, for it is the material constitution of our immediate environment. Similarly to Jameson, Frampton also identifies links between the production of architecture and economic and technical development; yet he not only discovers an affirmation of the prevailing postmodern tendency, but also a counter-moment. In his 1983 essay he adopts the term »critical regionalism« to describe the attempt to combine participation in modern civilization (science, technology, politics, etc.) with the cultural roots and particularities of a place. His theory is a response to the loss of culture due to the predetermination of buildings by the economy and high-tech production, and the »ubiquitous placelessness of our modern environment« (Frampton 1983: 24). It can also be read as an attempt to describe an architecture which links man to a pretemporal material reality.

Referring to Heidegger's 1954 lecture »Building Dwelling Thinking« (Heidegger 1951), Frampton argues that a building should be »bounded« to

---

3 ›Anwesenheit‹ means both presence and attendance and is synonymous to »Dasein«. Further, the stem ›Wesen‹ translates to the ›nature‹ and the ›being‹ (of a thing).

a »space/place« [German: ›Ort‹] (ibid.) by inscribing a place's »history in both a geological and agricultural sense [...] into the form and realization of the work« (ibid.: 26). Inscribing »history« into a building means making different stratifications of time simultaneously readable. In this overlap of eras, the things that exist separately in each era become indicators of a categorical supra-temporal existence, that which remains as an analogy after deducting all differences. They relieve us of the linear chronology, we experience these things and moments as present (cf. Suhrkamp 1978: 275–294). In response to that, Augé interprets the feeling that ruins can evoke as an impression of pure time – »le temps pur« – and compares this to the »permanence« we experience in the contemplation of »natural« landscapes (Augé 2003:38f).

One might argue that the experience of such pre-temporal presence stands in direct relation to the experience of the body, just insofar as chronological time relates to the principle of the mind. Since the »invention« of generations in ancient Greece, time has accelerated and turned into the modern age's concept of chronology, where it is no longer holistic and static and dependent on prophecy and religion, but divisible into past and future. Perceiving both requires consciousness,[4] for the past only exists in memory and the future only in anticipation – in return, predicting the future allows human reason to intervene and thus to produce future itself (Koselleck 1979: 17pp). And whereas past and future are a state of mind, presence is the physical condition (Gumbrecht 2012: 268).[5] Rational knowledge, on the other hand, gets abstracted from this physical condition, for the objective acceptance of subjective perception (that is, the knowledge deriving from our bodies' senses) is conditional and the condition is related to a certain moment in time: It is only valid for a specific subject within a specific context. In this

---

4 Wolfgang Pauli, who was fascinated by the theories of Kepler, drew the analogy between the dichotomy of self-awareness and time vs. the timeless and collective unconscious in human perception and the opposition of spatio-temporal processes and indistructible energy and momentum in physics, such as contained in the General Theory of Relativity or the Heisenberg Uncertainty Principle (Miller 2010: 183pp).

5 The word »Presence« derives from the lat. producere, which Gumbrecht translates to »bringing things within reach« and hence relates to the physical proximity of things. Gumbrecht 2012:268). Following this, the experience of fluent time has to be read as a series of different physical conditions, wherefore the temporal stands in opposition to the experience of the world as an indivisble whole.

act of abstraction, our bodily knowledge therefore becomes temporalized and the physical experience loses its eternal validity (cf. Koselleck 1979).[6]

Ultimately, it is the principle of the temporal which grants the possibility of making out of the universal existence of things something which is specifically existing in time. Adorno argues that this universal existence can impossibly be conceived by the mind. There is no way to assert its primacy over the existing by means of conceptual understanding, (Adorno 2002:95ff) and yet he admits: »Any existing is more than it is; existence, in contrast to the existing, reminds us of this« (Klein 2011: 365). This »more« to which he refers is the reality of the thing itself, which shines through on a pre-cognitive, non-intentional level (ibid.: 370); it is not the thing as a specific object but the profound nature of the thing, not the isolated thing existing as such, but the existence of the thing in this world. Its principle is paramount to that of the body and to that of cognition: Both of them manifest themselves only in the existence. But, while rationally, at best, only the existence of our isolated mind can be grasped – that is Descartes's sole certainty – the somatic experience provides us with a dull feeling for the existence of the world as a whole-because our senses are in direct contact with things and thus confirm that we are part of this physical reality. In other words, perceiving the universal existence of a thing, that is, its pre-temporal presence, presupposes a pre-cognitive state. In this condition, we not only experience the existence of this one thing, but of all things, including ourselves, as part of a comprehensive reality.

Frampton's concept of »critical regionalism« convolves both: the principle of the cognitive and that of the pre-cognitive. He describes Jørn Utzon's *Bagsværd Church* as follows: »a work whose complex meaning stems directly from a revealed conjunction between, on the one hand, the rationality of normative technique [expressed in the regular elevation] and, on the other, the arationality of idiosyncratic form [expressed in the organic section]« (Frampton 1982: 22) (fig. 6). But while the rational is established

---

6 Remarkably, also the idea of »happiness« is often connoted with a loss of the sense of time. Hesse defines happiness both as »being liberated from time« and as »being one with the world« (Hesse 2019). In his *Glass Bead Game*, the protagonist's story is told in four different periods of time as four different biographies, which are yet supposed to be understood as one life of one person. In analogy to the above descriptions, this superimposition of time relieves the character of his temporality In contrast to that, thoughtfulness and the perpetual search for meaning is more commonly associated with melancholy or sadness (cf. for instance Steiner 2006 and Camus 1942).

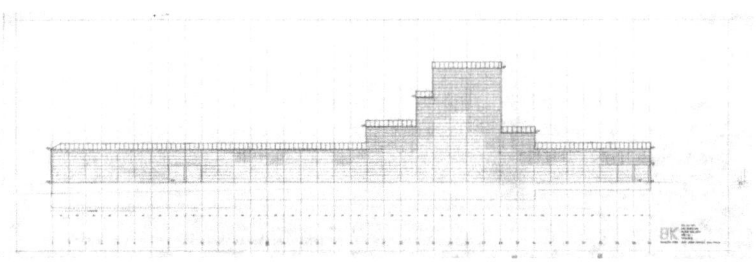

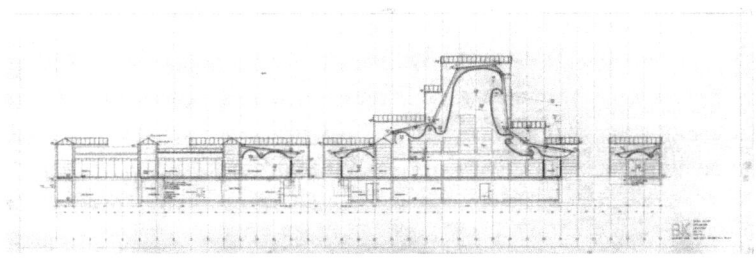

6.
Jørn Utzon. Bagsværd Kirke. Bagsværd, Denmark, 1976.
North Elevation, 1970.
Photo: Utzon Archives / Aalborg University & Utzon Center.

7.
Jørn Utzon. Bagsværd Kirke. Bagsværd, Denmark, 1976.
Longitudinal Section, 1970.
Photo: Utzon Archives / Aalborg University & Utzon Center.

as the fundamental condition of modernity, Frampton's essay must, above all, be understood as a plea for the irrational. It was the »rationalized sight« of modern man, he argues, which caused the »loss of nearness« in the Heideggerian sense (ibid.: 29).

So, while the – supposedly lost – »nearness« to Earth is thus expressed in the pre-cognitive and irrational moment of a building, Heidegger in his etymological-metaphysical reasoning recognizes cosmological connection to the world in the place [German: ›Ort‹]. He describes a building as creating a place, when bringing together the earthly (the material) with the heavenly (the essential), that is, existence in its entirety, quite in the meaning of Adorno. In this sense, he translates the German word for »building« [German: ›bauen‹] into »the way in which we humans are on earth« (Heidegger 1997: 139–156) – it contains the specific nature [German: ›Wesen‹] of a space, which, in return, derives from the place – just as the riverbank only emerges as a riverbank where the bridge crosses the river. In other words, »being-in-the-world« relates to perceiving the transcendental along with the material particularities of a place.

In accordance with, and in reference to, this concept, Frampton postulates that a building should be tied to the site through revealing its specific characteristics, its terrain and material, its climate, its light – and by presenting the specific character of a building, based on the local method of construction in its tectonics, rather than re-presenting it in the facade (Frampton 1983: 26–28). All these qualities only fully manifest themselves in bodily and, therefore, pre-cognitive experience:

> »The tactile resilience of the place-form and the capacity of the body to read the environment in terms other than those of sight alone suggest a potential strategy for resisting the domination of universal technology. [...] One has in mind a whole range of complementary sensory perceptions which are registered by the labile body: the intensity of light, darkness, heat and cold; the feeling of humidity; the aroma of material; the almost palpable presence of masonry as the body senses its own confinement; the momentum of an induced gait and the relative inertia of the body as it traverses the floor; the echoing resonance of our own footfall. [...] The liberative importance of the tactile resides in the fact that it can only be decoded in terms of experience itself: it cannot be reduced to mere information, to representation or to the simple evocation of a simulacrum substituting for absent presences.« (Frampton 1983:28)

Here, it becomes evident why Salingaros states that the concept of regionalism »proposes a post-Cartesian view of the universe. [...] The act of experiencing an artifact or building ties the observer with the observed« (Salingaros 2014). This link is expressed in the tie between building and place. Thence, the response to the postmodern condition of the disengaged body is an architecture which lets atmosphere dominate over concept and sign; the encounter between material space and senses rather than that between meaning and intellect. In this way, architecture bears the potential to respond to a very subjective need for irrational, pre-cognitive perception in a world overloaded with objective information and symbols. »It is precisely the disappearance of the experience of the body«, writes Gumbrecht, »that has intensified our attention to the body – and perhaps even indirectly evoked that new sensibility of space that characterizes contemporary architecture« (Gumbrecht 2012: 62). Now, if this sensibility is expressed in the physical experience of architecture, which is not entirely tangible for that reason, which implies that the building must also be conceived not only through thought, but also through feeling. To anticipate the building (more precisely, the way it will be perceived by the body), the architect cannot just reason but must be able to sense what it will be – to immerse itself in a space which has not yet been built. The next and final chapter will try to understand the implications this might have on the process of making architecture – and on the space that is thereby formed.

Constructing Material Reality

In his essay »Eye and Mind« (Merleau-Ponty 1961) Merleau-Ponty traces the matter of expressing the experience of the world in the phenomenological description of the emergence of a painting: »It is by lending his body to the world that the painter changes the world into paint« (Merleau-Ponty 1964: 16). The painter, he said, must sense his present and »operating« (ibid.) body in the world, meaning that he senses things not as objective re-presentations, but as acting components of one and the same space and thus is himself among these things; he is also within these things, visible for himself as much as for the things until the »indivision of the sensing and the sensed persists« (ibid.: 20). Immersed in space in such a way that it is impossible to say where »nature ends and man or expression begins« (ibid.: 86–87), the painting is painting itself through the hand of the painter as an act of auto-manifestation of the world itself. Here, the »mute being« comes to manifest its own »sense« (ibid.).

More than Heidegger, Merleau-Ponty bases the experience of being in the world on the perception of the body, for the connection between subject and space is primarily constituted in the sensory experience. Again, this is a strong critique of the Cartesian idea of space as an objective, geometrical »res extensa« – space, in Merleau-Ponty's sense, cannot be conceived without the own body within. The »world« thus might be described as Ernst Cassirer depicted it as an individual space of experience – »every organism is, so to speak, a monadic being. It has a world of its own because it has an experience of its own« (ibid.: 43).[7] Here, the mindfluently merges into the physical, yet the notion of the painting itself refers to an unreflected experience in which the painter is not rationally deciding how to set his brush, but where the brush itself, as an extension of the painter's hand and arm, »decides« where to go. In other words, the »body« produces the painting and without that the reason would intervene. We may conclude that pre-cognitive perception is a precondition of experiencing a painting's full presence, its own very reality – and this applies as much to the observer of the finished painting as to the painter while he is producing the painting (or even more to the latter).

Remarkably, this bodily experience of the world is linked to a dissolution of the body in things (»the indivision of the sensing and the sensed«). In Benjamin's words: »sensation does not nest in the head, [...] we do not sense a window, a cloud, a tree in the brain, but rather in the place where we see them« (Benjamin 1955).[8] The fragmented spatial experience of the isolated mind is contrasted here with the world as totality: While the sensing body is externalized, it merges into things which then become an entity. Accordingly, Heidegger notes that the state of mind which is »tuned« or »conditioned« [German: ›gestimmt‹] by space has always revealed »being-in-the-world as a whole« (Thomä 2013: 59) and that the »structural entirety of being« is of a unitary character (ibid.: 60). This means that when I perceive the »being« of

---

7 In *An Essay on Man: An Introduction to a Philosophy of Human Culture*, Ernst Cassirer, in his investigations into the symbolic nature of human existence (»animal symbolicum«) states: »Physical reality seems to recede in proportion as man's symbolic activity advances« (Cassirer 1953: 43).

8 In Walter Benjamin's *Einbahnstraße* (Benjamin 1955: 21), Heidegger says: »Even when we relate to things that are not in the tangible vicinity, we stay with the things themselves. [...] I am never only here as this encapsulated body, but I am there, i.e. already standing through the space, and only in this way can I walk through it« (Heidegger: 151–152).

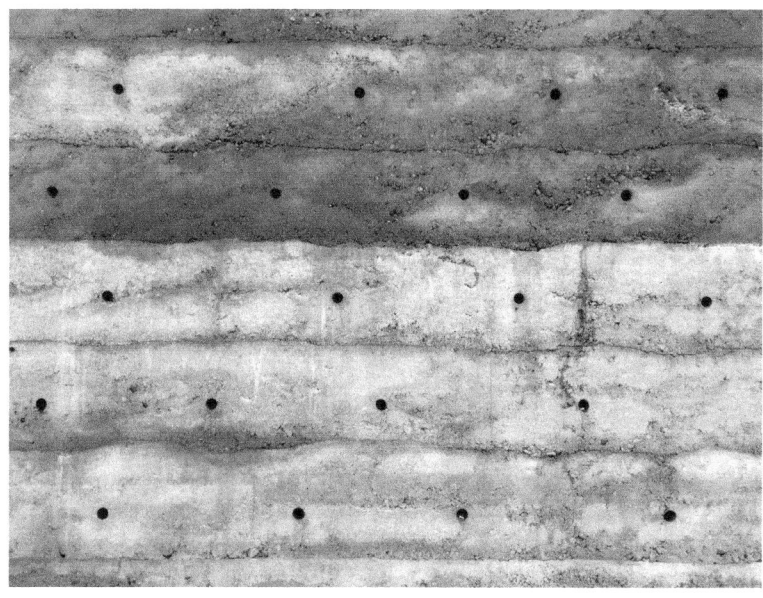

8.
Peter Zumthor: »Feldkapelle Bruder Klaus«, Wachendorf, Germany, 2007.
Photo: Victor Boye Julebæk.

a thing – when its nature is presenting itself to me – I experience something of the totality not only of this one but of all things, including myself. I am not »I«, I am also not the thing, I am not only mind, I am also not only body, for all these categories simply combine in how they belong to the entity of »being«.

Now, it is crucial that Merleau-Ponty describes the mergence of the painter not with the »real« physical world in which he lives, but with what he sees, or imagines, on his canvas. In this moment of immersion, things on the canvas, or in the imagination, are experienced as operational and present, and thus as part of the very same space as the painter himself. Following these descriptions, the architect must, analogously to the painter, perceive his building as real presence, even if it is still in the state of project. Gumbrecht's example of the eucharist illustrates this difference between presence and representation: In the medieval Catholic sense, bread and wine bring about the body and blood of Christ as a real presence insofar as they allow his real substance to appear within their form – and thus make the divine incorporable (Gumbrecht 2012: 127). Gumbrecht associates this conception of the sacrament with a »culture of presence«, where the principles of body and space are predominant and which stands in stark opposition to the »culture of representation« or »culture of meaning«, which is defined by the principles of intellect and time. He considers both types as coexisting with varying emphasis, yet the pre-Cartesian time is strongly associated with the first type where its »core element«, the human body, is still understood as an »internal element of a cosmology« (ibid.: 217). In contrast to that, the intellectualized Western culture has for centuries been primarily in the realm of the latter type (ibid.: 213pp). Therefore, in the modern reformed understanding, communion is only a sign-like memory, which means it is a re-presentation (and not presentation). In short, a thing that is present is perceived not as a mere bearer of meaning or as a signifier but as a signified, or in Adorno's words: not as an existing but as existence (Gumbrecht 2012: 126pp). Therefore, a drawing, image or model, for the architect who »sees« according to Merleau-Ponty, is not the re-presentation of a building, but must be understood as a presentation of the building itself, a coming-to-the-world of a comprehensive reality. The model is no longer a model in the sense of an abstraction of (or sign, or cognitive reference to) another reality, but is an evocation of the very reality of the project itself, an appearance and constitution of its real substance. At this point, the reality of the project merges with our own.

This notion of the »model as reality« becomes most evident when we think about full-scale mock-ups, where the distinction between an abstraction of the project and the actual building is nearly obsolete in so far as the mock-up may provide a real physical experience of the project space – it's tangible, it might look exactly like the represented building, smell like it, feel like it and sound like it. At this point, the distinction between »real« and »representation« can only happen in the mind, for the senses cannot perceive any difference. In addition, the mock-up, or some of its elements, might (theoretically or practically) be integrated, that is to say, turn into the later fabric of the building. Hence, the simple importance of mock-ups or large-scale models at a time when more and more steps in the process of making architecture are being transferred to the digital space anticipate the tactile experience and make the material reality of a building tangible before it has actually been built.

Another aspect begins to shine through here: How is it actually going to be built? The mock-up must find the same answer to this question as the later building and it shifts the focus to the construction process. Zumthor's Chivelstone House uses the historical construction method of Devonshire, where the project is located, for its walls (Zumthor 2014: 52). Building a mold of wooden planks into which, day by day, a rise of clay Zumthor used earthy concrete with a minimal quantity of cement) is filled, rammed down by a person and left to dry, while the mold is made to slide up (Laycock 1920: 179–182). This process not only reveals the regional method of construction and the ground of the site in the walls, as illustrated by Frampton's term »critical regionalism«, not only can the daily changes in climate during construction be read as they are reflected in the different texture and color of the material, but the physical impact of the worker can also be sensed in the irregularity of the layers (fig. 7). Herein the tie between building and place is expressed as much as the link between laborer and work; the observer, in turn, experiences all of these through his senses.

And while certainly the full scale mock-up comes closest to the building's physical appearance, it is important to stress that just like a mock-up can appear as a »real« part of the building, a drawing at an early stage of the process or even a mental image can be considered as »real«: Just like a small change in scale would make it impractical to reuse a mock-up for the later building, but would perhaps be barely perceptible to the senses (and therefore still allow us to experience the unbroken material reality of the project), also a larger change in scale, or in the medium, might still allow the senses to perceive the particularities of a space, even if only in memory or anticipation.

The bodily experience of a certain condition of space does not necessarily require this condition to be the external physical reality. Being in exchange with the material world means perceiving our own biological or biochemical response to the environmental conditions. Böhme describes how this response can be triggered not only externally, but also felt as our bodies latent potential to react to a representation or imaginary condition.

Perceiving this bodily potential is what he calls perceiving an atmosphere (Moravánszky 2015: 254–255). In this sense, atmosphere can also be defined as the mergence of subject and space. It is the direct impact of space – real or imagined – on our own felt condition, an affirmation of our senses that we exist as a body. Hence, perceiving an atmosphere through imagination means, to some extent, experiencing the physical reality of the imagined space, or perceiving the imagined space as physical reality.

To anticipate the impact of a space on the body is, however, only one part of the architect's work. Another part is to constitute this space, for which he must himself impact the labile space until it has found its stable condition. Here, reception is equal to production. And while Merleau-Ponty's painter could, at least theoretically, act unconsciously throughout to paint his picture, this would hardly be feasible for a building that must also fulfill practical, rational and at the same time quite complex requirements. This reveals a much greater contradiction: The subjective need for physical affiliation with the material world stands in opposition to the liberating forces of reason. Both principles operate in coexistence and both have their own merit. The pre-cognitive is the human primal state; the intellect, however, is no less than the foundation of human freedom. It is only outside this freedom that the pre-cognitive state is desirable again, because it is only the stable condition that allows for momentary oblivion.

In light of this contrast, Worringer describes how cultures that have built up a trust-based relationship with nature – perceiving the environment as safe rather than as an objective, alien space – feel an urge to immerse themselves in the things [German: ›Einfühlungsdrang‹] that is artistically expressed in naturalistic imitation. If, on the other hand, the environment appeared threatening, then inorganic, abstract and intellectualized objects would be produced, because in this case it would only be at a distance from the context of nature that man would find a »possibility to rest from the confusion and uncertainty of the world« (Worringer 1911: 49). On an aesthetic level, this feeling can be described using Kant's definition of the sublime: Becoming aware of one's own »strength of soul« when looking at natural violence from a safe distance. Here the subject, which would remain completely powerless as a pure natural being, becomes conscious of its freedom and superiority of reason. The sublime, for Kant, is also a »feeling of tension between the sensual and the rational which is projected onto the object« (Pöltner 2008: 101). The balance between the urge for immersion and its antagonist, the will to detach oneself and abstract the world, is impacted by external environmental conditions and their psychological interpretation.

With Worringer's theory in mind it becomes easy to understand why, in the tumultuous 1930s and 1940s, the critical theory surrounding Horkheimer and Adorno demanded that art be »disharmonic« in order to express the »cleft between the monadic individual and his barbaric environment« (Horkheimer 1988: 424). And yet Adorno has not given up on the idea of bodily perception. In his later work on aesthetics, he transfers Kant's idea of the sublime from nature to art – just as Humboldt and Schiller did. After man's alienation from nature has progressed so far that an immediate relationship is no longer possible, the once »mimetic« relationship can only be experienced in memory. It should be modern art's task to provoke this remembrance; not, however, by evoking an actual sense of unity, which at best would lead back to superstitious mythology, but by requiring constant rationalization, which reaches its limits in the simultaneous recognition of the irrational moment of art. Thus, art remains capable of criticism on the one hand, but on the other generates a »sublime« consciousness – in contrast to Kant, not that of the nature-subjugating power of the intellect, but the »self-consciousness of man of his naturality« (Peña 1994: 76).

Perhaps there is a slight inaccuracy in Adorno's theory: The understanding of oneself as a natural thing cannot be a matter of mere remembrance. It is acutely evoked by bodily perception. This becomes even clearer when looking at Lyotard's conception of the sublime. He criticises Adorno's »melancholic« attitude as he believes that the bodily is irretrievably lost, so that the »question of subject and object« is abstracted to a question of representability. This becomes particularly evident in non-objective art.

In his later publications, Lyotard increasingly speaks of the »present« instead of the »sublime«, because it eludes the structure of space and time (Peña 1994: 99pp). Again, it must be noted that, despite Lyotard's belief that the bodily is lost, this feeling for presence is provoked by the contemplation of art, i.e. by somatic perception. Moreover, his definition of the sublime is

Maybe the process of making architecture can be conceived as analogous to the experience of the sublime, as an alternation between thinking and feeling. The architect can trace his bodily experience in memory, as Adorno describes it in his concept of the »sublime«, (cf. Peña 1994: 76) to then act from memory, so as to reproduce his memory of the anticipated space. The challenge, however, is obvious: the rational side retains great weight here. There might be a first break between the anticipated and the remembered space and a second between the memory and its intellectual reproduction. To bridge this gap, a means is needed to act, that is, to impact the drawing or model with direct sensation to alternately form space without thought and to question the resulting space analytically. This is the same method as that used by the painter and sculptor. It might be self-evident, and yet, in light of the ever-increasing attention to digital design methods, it is worthwhile stressing that the pre-cognitive physical impact on the world requires the mediating tool to fade out of consciousness, to be »ready-to-hand«, in Heidegger's sense (cf. Thomä 2012: 48pp), and leave room for intuition. As opposed to most of today's digital planning tools, the hand drawing and the physical model might allow for such direct impact by the »operating« body.

The pencil can work as an extension of the hand and the model might also be subconciously formed or manipulated by the hand by cutting pieces, sculpting pieces, moving piecesand allowing the building to »manifest itself« through our hands. Eventually, the hand senses a space that would hardly have come about through rational calculation. It is also the material itself that decides how it wants to be formed. Certainly, a keyboard and mouse can step out of consciousness in equal measure. Yet, it is decisive that the digital drawing or model is based on parameters – abstract data which has to be controlled by reason. In order to manipulate the project, its digital parameters are usually altered first, for instance by entering verbal commands or numbers, an act that is rational by nature (and requests a precision that perhaps closes the room for the vagueness of imagination and intuition). It is only once this indirectness has been overcome that digital tools can be considered equal to analog tools in regard to their ability to support the making of tangible space, and yet another problem persists: The space's response to our body remains in the realm of the imagination. It can also be present this way, as set out by Böhme, but it is likely to remain less intense. Whereas the physical model is constituted in material space and can be touched and smelled, the digital model is primarily defined through form and thus perhaps contributes to the overestimation of the visual – it tends

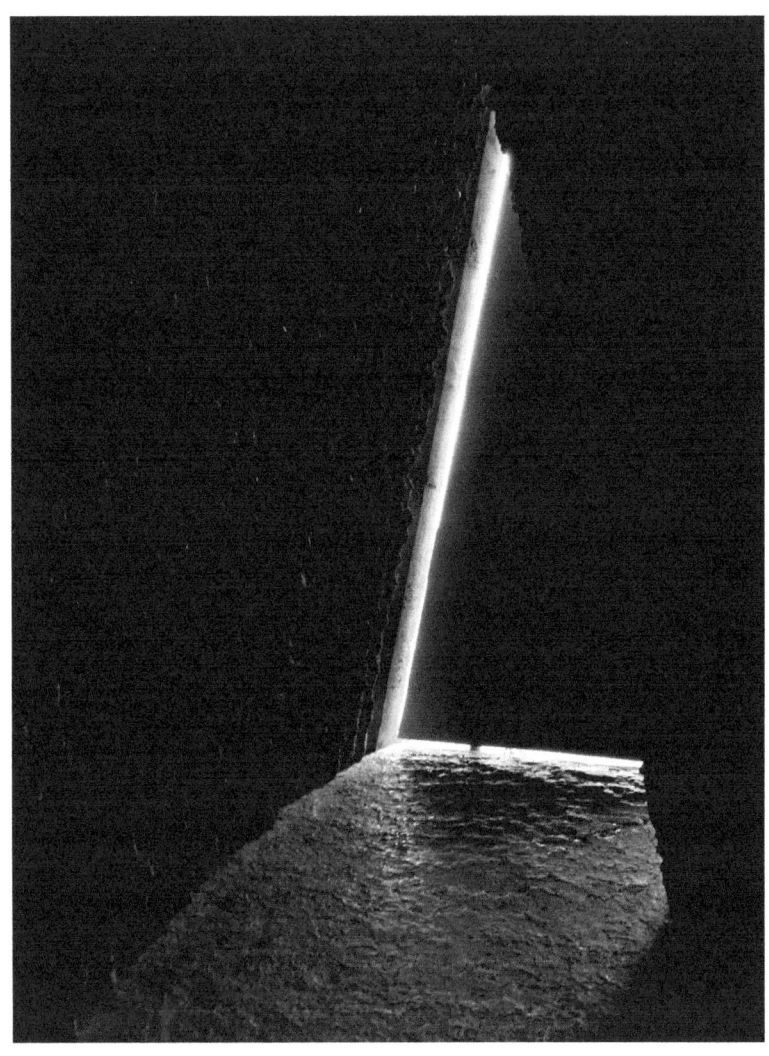

9.
Peter Zumthor. Feldkapelle Bruder Klaus. Wachendorf, Germany, 2007
Photo: Victor Boye Julebæk.

to be separated from the architect's world through the division provided by a screen, on which it appears as a flat, calculated and objective projection.

At a time when almost anything seems possible in the digital space, when virtual realities threaten to corrode what remains of our physical connection to the world and when artificial intelligence promises a rationalization of architecture that could take on a life of its own, the role of the analog model becomes clear in its sensory qualities. Firstly, it can be physically experienced and secondly, it can be physically manipulated, thus facilitating the development of a physically tangible architecture that can convey an affiliation to material reality upon an isolated postmodern subject. In the analog model, an architecture may thus emerge whose focus is less on the form than on the haptic qualities of the material and less on the assembly of individual building elements than on the process in which they are created, that is, the physical impact on the material and the physical exchange between man and space.

Perhaps this shift in focus, caused by the ever-increasing rationalization and fragmentation of space in our time, explains the emergence of seemingly primitive architecture over the past few years which tends to address our senses more than our reason. In some recent canonical works, the primacy of the material, the body and the atmosphere is so distinct that classical elements of »high-culture« architecture have almost entirely disappeared (to an extent that these buildings may not have been recognized as works of authorship some decades ago); instead of being composed of column and beam, wall and roof, window and façade, they instead form cave-like spaces. A few examples: Ishigami's house and restaurant in Yamaguchi Prefecture, completed in 2022, was created by pouring concrete into holes in the ground and excavating a space beneath, an act of »inverting the landscape«to »turn it into a dwelling« (Ishigami 2021: 227) and create the »distinctive atmosphere of something there since forever« (ibid.: 236).

Ensamble Studio turned an existing stone quarry into a house to inhabit the ground (Ca'n Terra 2018; Ensamble 2023). Zumthor describes his Thermal Bath in Vals, Switzerland, which was completed in 1996, as »an architectural structure, embedded in the slope, which in its architectural attitude and appearance is older than everything already built around it« (Hauser 2007: 23), a quarry-like space which »I immediately experience as a whole« (ibid.: 38). He built a chapel near Cologne, the Bruder-Klaus-Feldkapelle in 2007, which is entirely defined through the light and climate of the location, along with its material appearance. Zumthor refers to Heidegger's bridge when

very much in line with the descriptions of pre-cognitive bodily experience above. Eventually, the reason for this seeming contradiction is just a matter of focus.

The work of art is dialectical in nature. It has a subjective-irrational and an objective-rational moment« and our perception recognizes both in approximate simultaneity. It can convey both sensuality and meaningfulness with particular intensity. Thus, it may evoke a consciousness »ex negativo« of our rootedness in the physical world – a cognitive presence as opposed to the felt presence, a conceptual grasp of the material reality, provoked by a high-frequency alternation of somatic and rational perception. In this way, one might conclude that the sublime is an intended perturbation of the relationship between body and mind, an immediate experience of merging with the world, which does not last,[9] but is interrupted by the consciousness and then only grasped as such. It can be read as an expression of the ambiguity of our needs: To understand the world rationally and to merge with it in pre-cognitive, bodily perception, and while reason is the only guarantor of safety in the long term, but withdraws the body from the world, it can also be dispensable in the short term and a nuisance to our physical existence.

In his defence of regionalism and the body, Salingaros blames the Frankfurt School around Adorno for being responsible for the overvaluation of rationalizing progress thinking and thus for the insufficient consideration of the »tie between the observer and the observed« in today's architectural discourse – and even in Frampton's theories (Salingaros 2014).[10] And while the »critical« moment called for by Frampton in the sense of preserving a »critical self-consciousness« (Frampton 1983: 21) is indeed reminiscent of Adorno's attempt to outline an aesthetic that combines the experience of human naturalness with the simultaneous preservation of its capacity for social criticism (see above), one thing in Salingaros's critique is particularly relevant to us: It stands for the constant re-evaluation of two antagonistic moments of perception – the rational and the irrational. Ultimately, the question of weighting both factors in the process of making is decisive for the architectural result.

---

9 Accordingly, Jean-Luc Nancy points out that an absolute presence can never be experienced, for it exhausts itself in the shining of existence (Gumbrecht 2012: 302).

10 Unlike, in his view, in modern physics, i.e. quantum physics. Already Pauli drew parallels between quantum physics and the conscious/unconscious, see above.

describing how the tower-like building sits within the landscape. The client, a local farmer, felled trees from his own forest and transformed them into a tent-like structure that provided the formwork for the rammed concrete, which he then layered over 24 days. The wood was then burned away in a smoldering 30-day fire, which left behind a sooty, fire-scented surface (Zumthor 2014: 121–122) (fig. 9).

From the exterior, the builder's physical impact on the building can be read in the layers of concrete. From the interior, the construction process can be smelled and felt on the inclined walls, which equally form the ceiling. An overhead hole provides a view of the sky and light, rain and snow fall through this hole and on to the floor. There seems to be little symbolic meaning to this space, its experience is entirely informed by the senses. Rationally, its form can barely be grasped and we are reminded of the analogy that Giedion drew between the continuous change of direction between the vaulted, rocky surfaces of a cave (Giedion 1965: 345) and the pre-historic concept of space free from directionality or spatial boundaries (ibid.: 358).

Conclusion.

Primitive Architecture as Response to a Rationalized World? The German and Latin words for knowledge [German: ›wissen‹, Latin: ›sapere‹] once meant »to see« and »to taste« and thus refered to our body's senses (Grimm 1848). In the course of the development of human culture, the body's experiences have increasingly receded into the background. To the rational mind, space appears as a detached and objective geometry, as a fragmented condition in time. The built space reflects this global condition and reinforces itself the fragmented perception. Knowledge became abstracted from the physical reality, and yet, knowledge still derives from our senses. Our bodies are still embedded in the material world, they are labile, they are sentient, they are operating, they get impacted by this world and they impact this world. Our intellect has turned nature into an object while our bodies are drawn to merge with space. If conditions allow, we can lose ourselves in the physical reality and experience the world – our own subjective world of experience – as an entity, as a timeless whole, indivisible in itself and indistinguishable from ourselves. We can call this experience the assurance of our own existence, the pre-cognitive knowledge of our being-in-the-world. This knowledge is of a corporeal nature, not intellectual but sentient. And architecture also catalyzes – or contains – this knowledge. The process of making architecture decides how far it will be revealed in the building. To anticipate the material reality of a building, we must be able to sent the space, perceive its pre-cognitive presence and also impact it prior to cognition. It is both a matter of being open to inhabiting the space, which may not yet exist for others, but may be real in our imagination, and being able to constitute this space with our hands. Thus, eventually, our bodies' response to the rationalized and fragmented world we inhabit today are buildings that no longer look much like buildings and which appear as primitive spaces to the mind but offer an almost infinite experience to the senses.

The term »revolution« once symbolized French society's reversion to Greco-Roman antiquity. It was borrowed from astronomy – referring to the orbital motion of the planets – (The Age of Neo-Classicism, exhibition catalogue no. 1609) and actually comes from the Latin word »revolutio« (rotation or return) (Bertelsmann 1975: 3072). Today, Latour speaks of a »second revolution of science«: As opposed to the modern understanding of the world as an accumulation of objects without »agency« (that is to say without an independent existence), contemporary science realized that the world itself is alive. It is built from fungi, bacteria and viruses, which, instead of following calculated predictions, have their own effective power. Latour says: »We are no longer in a world of objects from which we are distant, but we are in the midst of beings that time superimposes with us« (De Chaney 2021). The »operating body« of Merleau-Ponty's painter is in the midst of things which he sees as acting components (Merleau-Ponty 1964: 20). Perhaps an architecture in Frampton's sense of »regionalism« – which draws its space from the place of a building, from its climate and material, and which ties the observer to the observed can go hand in hand both with a very ancient experience of space and with Latour's new ecological understanding of the world.

References

Achenbach, Sigrid (2009): *Kunst um Humboldt: Reisestudien aus Mittel- und Südamerika von Rugendas, Bellermann und Hildebrandt im Berliner Kupferstichkabinett*, München: Hirmer.

Adorno, Theodor W (2002): »Ontologie und Dialektik«, in: Rolf Tiedemann (ed.), *Nachgelassene Schriften, Abt. IV, Bd. 7.* (1960/61), Frankfurt am Main: Suhrkamp.

Allen, R. E., Fowler, H. W. and Fowler, F.G. (1990), in: T*he Concise Oxford Dictionary of Current English*, 8th ed., Oxford: Clarendon Press.

Arts Council of Great Britain, (1972): *The Age of Neo-Classicism (Exhibition Catalog no. 1609)*, London: Victoria and Albert Museum.

Augé, Marc. (1992): *Non-lieux: introduction à une anthropologie de la surmodernité*, Paris: Seuil.

Benjamin, Walter (1955): *Einbahnstraße*, Frankfurt am Main: Suhrkamp.

Böhme, Gernot (2013): *Atmosphäre: Essays zur neuen Ästhetik*, 7th ed., Berlin: Suhrkamp.

Burgdorff, Stephan/Bernhard Zand (2008): »Zwang zum Spektakel«, in: *Der Spiegel*, 24 June.

Camus, Albert(1942): Le mythe de Sisyphe, Paris: Gallimard.

Cassirer, Ernst (1953): An Essay on Man: An Introduction to a Philosophy of Human Culture, New York: Doubleday.

De Chaney, Camille/Truong, Nicolas (2021): »Nous avons changé de monde«, *Entretiens avec Bruno Latour* (1/12), ARTE France, https://www.arte.tv/fr/videos/106738-001-A/entretiens-avec-bruno-latour-1-12/, accessed July 23, 2024.

Descola, Philippe (2011): *Leben und Sterben in Amazonien: Bei den Jívaro-Indianern*, transl. Grete Osterwald, Berlin: Suhrkamp.

Descola, Philippe (2013): *Jenseits von Natur und Kultur*, transl. Eva Moldenhauer, Berlin: Suhrkamp.

Dieter, Thomäs (2013): *Heidegger-Handbuch: Leben, Werk, Wirkung*, 2nd ed., Stuttgart: J.B. Metzler.

Ensamble Studio (2018): »Ca'n Terra: House in Menorca«, https://www.ensamble.info/canterra-house-in-menorca. accessed July 23, 2024.

Fischer, Norbert (2010): »Landschaft als kulturwissenschaftliche Kategorie«, lecture, Paris, January 8, 2010, http://www.n-fischer.de/landschaft_kultur_4.html, accessed July 23, 2024.

Frampton, Kenneth (1983) »Towards a Critical Regionalism: Six Points for an Architecture of Resistance«, in: Hal Foster (ed.), *The Anti-Aesthetic: Essays on Postmodern Culture*, Seattle: Bay Press.

Gehrke, Hans-Joachim (2003): *Geschichte des Hellenismus*, 3rd ed, München: Oldenbourg.

Giedion, Sigfried (1965): *Ewige Gegenwart: Der Beginn der Architektur*, Köln: Du Mont.

Grimm, Jacob (1848): »Die fünf Sinne«, in: Zeitschrift für deutsches Altertum 6, 1–15. https://www.jstor.org/stable/20650096.

Gumbrecht, Hans Ulrich (2012): *Präsenz*, Berlin: Suhrkamp.

Hauser, Sigrid/Peter Zumthor/Hélène Binet (2007): *Peter Zumthor: Therme Vals*, Zürich: Scheidegger & Spiess.

Heidegger, Martin (1997): »Bauen Wohnen Denken«, in: *Vorträge und Aufsätze*, 8th ed, Stuttgart: Neske.

Hesse, Hermann (2013): *Das Glasperlenspiel*, 40th ed., Berlin: Suhrkamp.

Hesse, Hermann: »Über das Glück«. 2019, https://www.suhrkamp.de/mediathek/hermann_hesse_spricht_ueber_das_glueck_489.html, accessed July 23, 2024.

Horkheimer, Max(1988): »Neue Kunst und Massenkultur«, in: *Gesammelte Schriften in 19 Bänden*, Bd. 4: Schriften 1936–1941, Frankfurt am Main: Fischer.

Ishigami, Jun'ya (2021): *Freeing Architecture*, Paris: Fondation Cartier pour l'art contemporain.

Jameson, Fredric (1991): *Postmodernism or The Cultural Logic of Late Capitalism*, Durham, NC: Duke University Press.

Klein, Richard, ed. (2011): *Adorno-Handbuch: Leben, Werk, Wirkung*, Stuttgart: J. B. Metzler.

Koselleck, Reinhart (1979): *Vergangene Zukunft: Zur Semantik geschichtlicher Zeiten*, Frankfurt am Main: Suhrkamp.

Kuhn, Thomas S. (1957): *The Copernican Revolution: Planetary Astronomy and the Development of Western Thought*, New York: Vintage Books.

Laycock, Charles H. (1920) : »The Old Devon Farm-House«, in: *DA Transactions, Vol. 52*, 158–191.

Leupen, Bernard (1990): »Fragment als Strategie«, in: *Werk, Bauen + Wohnen, Vol. 3*, 24–31.

Lewis, Charlton/Short, Charles (1879): *A Latin Dictionary: Founded on Andrews' Edition of Freund's Latin Dictionary. Revised, Enlarged, and in Great Part Rewritten*, Oxford: Clarendon Press, 1879.

Michaelsen, Sven (2018): »Fast die ganze Welt hat sich der Diktatur der Marktwirtschaft unterworfen«, in: SZ Magazin, 18 May.

Miller, Arthur I.(2010): 137: *Jung, Pauli and the Pursuit of a Scientific Obsession*, New York: W. W. Norton & Co.

Pauli, Wolfgang(1955): »The Influence of Archetypal Ideas on the Scientific Theories of Kepler«, in: *The Interpretation of Nature and the Psyche*, transl. Priscilla Silz, New York: Bollingen Series LI, Pantheon Books.

Peña Aguado, María Isabel (1994): Ästhetik des Erhabenen: *Burke, Kant, Adorno, Lyotard*, Wien: Passagen-Verlag.

Pöltner, Günther (2008): *Philosophische Ästhetik*, Stuttgart: Kohlhammer.

Ritter, Joachim (1974): *Subjektivität: Sechs Aufsätze*, Frankfurt am Main: Suhrkamp.

Rowe, Colin/Fred Koetter (1979): *Collage City*, Cambridge, MA/London: MIT Press.

Salingaros, Nikos (2014): *Unified Architectural Theory, Chapter 6*, July 26. https://www.archdaily.com/530829/unified-architectural-theory-chapter-6.

von Schiller, J. C. Friedrich (2002): »Letters Upon the Aesthetic Education of Man: Letter XXV«, in: *The Aesthetical Essays*, https://www.gutenberg.org/files/6798/6798-h/6798-h.htm.

Schuller, Wolfgang (2002): *Griechische Geschichte*, 5th ed, München: Oldenbourg.

Steiner, George (2006): *Warum Denken traurig macht. Zehn (mögliche) Gründe –* English translation: Ten (Possible) Reasons for the Sadness of Thought, transl. Nicolaus Bornhorn, Frankfurt am Main: Suhrkamp.

Szondi, Peter(1978): »Hoffnung im Vergangenen: Über Walter Benjamin«, in: *Schriften II*, Frankfurt am Main: Suhrkamp.

Wahrig, Gerhard ed. (1975): *Deutsches Wörterbuch*, München: Bertelsmann.

Worringer, Wilhelm (1911): *Abstraktion und Einfühlung: Ein Beitrag zur Stilpsychologie*, 3rd ed., München: R. Piper & Co.

Zumthor, Peter (2010): *Architektur Denken*, 3rd ed., Basel: Birkhäuser.

Zumthor, Peter (2014): *Peter Zumthor: Bauten und Projekte 1985–2013*, Zürich: Scheidegger & Spiess.

Places of Rural Practice

Niklas Fanelsa

Abstract: Places of Rural Practice is an innovative learning environment that embraces multiple disciplines and seeks to expand the application of architectural and design practices. Through a series of workshops, participants engage in hands-on exploration, focusing on the practical aspects of design. These workshops take place in rural spaces, which serve as productive settings for experimenting with spatial concepts and creating unique architectural experiences. This project reimagines rural environments as lively hubs for pushing the boundaries of design and fostering creative collaboration.

Keywords: Workshop; Experience-Based Learning; Embodied Knowledge; Practice-Based Design; Commoning; Rural Reality.

Introduction

The limitations of our global neo-liberal economy, which relies heavily on the extraction of non-renewable natural resources, have sparked a strong desire for societal changes, particularly in our everyday routines and behaviors. Crises like the recent Covid-19 pandemic have exposed the vulnerability of lifestyles that depend on fossil fuels and the production of goods from distant locations. With the concentration of global capital in rapidly growing urban areas, cities have become more expensive and less appealing, leading more people to seek a simpler way of life in smaller communities (Fanelsa 2020). With home offices becoming more popular, the notion that cities are the sole source of creativity has become obsolete. The countryside is gaining attention as a place that generates desirable patterns of life, work, and production. In rural areas, specific places are emerging as hubs that bring together expertise, skills, and inhabitants to create communal initiatives that prioritize local built environments and social networks (Kayoko 2018). In the countryside, groups gather to develop and expand upon the local context and have

---

Corresponding author: Niklas Fanelsa (Technical University of Munich, Germany), niklas.fanelsa@tum.de.
Open Access. © 2024 Niklas Fanelsa published by transcript Verlag.
This work is licensed under the Creative Commons Attribution 4.0 (BY) license.

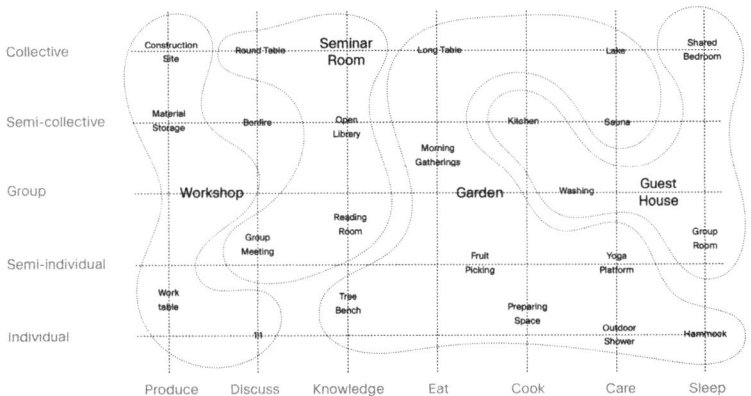

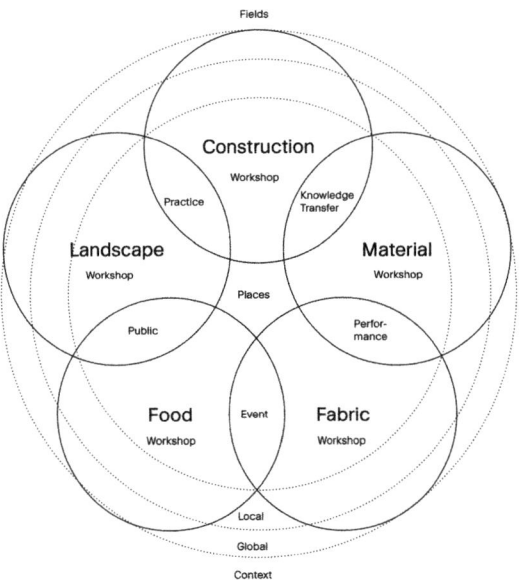

1.
Learning Spaces. Illustration by the author.

2.
Five Fields. Illustration by the author.

a holistic approach to living and working. The village's smaller scale allows for practical experimentation and shared activities.

In such a close-knit environment, the impact directly influences the entire community's daily life, promoting development based on the unique characteristics of the place.

Methodology

Places of Rural Practice is a series of co-creation workshops, with each session rooted in a specific location, a local framework, and a network of people. Drawing inspiration from the historic *Black Mountain College*, it aims to develop an understanding of the countryside from within (Fanelsa 2020). At *Black Mountain*, its work program combined building construction, farming, and learning classes at the rural site of Lake Eden in North Carolina (Blume et al. 2015). An important aspect of these workshops is that they occur in an inspiring environment where participants can live and work for the duration of the workshop. There must be the necessary infrastructure to host events and exchange ideas within the group (fig. 1).

Each workshop series has at least two thematic fields that are led by an expert with a connection to the local area. Preparation is integrated into the workshop, with specific topics and frameworks developed in collaboration with the experts. In most cases, a thematic field is assigned to each workshop every day and the last day is dedicated to organizing a joint concluding event. Similar to *Global Tools* (Borgonuovo and Franceschini 2022), during this event, the individual thematic fields form as many intersections and collaborative constellations as possible. What was initially independent is transformed into a holistic artifact in the final event (*Construct Lab*, 2023). This occurs through a joint negotiation process involving the group, which is continuously guided by the tutors.

The Places of Rural Practice workshop series draws on five main fields: construction; material; landscape; fabric and food. These are not exhaustive, however, and may be adapted in the future. Each workshop is based locally, but over time they will generate a network of international rural places (fig. 2).

The field of construction (fig. 3–6) deals with traditional techniques of joining, the circular use of building elements, and the creation of constructional spatial structures. This can include the framework for a wooden pavilion or a new interpretation of old building components.

3.
The first workshop day in CONSTRUCTION starts at a former garage, Ronald Klemmer, the local carpenter, transformed into a professional workshop. Participants learn about the concept of the journeyman years, where international experience combines with local tradition. Using hand tools, individuals prepare mortise and tenon joints for the main structure with chisels and hammers. Photo: Zara Pfeifer, 2020.

In the material field, bioregional building materials (*Atelier Luma* 2023) are used in the sense of climate-positive architecture and make its haptic qualities accessible. Ranging from the traditional use of lime as a versatile building material to new insulation materials, such as hemp or straw, the joint collaboration between craftspeople, clients, and architects on specific prototypes is its essential feature.

Landscape examines the contextual design of outdoor spaces with regard to vegetation, climate, and the seasons. This includes maintaining a kitchen garden, the pruning of old fruit treesand the introduction of new elements into the grounds of a listed park.

Food (fig. 7–8) treats eating as a means of communicating hospitality, as regional production and as a performative activity. Through culinary practice, the participants are able to come into contact with the local community and map existing practice.

Fabric (fig. 9) describes textiles as everyday objects and an ephemeral design resource. This can involve designing work clothes, or wall hangings using blueprint techniques.

Results

The methodology outlined above shapes a spatial learning environment and facilitates the collaborative creation of diverse artifacts. These artifacts, including the wooden pavilion, naturally dyed fabrics, sun blinds, and fermented food (fig. 10–11), emerged as tangible outcomes of the CCA Emerging Curator program in Gerswalde in 2020. At the concluding event, these artifacts undergo a collective presentation and evaluation. This culminates in a gathering of villagers, tutors, spontaneous guests, and workshop participants and goes beyond a mere assessment; it evolves into a reunion of those who encountered each other during the workshop and fosters meaningful connections and deepens mutual understanding. For many, this event is not just an endpoint but a starting point for continued exploration of the countryside and its potential. Moreover, this workshop series has been the catalyst for subsequent initiatives in rural areas of France, Italy, and elsewhere in Europe. Collaborating institutions included the *Biennale Versailles*, *Villa Massimo*, and *The Technical University of Munich*. These further iterations extend the original endeavor's impact and ethos to a network of diverse rural landscapes.

4.
In four small groups, work continues in the workshop and its exterior space. Some test the joints and mark the individual elements for later construction. Others cut notches into lighter wooden beams for the floor and roof grid using hand saws. Some of the joints need to be cut in place, so the cooperation of three to four people is required. Photo: Zara Pfeifer, 2020.

Discussion

This workshop series has significant implications for contemporary society and addresses pressing challenges and trends while also offering potential solutions and insights. The workshops emphasize sustainable practices, the circular use of materials, climate-positive architecture, and regional production. In the face of the climate crisis, there is a growing recognition of the need to transition toward more sustainable lifestyles and built environments. The workshops provide practical examples and hands-on experiences that showcase sustainable approaches to construction, material usage, and food production. By promoting climate-conscious practices, the workshop series contributes to the larger goal of mitigating the impact on the environment and fostersecological resilience. The presented workshop focused on professionals and students from the field of architecture and design, with less focus on involving other groups, such as children or professionals from other disciplines. Recognizing this bias is essential for a more inclusive and comprehensive approach to the workshop concept.

Design in Dialogue formats (ETH Newrope 2021) encourages participants to engage with local communities and establish connections with experts who have a strong connection to the local area. This approach fosters a sense of community, promotes the intergenerational transfer of knowledge, and empowers individuals to actively contribute to their surroundings. In an increasingly globalized and individualistic world, community engagement is crucial for creating cohesive societies and addressing social challenges. Workshops, as in *Granby Four Street* (Assemble 2017) can serve as a platform for building community and collective action by nurturing a sense of belonging and shared responsibility.

Rural areas often face depopulation, economic challenges, and the loss of cultural heritage. Workshop series like *Satoyama School of Design* (Tsukamoto Laboratory 2021) bring attention to the unique qualities and potential possessed by rural environments and highlight their value as spaces for creative exploration, cultural exchange, and sustainable practices. By investing in rural areas and fostering collaboration between urban and rural communities, workshops contribute to revitalizing these regions and create opportunities for economic growth, cultural preservation, and innovation.

The workshop series' methodology embraces an alternative approach to education and emphasizes embodied learning, interdisciplinary collaboration, and experiential knowledge. This resonates with the evolving

5.
To fix the joinery, two to three people hold the joint in a good position, and one person drives in a dowel made from oak. Having prepared the wooden beams precisely, the group builds the structure in less than one hour. Once done, everybody has different ideas for its potential use. Photo: Zara Pfeifer, 2020.

understanding of education in today's society, where there is a need for more holistic and practical forms of learning.

As in the *Floating University* (Raumlaborberlin 2021) workshop formats can grow into a platform for lifelong learning and the development of skills, where participants are empowered to become active agents in their own education and personal growth. This approach challenges didactic teaching models and encourages a shift toward more experience-based and participatory learning methods.

Conclusion

In conclusion, co-creation workshop series like *Places of Rural Practice* hold an important position in today's society. They address pressing challenges, such as sustainable practices, community engagement, rural revitalization, and alternative education. As such, the workshops contribute to a more sustainable, inclusive, and resilient society. The workshop format offers practical examples and hands-on experiences that showcase sustainable approaches to construction, material usage, and food productionand aligns with the urgent need to address the climate crisis. By connecting participants and local communities and experts, the workshops foster a sense of community and empower individuals to actively contribute to their surroundings, while also nurturing a collective sense of responsibility.

Furthermore, the workshops illuminate the unique qualities and potential of rural environments, contributing to their revitalization and offering opportunities for economic growth, cultural preservation, and innovation. In addition, the workshops embrace an alternative approach to education and promote embodied learning and interdisciplinary collaboration, which aligns with the evolving knowledge of education in today's society.

Overall, the workshop series, *Places of Rural Practice*, serves as a catalyst for positive change. It inspires participants to apply their newfound knowledge and skills to their personal and professional livesand contributes to a more sustainable future. By addressing critical issues and fostering a deeper connection between individuals, communities, and their environment, the workshops have the opportunity to create a lasting impact that will extend far beyond their immediate context.

6.
The second day on FOOD is tutored by fermentation producer Markus Shimizu. A tour of local gardens includes a visit to the garden of Renate. She is always open to showing visitors around her garden and sharing her knowledge on gardening. Various vegetables and herbs are harvested. Photo: Zara Pfeifer, 2020.

7.
The group divides into teams, each preparing one fermented product or liquid. In the beginning, the process is complex, but through collective activity, each person finds their role in the group. Together a culinary mapping of the local gardens is created, and by the process of fermentation, the findings are archived in jars, forming a sensory archive. Photo: Zara Pfeifer, 2020.

8.
The third day focuses on FABRIC. Group member and textile artist Anne Schwalbe fill three large aluminum pots with water from a nearby stream and place them to boil over the fires. Photo: Zara Pfeifer, 2020.

9.
»This is the practical way of learning. No theory, just hands-on.« – Frank.
Photo: Zara Pfeifer.

Places of Rural Practice 237

10.
The group prepares the concluding event by dressing the pavilion with the fabrics from the dye baths. The large fabric becomes a canopy, and the smaller ones, a surface. The blind of goldenrod serves as a backdrop for the closing event.
Photo: Zara Pfeifer.

11.
»We open the jars in a common ceremony and share the experience of tasting flavours you wouldn't have expected.« –Enno.
Photo: Zara Pfeifer.

12.
The concluding event starts as villagers, experts, and spontaneous guests join the workshop participants in the Kalklaube garden. The pavilion, in its completion, is now a structure that gathers the group's experience, knowledge, exercise, and their physical results. What began as a group of anonymous participants has evolved into a collective, bonded by shared experiences, communal living, collaborative work, and the realization of the pavilion itself. Photo: Zara Pfeifer.

References

Atelier LUMA (2023): *Bioregional Design Practices / Practiques de design bioregional.* Arles: Luma.

Blume, Eugen/Nichols, Catharine/Felex, Matilda/Knapstein, Gabriele (eds.) (2015): *Black Mountain: An Interdisciplinary Experiment 1933–1957*, Leipzig: Spector.

Borgonuovo, Valerio/Franceschini, Silvia (eds.) (2018): *Global Tools 1973–1975: When Education Coincides with Life*, Rome: Nero Editions.

Constructlab (2023): *Convivial Ground: Stories from Collaborative Spatial Practices*, Berlin: Jovis.

ETH Newrope (2021): *Design in Dialogue: 51N4E*, Berlin: Ruby Press.

Fanelsa, Niklas (2020): »Countryside Narrative«, in: *What About the Provinces*. https://www.cca.qc.ca/en/articles/issues/26/what-about-the-provinces/76638/countryside-narrative.

Fanelsa, Niklas (2020): »Patterns of Rural Commoning«, in: *What About the Provinces*. https://www.cca.qc.ca/en/articles/issues/26/what-about-the-provinces/74210/patterns-of-rural-commoning. https://www.cca.qc.ca/en/articles/issues/26/what-about-the-provinces/74210/patterns-of-rural-commoning.

Fitz, Angelika/Ritter, Katharina/Architekturzentrum Wien (eds.) (2017). *Assemble: Wie wir bauen / How We Build*, Zurich: Park Books.

Kayoko, Ota: The Posturban Phenomenon. https://www.cca.qc.ca/en/articles/issues/26/what-about-the-provinces/56442/the-posturban-phenomenon, accessed July 23, 2024.

Pfeifer, Zara (2020): *Countryside Narrative*, Montréal: Canadian Center for Architecture.

Raumlaborberlin (2021): *Instances of Urban Practice*, exhibition contribution to the 17th Biennale Architettura, How will we live together? Venice, 23 May to 21 November 2021.

Tsukamoto Laboratory (2021): »Satoyama School of Design«, in: *DOMa* 5: 69–108.

Handscapes
Gestures as Agents of Change and Mimetic Awareness

Otto Paans

Abstract: While a sizable literature on meaning and knowledge in design processes has focused on objects or designed artefacts, this article proposes to shift the emphasis of meaning-making towards the embodied »designing subject«. Specifically, gestures made in the course of sketching, shape the designing subject as much as the designed object. Gesturing literally in-forms the world and consequently shapes and directs thinking processes. Moreover, gesturing involves the entire body in the process of understanding and opens up an alternative pathway for understanding how meaning is created and how one's affective frame widens and develops while designing. Gestures develop a mimetic awareness anchored in the body of architectural contents. They enable a phenomenologically rich and layered form of meaning-making and understanding alike – an evocative »handscape« that is actively and purposively created. Through a case study in landscape architecture, the efficacy, potential, subtlety and layered structure of the relationships between embodiment, gesturing, thinking, sketching and meaning-making are illustrated and explained.

Keywords: Gestures; Landscape Architecture; Mimesis; Drawing; Phenomenology; Embodiment; Design Cognition; Sketching.

Introduction

Over recent decades, there has been a tendency in design literature to locate the locus of meaning-making in the objects or artefacts that emerge during such processes. Examples include the use of visual and/or spatial representations as spaces one could imaginatively inhabit (Zumthor 2014), the role of creating variations and differentially exploring possibilities (Rittel 2014; Rheinberger 2008), the way knowledge is embodied in artefacts (Ballestrem/Gasperoni 2023) and the role that a certain »fuzziness« or »openness« plays in conceiving objects.

In the »object-focused« line of thinking, the artefact is treated as a physical focal point that directs, influences and aids decision-taking. When Donald Schön expanded the debate toward the social dimension surrounding artefacts, the focal point of the »conversation with the situation« was still the sketch (Schön 1983, 1992). More recent notions, for instance »epistemic dissonance« (Farias 2013) still utilize a similar approach: Meanings are held to be »read into« artefacts and so it is the act of »beholding« that drives the process of designing and deciding. This line of thinking leads to two dead ends simultaneously:

First, it unwittingly accepts so-called »ocularcentrism«, the predominantly Western notion whereby visual perception in the form of the glance (or the Platonic eidos, perhaps) is taken as the pinnacle of knowledge, and consequently techniques of »making visible« or »making explicit« assume center stage (Pallasmaa 2012: 18–22).

Second, in focusing on objects, there is a tendency to reconstruct the processes of reasoning that occurred when they were created. However, this has the (often unintended) consequence that any form of meaning-making is retrospectively reduced to deliberative reasoning or to the practice of logic more generally at the expense of lived, embodied experience.

The idea that understanding resides only in grasping theoretical concepts, or that the center of cognition merely resides in the brain exemplifies the intellectualism and associated conceptualism inherited from the Enlightenment. These ideas subsequently found their way into the works from the first generation of researchers that laid the foundations for the post-World War II developments in design theory (cf. Asimow 1962; Eastman 1969; Simon 1996). By and large, their logic-centered approach discounted the lived and experienced body, its mnemonic capacities, its haptic operation, its gestural capacities and its proprioceptive, situated, oriented being in favor of abstract conceptualization.

Given its emphasis on logic and conceptualism, the object-focused line of thinking owes a certain debt to the philosophy of language and linguistic notions of meaning-making that were prevalent in architectural theory during the 1970s and 1980s: Like a text, an artefact was held to be read or interpreted and so, a variety of overlapping meanings emerge and enrich the its meaning (Pirolli 1992; Peréz-Goméz 2007; Eisenmann 1995; Knorr-Cetina 2006; Rheinberger 2005). We can easily detect the influence of notions like Derridean *différance* or hermeneutic theory in this line of thought. The underlying idea that meaning emerges through an ever-shifting play of interpretations has claimed a prominent place in the pantheon of design theory.

The recent move to regard architectural sketches as traces that can be read or interpreted afterward places the emphasis mostly on the object or its production process (Krämer et al. 2016; Krämer 2015, 2016). This direction of thought is clearly indebted to the idea that language-use is inherently performative.

In the next section, I introduce my argument, as well as four remarks that provide the theoretical foundation for thinking about the links between gesture and meaning. In the third section, I introduce a case study in landscape architecture in which gestures played an important role in creating mimetic awareness. In the concluding section, all thematic lines are drawn together in a concise reflection.

Gestures as Agents of Change: Four Remarks

Drawing on the perspectives of (i.) embodied cognition, (ii.) architectural phenomenology and (iii.) gesture theory, I propose to temporarily shift the perspective away from object-focused thinking. I do not imply that the object-focused perspective is somehow superfluous or useless. Instead, I intend to invoke a »subject-focused approach« in order to supplement it. Since we fully engage our biological, living bodies while designing (especially when sketching and/or building models or prototypes), a significant part of the meaning-making process involves our embodied cognition, in particular our capability to use our hands in gesturing. Together, these gestures form a »handscape«: a bodily anchored complex of affordances, understandings, and evocations broadly similar to what Marco Frascari has called »a genetic analysis which forms a continuation of the architectural imaginative act« (Frascari 2009: 204).

The turn toward embodied cognition was largely, although not exclusively, initiated by Maturana and Varela (Maturana/Varela 1980; Varela/Thompson/Rosch 2016; Hanna/Maiese 2009; Gallagher 2005) and has developed steadily ever since. Closely related to J. J. Gibson's ecological psychology (Gibson 1966), it frames cognition as a fully embodied capacity, locating the mind not just in the brain, but in a network of sensory capacities, including the ability to sense moods and atmospheres, pick up on perceptual clues, and to cognize through gesturing. Likewise, it was cemented in architectural theory due to the pioneering work of Pallasmaa (2009, 2011) and Zumthor

(2014), acquiring prominence as the »phenomenological approach« (cf. Mallgrave/Goodman 2011: 201–14).

With this in mind, we shift our attention from the »object of design« to the »subject of design« (Carbon 2016) to emphasize different aspects of what transpires when meaning is created through designing. In line with this intention, I suggest that the gestures involved in drawing may be read as epistemic operations all their own, in the sense that they deepen understanding through gestural enactment. This enactment changes the designer in the process.

First, we must liberate ourselves from the assumption that gestures are mere embellishments of speech acts. Mental processes are externalized by two distinct modes of expression: speech and gesture. Gestures are distinct from speech, but they form an integral part of language (McNeil 2005: 13). Because gestures are performed in a three-dimensional space, they are naturally closely allied to imagery. For instance, we may assert that »we would like to follow the natural contours of the slope in laying out the sidewalk«, while tracing this spatial connection and slope angle with our hands, pulling it from the realm of the verbally expressed idea into the realm of spatial orientation.

Second, gestures change the person making them. We touch the world, but our understanding of it is mediated and negotiated through words and gestures, utilizing them as probes or instruments (Flusser 1994: 49–52). They literally »in-form« the world. Flusser plays on the terms »inform« and »in-form«, emphasizing that our understanding of the world is action-oriented and dialectic (ibid.: 50). Hands in-form the world between them and shape our image of the world accordingly.

Flusser echoes the Kantian insight that: »[One] orients [one]self geographically only through a subjective ground of differentiation« (Kant 2001: 9). We might here exchange »geographically« for »spatially«. The very subjective ground of understanding is constituted by our bodies, through which we gesture and act on possibilities. Moreover, every act of thinking-through-making shapes thought patterns and the foundational images and ideas that direct and inflect our thinking. These foundational images influence our thinking and they change and develop over time, leading to (thought) habits, preferences and values (Hanna/Paans 2021). Through making practices, one can actively prime the mind to regard certain images or ideas as rich in meanings, allowing designers to gradually explore their own thinking. As Pallasmaa (2009) worked out in his study on the »thinking hand«, gestures enable us to »fuse« to some degree with the subject matter that we investigate through tactile and haptic qualities.

The gestures in architectural designing are »invented gestures« (Kang and Tversky 2016). They belong not only to the category of movements that speakers use to communicate thoughts. Instead, they are deliberately invented for the purpose of working on a specific idea. They are unique, responsive and context-sensitive.

Such invented gestures indicate a »deep understanding«: They are unique creations by individuals, used in the course of probing and exploring the space of possibilities. This is especially important as (landscape) designers often deal with dynamic systems, such as erosion pattern, agricultural cycles, water runoff and developing settlement patterns. Gestures that »explain« or »highlight« how dynamic systems function over time and in conjunction, exert important cognitive effects. One effect is that a person working gesturally with a dynamic system (say, in sketching its structure) develops the skill to explain the fundamental features to him or herself or to other parties (Kang and Tversky 2016).

There is an intimate link between gesturing, language (cf. Harrison 2018) and procedural memory – that is, knowledge of how to perform certain actions (cf. Klooster et al. 2016). Patients with impaired procedural memory experienced problems in learning from watching gestures or their own gestures, suggesting that »knowing-how« is activated and directed through bodily movement.

Literally, to understand through the body, one must move: »[The] spatial reality [of imaginative patterns] is such that they cannot be perceived. The patterns emerge in the form of imagined trajectories, moving lines of force, that a moving body draws in the process of moving, as when a dancer runs across a stage, jumps in the air, and in landing, turns upstage and moves in a series of spirals downstage – or more simply, when we ourselves, in walking, turn a corner and proceed on our way down the different street« (Sheets-Johnston 2013: 24).

To deeply understand a spatial reality, it must be actively created through lines of force – embodied projections in a three-dimensional space. The body draws the line through gesture and creates its own space, delineating and orienting itself in the world.

Third, resulting from the double tension between speech and gesture or word and image, a »growth point« emerges:

»A growth point [...] is a minimal unit of dialectic in which imagery and linguistic content are combined. A GP contains opposite semiotic modes of meaning capture—instantaneous, global, nonhierarchical imagery with temporally sequential, segmented, and hierarchical language. The GP is a unit with demonstrable self-binding power (attempts to disrupt it, for example, with delayed auditory feedback do not succeed), and the opposition of semiotic modes within it fuels the dialectic.« (McNeil 2005: 18)

Oppositions, tensions, fuzziness, sketchy lines etc. invite a kind of playful speculation that shapes subject as much as object. Gesturing as sketching is not just embellishment, but a continuous »update of a speaker's cognitive state of being« (McNeil 2005: 19). As Marco Frascari has argued, in the context of architectural creation, the drawn line is the materialization of a sequence of cognitive states that shape thoughts and thinking habits alike (Frascari 2009). In tracing an intricate or dynamic line, the gesture in its entirety is felt as a sequence of varying cognitive states, a kind of free hypothesizing, a playful, yet directed and inquisitive »what if?« question (Cocker 2013).

Fourth, all this confirms a further finding from cognitive science: Representations of objects are built out of systems of activations. During gesturing, the body actually creates and refers to perceptual symbol systems (PSS). Put concisely, PSS are layered neural traces that contain some of the motor information of the gesture that was being made in the attempt to work out a thought or idea (Goldin-Meadow 2010: 665).

Sketching is a means by which thought is oriented toward an idea through gesturing and tracing. As such, it leaves neural traces (PSS) in the brain, opening a gestural connection to conceive of something not (yet) imagined, but that operates via a non-intellectual pathway. It allows one to treat lines as if they were processes instead of depictions or pieces in a logical puzzle (Paans 2024). This introduces an important cognitive change: A re-ordering of one's »affective frame« (Hanna/Maiese 2009), or the way in which someone relegates certain visual aspects to the cognitive periphery while pulling others toward the center of cognition. This associative ordering is not random: It is importantly influenced by bodily states, including memories, feelings, emotions, and affects. Literally, gestures change what we perceive and what we deem important or merely secondary. Even more poignantly, tool-use in general (including sketching) changes the conception of the body image, thereby altering one's own view of what one is bodily capable of (Martel et al. 2016).

From Landscape to Handscape

I illustrate some of the notions discussed previously by way of a case study. It concerns a »cloud of sketches« made during a single project that lasted around 18 months. The project's goal was to provide a new landscape vision for the municipality of Beekdaelen in South Limburg, the Netherlands. The vision was considered as an »architectural agenda« that would address threats and developmental possibilities within the landscape. The topics included were agriculture, water management, tourism, residential quality, and natural development.

The problem we ran into was that the main themes relentlessly fused with one another. In this case, the geographical features of the landscape tied into our conceptual difficulties. The region of Southern Limburg has unique geographical features, including hills and a natural network of small streams. During its agricultural development, a network of villages and traditional farms emerged in reciprocal relationships with these features.

It literally took meters of sketch paper to present our strategic ideas in ways that did justice to the fine-grained, interlinked, and legally protected features of the physical landscape (fig. 1). The resulting sketches were often halfway products depicting (a.) unfinished, quick design ideas, (b.) landscape structures with which they interacted and (c.) an idea's connection to adjacent themes.

An example of such a sketch concerned the relationship between the altitude, the resulting network of fine-grained streams, and the traditional settlement pattern. Southern Limburg has long been an agricultural region and so, small clusters of farms grew into villages. Since this process already started before medieval times, the villages were located within walking distance of each another. Larger farms, religious structures, and family estates complete the settlement pattern. When tracing these old, yet tangible structures, the first thing we noticed is that precision is essential. One has to acquire a bodily sensibility to the subtle twists and turns of the water network, just as one must acquire a feeling for how the old roads connect the villages and isolated structures. Nothing is coincidental – everything has a reason (fig. 2).

Through gesture, a newly developed sensibility or cognitive attention emerges from reproducing and superimposing existing patterns. The exact geographical data is also available in a GIS-format, but merely seeing it does not result in comprehension, let alone in intimate, felt knowledge. The key is

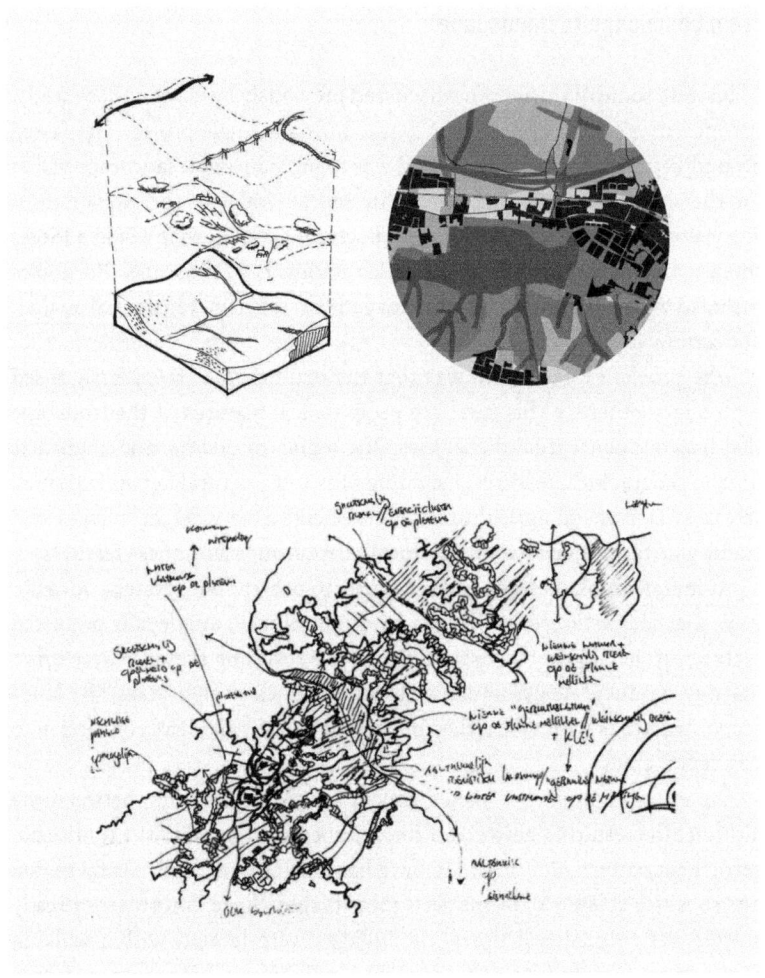

1.
Isometric depiction of the main landscape systems and processes (left) and how it appears in GIS-data (right). Illustration by the author, 2022.

2.
Tracing of multiple systems led to intricate drawings dealing with scale, subtle spatial features and interconnections rather than analysis.
Illustration by the author, 2022.

that in the process of familiarizing oneself with the contents and developing a sensibility, the body is gesturally, and not just cognitively, involved.

While the representational contents of the data and the tracing are largely identical, the process of interiorizing them in the body, and therefore establishing a sensible, felt, and haptic relation with it, unlocks a level of intimate knowledge that exerts a very tangible effect on how the next design steps unfold (fig. 3).

Rather than absorbing contents informationally, it is drawn into being. It is »in-forming« rather than being informed. The body's full involvement through gesture organizes knowledge. In doing so, it affectively frames meanings that emerge during the drawing process. The process-based character of gesturing and sketching recreates and mimics processes rather than looking at them resulting in a rich handscape of affordances. When investigating the natural flow of precipitation downhill, sketching and tracing the main streams recreates a real-life movement, and causes one to think through the landscape structures (fig. 4).

One »fuses« with the behavior of the water by tracing its pathways and evoking a process that shapes the world emerging under the pen. In making such drawings and highlighting a single aspect, the processes occurring in the landscape acquire a rhyme and reason, as the relation between their unfolding and the physical features of the environment are drawn into the center of the affective frame.

Discussion: Mimetic Awareness and Meaning

The deep connections that shape the landscape were gradually made tangible by drawing multiple sketches in which we attempted to superimpose all layers. To create an image that is understandable, a lot of fine-tuned drawing was required. No sweeping gestures, but a careful overlapping of layers to ensure that every element was intelligible as part of a larger, integral story.

The gestural approach made it far easier to devise strategies that interacted with the features we had mapped out before. We easily built on the connections that we had identified earlier, but now with an eye to solve recurrent problems like loss of biodiversity, drought, the disappearance of small elements of the landscape, or messy built-up village edges.

Gestures make it easier to cement knowledge about the interconnections that constitute landscapes. To our surprise, we found we had them cognitively »ready« when thinking about solutions to systemic problems. Tracing

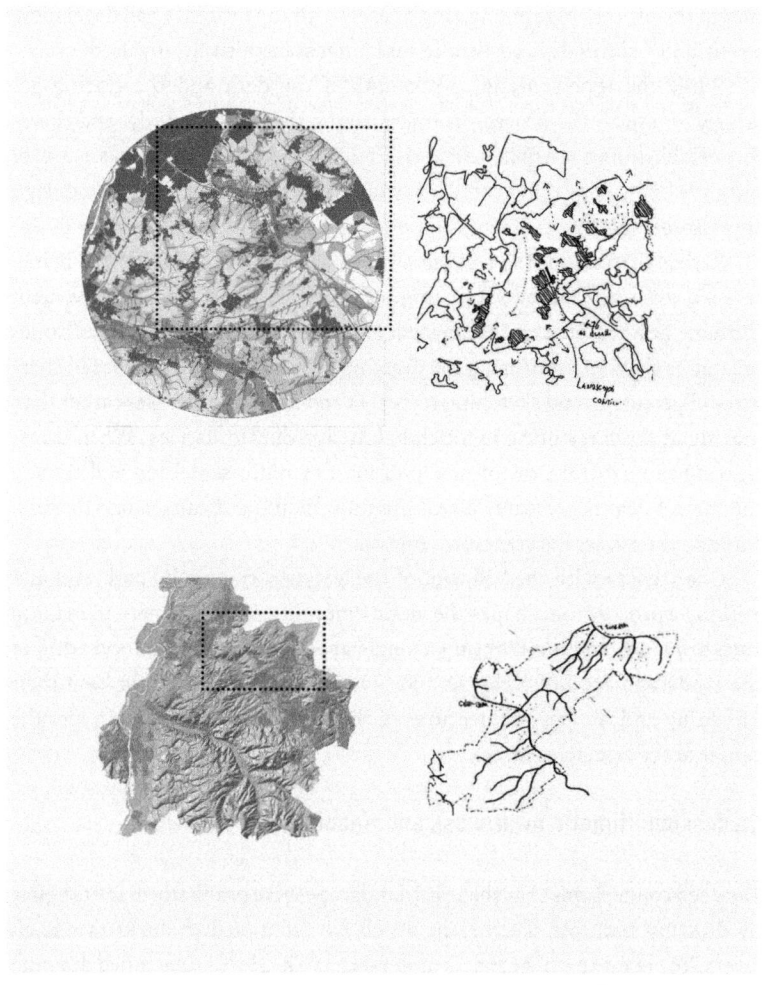

3.
Multiple tracings are required for deep familiarization with the content. The dotted rectangle on the GIS drawing (left) corresponds to the area of the hand drawing (right). Author, 2021. Illustration by the author.

4.
The subtlety and fragility of the vein-like water system (right) shows the underlying geomorphology (left). Mimetic awareness creates a deep understanding of the relation between geological features and water management. The dotted rectangle (left) corresponds to the area of the drawing. Illustration by the author.

connections by hand stores the acquired information in the body and so it becomes readily accessible while sketching. We customarily think of information as something to be obtained by viewing or reading, while we think of a skill as something to be acquired by practicing. Some information, however, is acquired by doing.

I would suggest that gestural involvement in architectural design creates a mimetic awareness. It has been argued that architectural drawings are non-mimetic (Emmon 2019: 192). That is, they are not aiming for the faithful visual reproduction of an object. However, in this case, mimetic quality played an indispensable role. Like the invented gesture, tracings and orderings resulted in a deep familiarization with the subject matter. Reproducing a pattern or landscape feature stimulates a thought process about the logic of what is gesturally experienced. Why are the twists and turns in the road this way rather than that? Why are these estates located here instead of there? This information is uncovered when one reconstructs these features with a certain mimetic acumen (fig. 5), as in this manner, anomalies and unique features quickly stand out as the underlying structure discloses itself (Paans 2022: 12–31).

In a theory titled the »cognition-action transduction hypothesis«, Nathan (2017: 191) proposed that repeated bodily actions lead to long-term, generalized learning. This may explain the relative cognitive ease with which we could navigate the complexity of physical landscape features, issues, and solutions. The action of tracing is a bodily activity that stimulates a learning process in which spatial features are related and cohere in an increasingly meaningful whole.

Meaning and comprehension emerges in a gestural process not just by receiving information, but by creating it. The handscape literally changes the mind, shaping its cognitive and affective pathways, and its procedural memory:

> »Epistemologically, hypothesizing a reciprocal action-cognition system challenges deep-seated notions that place intellectual processes atop physical actions. There is a broad, societal bias favoring explicit, verbal ways of describing and assessing knowledge.« (Nathan 2017: 191)

Mimetic awareness aims not at visual imitation or verbal forms of description and assessment. Instead, through gesture, one becomes acquainted with the subtleties that underlie form and function. In sketching and

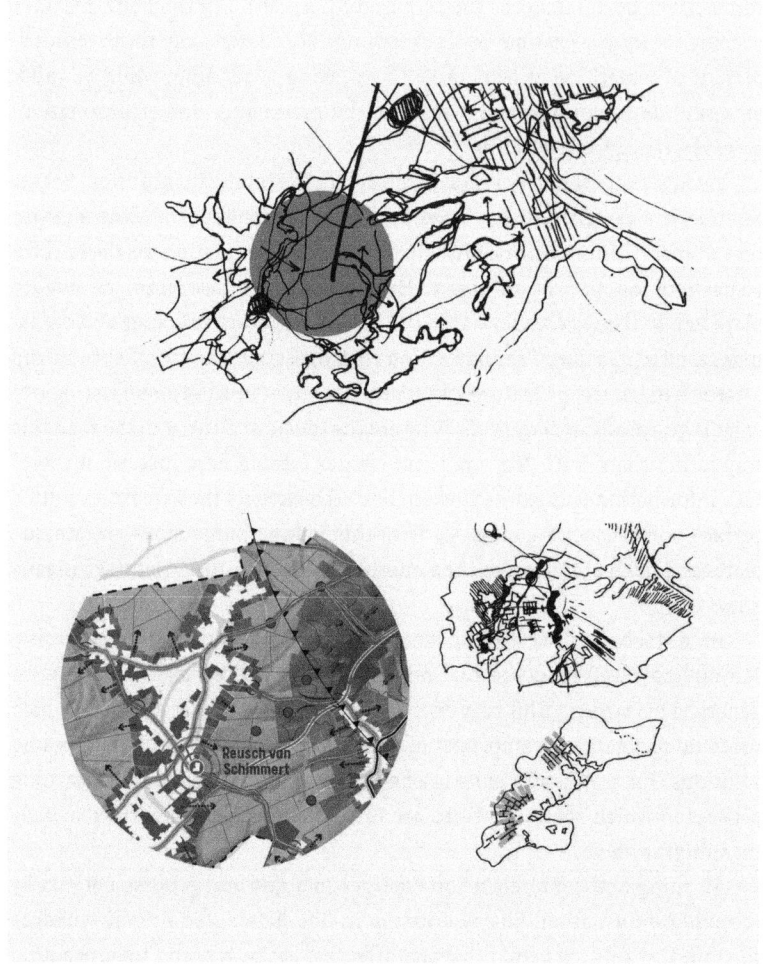

5.
The highlighted area shows how intricate the road network is. Its twists and turns respond closely to geographic landscape features and functional demands alike. Illustration: The author, 2021.

6.
Two types of parcellation and their orientation (left, below), settlement patterns and road networks (left, top) considered with the altitude in mind. In the end, we proposed a new type of parcellation derived from characteristic features in the geomorphology and existing structures (right).Illustration: The author, 2022

tracing, this information is stored in the body for easy retrieval, but also for changing thinking habits, which thereby changes the designing subject as the line unfolds.

Here, we find a link to the orientation of our embodied cognition. As a bipedal species with two eyes, we perceive depth, and intuit a clear up-down orientation (cf. Koffka 1936). These physical features enable us to situate our perceptual system and proprioceptively experienced body in an organized, oriented space of cognition. We can trace out a gesture space within the limits of our bodily capabilities. A sweeping architectural gesture or delicate line is not merely drawn as a way of visually representing an idea; instead, it is acted out bodily.

Our perceptual field is never undisturbed or homogeneous (ibid.: 281–282). If we gesture (by carefully tracing a line, or interacting with what we have already drawn), we deliberately disturb the tranquility of the perceptual field. If we do so purposely, we re-orient the entire field and consequently, we literally change our outlook on the subject matter. The »growth point« emerges due to these disturbances, and exactly there, the dialectic between gesture and thought unfolds. For architectural design, the drawn lines, and therefore the gestures, conjoin into a graphesis, or generative process of visual understanding (Frascari 2009: 202).

A further point concerns precision. In a landscape where nothing is coincidental and where searching for historical clues is necessary to make any proposed change appropriate and meaningful, the first thing to do is train the body to achieve a heightened, mimetic awareness of features that might elude the innocent eye. Often, these innocuous clues provide fundamental motives to propose changes.

An example is the relation between the angle of the hillsides and the runoff speed of precipitation. On a steep slope, water runs off quickly, dragging fertile soil with it and causing erosion, as well as flooding down the slope. However, steep slopes are often flanked by gentle slopes. Because the water reaches a lower speed on such slopes, it takes longer to traverse them. During that time, it is possible to »trap« the water in hedges, bushes, or artificial cascades. Once we realized this possibility, it became the basis for a new spatial order, in which shallow slopes were designated as areas where small elements of the landscapes are added and traditional visual features are revived (fig. 5).

This insight made it possible to perceive a new set of potentials in the landscape, apprehending a possible order that was immanent in it, but that could only be recognized through a careful, mimetic, and above all, gesture-based form of engagement.

Gestures, as carriers of meaning, emerge within an integral sequence of thoughts, gestures, concepts, and representations that are experienced as a more-or-less continuous tapestry of meaning. Each gesture is oriented toward action and the future (Gallagher/Martínez/Gastelum 2017). Simultaneously, the gesture already retains content from former experiences. Through this in-forming dialectic, meaning emerges in the present through the interplay of past and future.

The epistemic process implied here progresses via a phenomenological, lived method for meaning-making. It is an unfolding of understanding, remembering, and learning through gestures. Any concepts emerging from such a practice bear little resemblance to »concepts« in the sense of systematic abstractions. Sheets-Johnstone calls them »concrete concepts« or »corporeal concepts« (Sheets-Johnstone 2010). Gesturing activates and embodies knowledge through bodily, lived experience and shapes thoughts, thinking habits, sensibility, and ultimately, one's creative space. Knowledge acquired through a gestural process possesses a phenomenological depth that far surpasses theoretical abstractions. It imbues newly acquired knowledge with a bodily, grounded, first-person aspect, thereby becoming lived meaning rather than dry fact. In this context, Haarmann has spoken of an »aesthetic epistemology« – a way of acquiring and evoking insights via an aesthetic rather than logic-based pathway (cf. Haarmann 2019; Root-Bernstein 2002).

The design outcomes of a high mimetic awareness are not straightforwardly replicable across all contexts and cases, as much depends on the individual's design skill, the changed plasticity of the body, brain, and mind, and the context in which they apply them. However, the efficacy of this method is able to be generalized as a skill. A competent piano teacher may teach students all the techniques to foster performative excellence but cannot expect that all the students will become concert pianists. Yet, without providing these techniques, any chance of becoming skilled is forestalled from the very beginning. A similar case can be made with regard to mimetic awareness. Just like a feeling for composition, process control, and aesthetic acumen, this skill exerts a diffuse, yet essential practical effect, expanding design competence for the better.

First, it has been established that gesturing while describing design features facilitates perspective-taking. (Mittelberg/Schmitz/Groninger 2017;

Paans/Pasel 2020). For instance, someone may – supported by gestures – describe the properties of their design to someone else, or they may describe it from a first-person perspective (or even multiple perspectives). This way of gesturally »simulating« certain features of the design aids comprehension, as it engages with multiple embodied, perspectival and functional aspects of the design proposal. In turn, this deeper understanding changes the designing subject, as they come to grips with what their decisions entail.

Second, gesturing – like sketching – transfers mental content (thoughts, notions) from the mental domain into the realm of semantic content. So, fluid and open ideas are (partially) materially fixed and thereby become the object of (collective) inquiry. Through such translation, ideas, assumptions, or tacitly accepted notions often come to light, as well as anomalies, that underlie patterns or inconsistencies. By visually and gesturally »working through« the material, the process of mimetic awareness gradually progresses, as formerly subconscious mental content is drawn into the conscious domain, thereby fully assimilating itself into the body's repertoire of awareness.

Conveying the development of awareness presents challenges, but also invites opportunities to engage in auto-ethnography or the first-person reporting of design experiences (cf. Schouwenberg/Kaethler 2021). By describing, analysing, and carefully reflecting on how the interplay of gesture, thought, and drawing aids comprehension, embodied experiences that are otherwise difficult to communicate can be made intelligible. This practice is irrevocably subjective, but we might consider this an advantage: Who else but the people themselves can better describe the process of understanding that unfolds in and through them?

Working through gestures situates knowledge through a familiarization that is thoroughly context-bound. In Southern Limburg, the geomorphology is a determining factor underpinning a variety of landscape processes. It influences water runoff, the distribution of vegetation, erosion patterns, spatial contrasts, and microclimate. In abstracting these features and surgically tracing them, one acquires a bodily sensibility that is layered, yet not fragmentary; context-sensitive yet largely able to be generalized; local but amenable to various scale levels. Walking through the landscape one traced, it begets depth, relationality, and a logic all its own. It becomes active and organic rather than abstract and visual.

Only through corporeal entanglement with the subject matter can the embodied mind acquire and actively »hand-scape« the sharpness, sensitivity, and acumen required to judge whether a given design proposal is effective or desirable. This knowledge is acquired through a phenomenological pathway and is deep, layered, and laden with meaning. There is a single phrase by Pallasmaa (2009) in his study on the thinking hand that catches it with breathtaking precision: the new, he says, »continuously emerges« under our hands. And, we should add, under the inquisitive tip of the pen as well.

References

Asimow, Morris (1962): *Introduction to Design*, Englewood Cliffs, NJ: Prentice Hall.

Ballestrem, Matthias/Gasperoni, Lidia (2023): *Epistemic Artefacts: A Dialogical Reflection on Design Research in Architecture*, Baunach: Spurbuchverlag/AADR.

Carbon, Claus-Christian (2016): »Psychology of Design«, in: *Design Science* 5/e26. DOI: 10.1017/dsj.2019.25.

Cocker, Emma (2017): »Hypothesis #6. Distancing The If and Then«, in: Nikolaus Gansterer (ed.), *Drawing a Hypothesis: Figures of Thought*, New York, NY: Springer, 97–108.

Eastman, Charles (1968): *Explorations of the Cognitive Processes in Design*, Pittsburgh: Carnegie Mellon University.

Eisenmann, Peter (1996): »Architecture and The Problem of the Rhetorical Figure«, in: Nesbitt, Kate (ed.), *Theorizing a New Agenda for Architecture: An Anthology of Architectural Theory 1965–1995*, Princeton, NJ: Princeton Architectural Press, 174–81.

Emmon, Paul (2019): *Drawing Imagining Building: Embodiment in Architectural Design Practices*, Oxford: Routledge.

Farias, Ignacio (2013): »Epistemische Dissonanz. Zu Vervielfältigung Entwurfsalternativen in der Architektur«, in: Sabine, Ammon/Eva-Maria, Froschauer (eds.), *Wissenschaft Entwerfen*, München: Wilhelm Fink Verlag, 76–107.

Flusser, Vilém (1994): *Gesten. Versuch einer Phänomenonologie*, Frankfurt am Main: Fischer Taschenbuch Verlag.

Frascari, Marco (2009): »Lines as Architectural Thinking«, in: *Architectural Theory Review* 14, 200–212. DOI: 10.1080/13264820903341605.

Gallagher, Shaun (2005): *How the Body Shapes the Mind*, Oxford: Oxford University Press.

Gallagher, Shaun/Martínez, Sergio F./Gastelum, Melina (2017): »Action-Space and Time: Towards an Enactive Hermeneutics« ,in: Bruce B. Janz (ed.) *Place, Space and Hermeneutics: Contributions to Hermeneutics* 5, 83–96. doi: 10.1007/978-3-319-52214-2_7.

Gibson, James J. (1966): *The Senses Considered as Perceptual Systems*, Boston, MA: Houghton Mifflin.

Goldin-Meadow, Susan/Beilock, Sian L. (2010): »Action's Influence on Thought: The Case of Gesture«, in: *Perspectives on Psychological Science* 5, 664–674. DOI: 10.1177/1745691610388764.

Haarmann, Anke (2019): *Artistic Research: Eine Epistemologische Ästhetik*, Bielefeld: Transcript Verlag.

Hanna, Robert/Maiese, Michelle (2009): *Embodied Minds in Action*, Oxford: Oxford University Press.

Hanna, Robert Alan/Paans, Otto (2021): »Thought-Shapers«, in: *Cosmos and History* 17/1, 1–72.

Harrison, Simon (2018): *The Impulse to Gesture: Where Language, Minds and Bodies Intersect*, Cambridge: Cambridge University Press. DOI: 10.1017/9781108265065.

Kang, Seokmin/Tversky, Barbara (2016): »From Hands to Minds: Gestures Promote Understanding«, in: *Cognitive Research: Principles and Implications* 1/4. DOI: 10.1186/s41235-016-0004-9. doi: 10.1186/s41235-016-0004-9.

Kant, Immanuel (2001): »What Does It Mean to Orient Oneself in Thinking?«, in: Allen W. Wood/Giorgio Di Giovanni (eds.), *Religion and Rational Theology*, Cambridge: Cambridge University Press.

Klooster, Nathaniel B./Cook, Susanne W./Uc, Ergun Y./Duff, Melissa C. (2015): »Gestures Make Memories, But What Kind? Patients with Impaired Procedural Memory Display Disruptions in Gesture Production and Comprehension«, in: *Frontiers in Human Neuroscience* 8. DOI: 10.3389/fnhum.2014.01054.

Knorr-Cetina, Karin (2006): »Objectual Practice«, in: Theodore R. Schatzki//Karin Knorr-Cetina, Karin/Eike von Savigny (eds.) *The Practice Turn in Contemporary Theory*, Oxford: Routledge, 175–88.

Koffka, Kurt (1936): *Principles of Gestalt Psychology*, London: Kegan Paul.

Krämer, Sybille (2015): »Sprache – Stimme – Schrift. Sieben Gedanken über Performativität als Medialität«, in: Uwe Wirth (ed.) *Performanz. Zwischen Sprachphilosophie und Kulturwissenschaften*, Berlin: Suhrkamp, 323–47.

Krämer, Sybille (2016): *Figuration, Anschauung, Erkenntnis. Grundlinien einer Diagrammatologie*, Berlin: Suhrkamp.

Krämer, Sybille/Kogge, Werner/Grube, Gernot (eds.) (2016): *Spur. Spurenlesen als Orienterungstechnik und Wissenskunst*, Berlin: Suhrkamp.

Mallgrave, Henry Francis/Goodman, David (2011): *An Introduction to Architectural Theory: 1968 to the Present*, Chichester: Wiley-Blackwell.

Martel, Marie/Cardinali, Lucilla/Roy, Alice C./Farné, Alessandro (2016): »Tool-Use: An Open Window into Body Representation and Its Plasticity«, in: *Cognitive Neuropsychology* 33/1–2, 82–101. DOI: 10.1080/02643294.2016.1167678.

Maturana, Humberto/Varela, Francesco (1980): *Autopoiesis and Cognition*, Dordrecht: D. Reidel Publishing Company.

McNeill, David (2005): *Gesture and Thought*, Chicago, IL: Chicago University Press.

Mittelberg, Irene/Schmitz, Thomas/Groninger, Hannah (2017): »Operative Manufacts: Gestures as Embodied Sketches in the Early Design Process«, in: Sabine Ammon/Remei Capdevila-Werning (eds.), *The Active Image: Architecture and Engineering in the Age of Modeling*, Cham: Springer, 99–132. DOI: 10.1007/978-3-319-56466-1.

Nathan, Mitchell J. (2017): »One Function of Gestures is to Make New Ideas: The Action-Cognition Transduction Hypothesis«, in: R. Breckinridge Church/Martha W. Alibali/Spencer D. Kelly (eds.) *Why Gesture? How the Hands Function in Speaking, Thinking, and Communicating*, Amsterdam/Philadelphia: John Benjamins Publishing Company, 175–96. DOI: 10.1075/gs.7.

Paans, Otto/Pasel, Ralf (2020): »The Simulative Stance: An Essay on Architectural Design as Epistemic Enactment«, in: Rikke Lyngsø Christensen/Ekkerhard Drach/Lidia Gasperoni/Doris Hallama/Anna Hougaard/Ralf Liptau (eds.), *Artefakte des Entwerfens. Skizzieren, Zeichnen, Skripten, Modellieren*, Berlin: Universitätsverlag der TU Berlin, 58–74. DOI: 10.14279/depositonce-8508.

Paans, O. (2022): *Field Notes from Design Space: Essays in Design Theory*, Berlin: Universitätsverlag der TU Berlin. DOI: 10.14279/depositonce-16309.

Pallasmaa, Juhani (2009): *The Thinking Hand: Existential and Embodied Wisdom in Architecture*, Chichester: John Wiley and Sons.

Pallasmaa, Juhani (2011): *The Embodied Image: Imagination and Imagery in Architecture*, Chichester: John Wiley and Sons.

Pallasmaa, Juhani (2012): *The Eyes of the Skin: Architecture and the Senses*, Chichester: John Wiley and Sons.

Peréz-Goméz, Alberto (2007): »Questions of Representation: The Poetic Origin of Architecture«, in: Marco Frascari/Jonathan Hale/Bradley Starkey (eds.), *From Models to Drawings*, London: Routledge, 11–22.

Pirolli, Pietro (1992): *Knowledge and Processes in Design*, Berkeley: University of California Press.

Rheinberger, Hans-Jörg (2005): *Iterationen*, Berlin: Merve Verlag.

Root-Bernstein, Robert S. (2002): »Aesthetic Cognition«, in: *International Studies in the Philosophy of Science* 16/1, 61–77.

Schön, Donald (1983): *The Reflective Practitioner*, Cambridge, MA: The MIT Press.

Schön, Donald (1992): »Designing as Reflective Conversation with the Materials of a Design Situation«, in: *Knowledge-Based Systems* 6/1, 3–14. DOI: 10.1016/0950-7051(92)90020-G.

Schouwenberg, Louise/Kaethler, Michael (eds.) (2021): *The Auto-Ethnographic Turn in Design*, Amsterdam: Valiz.

Sheets-Johnstone, Maxine (2010): »Thinking in Movement: Further Analyses and Validations«, in: John Stewart/Olivier Gapenne/Ezequiel di Paolo (eds.) *Enaction: Toward a New Paradigm for Cognitive Science*, Cambridge, MA: Bradford Books/The MIT Press, 165–182.

Sheets-Johnstone, Maxine (2013): »Bodily Resonance«, in: Helena De Preester (ed.) *Moving Imagination: Explorations of Gesture and Inner Movement*, Amsterdam: John Benjamins Publishing Company, 19–36.

Simon, Herbert (1996): *The Sciences of the Artificial*, Cambridge, MA: The MIT Press.

Thompson, Evan (2007): *Mind in Life. Biology, Phenomenology and the Sciences of Mind*, Cambridge, MA: Harvard University Press.

Varela, Francesco/Thompson, Evan/Rosch, Eleanor (2016): *The Embodied Mind: Cognitive Science and Human Behaviour*, Cambridge, MA: The MIT Press.

Zumthor, Peter (2014): *Architektur Denken*, Basel: Birkhäuser.

CONTRIBUTORS

Biographies

Nicolai Bo Andersen
Nicolai Bo Andersen is an architect and professor at the *Royal Danish Academy Centre for Sustainable Building Culture*. He has studied at *The Cooper Union* and graduated from the *Royal Danish Academy of Fine Arts, School of Architecture* in 1998. In his teaching, research and practice, a critical question is how a phenomenological, first-person aesthetic experience may inspire ecological awareness and protection of the environment while respecting the planetary boundaries. He is head of the master's degree programme *Sustainable Building Culture*, and head of the *Centre for Sustainable Building Culture at the Royal Danish Academy Institute of Architecture and Culture*.

Eva Sievert Asmussen
Eva Sievert Asmussen is an architect and industrial PhD fellow at the *Royal Danish Academy Centre for Sustainable Building Culture* working within the field of cultural heritage. She graduated from the *Royal Danish Academy Cultural Heritage, Transformation and Conservation* in 2016. Since her graduation, she has worked intensively with cultural heritage management at the *Danish Agency for Culture and Palaces*. Exploring the relation between the human body and the body of the building, her PhD project investigates potentials and challenges in working with universal design and accessibility in the built cultural heritage.

Jacob Sebastian Bang
Jacob Sebastian Bang is Associate Professor and the head of program at *Helhed og Del* at the *Royal Danish Academy, School of Architecture*. He is a member of *The Royal Danish Academy of Fine Arts*, member of the *Society of Artists*. His research interests are architecture and representation, and artistic methodology. He works within multiple media – painting, drawing, model-making and graphical techniques.

Zijing Deng

Zijing Deng is a landscape architect with experience in both Asia and Europe. She earned her bachelor's degree in landscape architecture from *South China Agricultural University* in 2019. Collaborating with her colleagues, their research project, »From Risk to Resilience: Assessment and Strategy of Complex Urban Systems to Future Sea-level Rise in Guangzhou«, won the *Award of Excellence* in the *IFLA Asia-Pac LA Awards in the Analysis and Master Planning* category. She holds a master's degree in landscape architecture from *Technical University of Munich*. Her master's thesis envisions the future urban space in Guangzhou, China, emphasizing both human citizens and urban banyan trees as active stakeholders. Alongside her studies, she as professional experience in various types of architecture and landscape architecture offices, including a government-led architectural office in China, the Chinese office of a Netherlands-based landscape architecture firm, and a German landscape architecture firm.

Hisham El-Hitami

Hisham El-Hitami studied architecture and urbanism at the *University of Stuttgart*, where he completed his M.Sc. degree in 2017. After working in several architecture offices in Berlin and London, he started his own practice in 2020. In 2021, he became a research fellow at the *HafenCity University* in Hamburg and a team member of the *CRC 1244 Adaptive Skins and Structures*. Since 2022, he has been working as a researcher at the *Faculty of Architecture of the Bauhaus-Universität* in Weimar. In his research he focuses on spatial adaptivity and its ecological potential in architecture.

Niklas Fanelsa

Niklas Fanelsa studied architecture at *RWTH Aachen University* and the *Tokyo Institute of Technology*. After his studies he worked with *De Vylder Vinck Taillieu* in Gent and *Thomas Baecker Bettina Kraus Architekten* in Berlin. In 2016 Niklas Fanelsa founded the architecture practice *Atelier Fanelsa* based in Berlin and Gerswalde. He was a Teaching and Research Associate at *RWTH Aachen University, BTU Cottbus-Senftenberg*, and *Bauhaus-Universität Weimar*. Niklas Fanelsa was *Emerging Curato*r at the *Canadian Center for Architecture* in Montreal in 2019/20. In 2022 he received the *German Academy Rome Casa Baldi Fellowship*. Niklas Fanelsa holds the *Professorship of Architecture and Design* at the *Technical University of Munich*.

Ida Flarup and Maria Mengel

Ida Flarup (1978) and Maria Mengel (1977) are architects and Associate Teaching Professors at the *Royal Danish Academy*. They are both studio leaders at the bachelor program *Finder Sted* at the **Institute of Architecture and Culture**. Alongside their teaching collaborations they have founded the studio *VAERK>STED* and co-founded the exhibition space »Modtar projects«. Their project Motherboard is part of their artistic research project conducted at the *Royal Danish Academy*, in which reflect their shared interest in pedagogy, craft and collective practice. Their work is characterized by making – by insisting on hands on experimentation and sketching in 1:1 as a method for developing architecture. The Danish word »omforandring« can be seen as a common denominator for their practice. The word is not easily translated to English but can be understood as updating something that already exists. To some extent it means »change« and 'transformation', but it also carries connotations to handicraft and can therefore be explained with words like alter, re-organize, renovate, adapt, repair and modernize. Their work which include large scale installations, exhibition design, furniture and objects is supported by the *Danish Arts Counsil, Danmarks Nationalbank's Anniversary Foundation* and others, and have been exhibited extensively both in Denmark and internationally.

Bernhard Leopold Geiger

Bernhard Geiger is an architect living and working in Basel. He studied at the *Technical University of Munich* and completed his master's degree in 2019 at the *Academy of Architecture of Mendrisio*, where he developed a strong – theoretical and practical – interest in the phenomenology of space and the mutual impact of subjective perception, ontological matters and building practice. He is currently pursuing a *Master of Advanced Studies in History and Theory of Architecture* at the *ETH Zürich*.

Jonathan Meldgaard Houser

Jonathan Meldgaard Houser is a Teaching Associate Professor and head of the BA program *Taking Place* at the *Royal Danish Academy*. Jonathan also runs an award-winning independent architecture practice rooted in artistic research and focused on transformations, installations, and exhibitions. Results of his practice, where art, architecture and landscape meet have been published and widely exhibited across Scandinavia. He holds an M.Arch. and a B.Arch from the *Royal Danish Academy*.

Aileen Iverson-Radtke

Aileen Iverson-Radtke is an American architect based in Berlin, Germany. She has studied and practiced architecture for over 30 years and recently received her doctoral degree in *Design Driven Research Program (PEP)*, TU Berlin. Dr. Iverson's research focuses on the function of architectural modeling as analytic making. The research position is that the analytic function of modeling is compromised in digitization due to the isolation of the design subject (model) from its spatial context and from the hands of the architect. Dr. Iverson examined her subject by developing a hybrid analogue-digital modeling technique improvised from current technologies. This hybrid modeling technique uses »Sensor Models«, analogue models embedded with microsensors, as the interface to digital design, replacing mouse and keyboard. Hybrid modeling differentiates from Virtual Reality (VR) by seeking to interface digital and physical through architectural modeling; and from Artificial Intelligence (AI) since the goal of hybrid modeling is to increase human corporeal intelligence within digital design.

Victor Boye Julebæk

Victor Boye Julebæk is an architect PhD and assistant professor at the *Royal Danish Academy, Centre for Sustainable Building Culture*. He has studied at the *Swiss Federal Institute of Technology* in Lausanne and graduated from the *Royal Danish Academy of Fine Arts, School of Architecture* in 2011. His academic work explores the material practices, cultures and ecologies of architecture from both a theoretical and a hands-on, applied perspective through research, teaching and practice. He is head of the master's programme for *Cultural Heritage, Transformation and Conservation* at the *Royal Danish Academy Institute of Architecture and Culture*.

Ferdinand Ludwig

Ferdinand Ludwig is Assotiate Professor for *Green Technologies in Landscape Architecture* at the *Technical University of Munich* where he leads the research group *Baubotanik*. He is founding partner at *OLA – Office for Living Architecture* in Stuttgart, Germany. His interdisciplinary research, practice and teaching focuses on architectural concepts in which plants play a central role.

Mona Mahall

Mona Mahall studied art and media theory as well as architecture in Karlsruhe, where she obtained her M.A. degree in 2004. She completed her doctorate at the *University of Stuttgart* in 2009, where she continued to work as a scientific associate until 2017. During this time, she held several teaching assignments, among others a guest professorship at *Cornell University*. In 2017, she became a professor for architecture and art at the *HafenCity University* in Hamburg and a member on the board of the *CRC 1244 Adaptive Skins and Structures*. Since 2022, she is a professor for *Politics of Representation* at the *Faculty of Architecture* of the *Bauhaus-Universität* in Weimar. As a collective, she and Asli Serbest work at the intersection between art and spatial practices.

Elahe Mahdavi

Elahe Mahdavi is an Architectural Engineering graduate from *Islamic Azad University of Tehran*, Iran, currently pursuing a Master's degree in Architecture at the *Technical University of Munich* in Germany. She is also working as a project management student at *EDR GmbH*. Her academic work focuses on sustainable architecture and urban design. She has received the *Oskar von Miller Forum* scholarship for the *Leadership Program in the Building Industry* and has been awarded the *TUM Scholarship for International Students* three times. Elahe has worked as an architect in both Iran and Germany since 2015, including managing and designing housing projects as a self-employed professional.

Wilfrid Middleton

Wilf Middleton's research explores the combination of vernacular and computational techniques in design. In particular, his work involves the use of point clouds for analysing and designing trees in built structures and the built environment. During his PhD (*Technical University of Munich* 2023), he focused on Meghalaya's living root bridges, developing workflows for their analysis in terms of regenerative design, mechanics, and topology.

Otto Paans
Otto Paans studied horticulture and gardening in the Netherlands, followed by landscape architecture at the *Erasmushogeschool Brussel* (BE). Subsequently, he studied urban/public space design at the *Utrecht School of the Arts* and the *Utrecht Graduate School for Visual Art and Design* (NL) and philosophy at the *Open University* (UK). Upon completion of his urban design studies, he worked as a landscape designer. He has collaborated in several European FP7 and H2020 projects in urban design, circular building, renewable energy, recycling, medical science, material science, and product design as concept developer, visual designer and dissemination manager. Since 2014, he has published various articles and books on design theory and philosophy. In 2020, he received his PhD summa cum laude from the *Technische Universität Berlin* (DE), and currently works as spatial strategist/concept developer, visual designer and philosopher.

João Quintela
João Quintela studied architecture at the *UAL Lisboa* and the *Politecnico di Milano* and gained practical experience at the firm of *Pezo von Ellrichshausen* in Concepción, Chile. He was a teaching assistant at UD Campo Baeza at the *ESTAM Madrid* and *UAL Lisboa* with Carlos Nogueira. Since 2017 he is professor at the *UAL Lisboa*.

Mario Rinke
Mario Rinke is a Professor at the *Faculty of Design Sciences* at the *University of Antwerp*. Trained as a structural engineer and working in the field of architecture for some years, he researches and teaches structures and construction in architecture. Mario holds a Diploma degree in civil engineering from the *Bauhaus-Universität Weimar* and a PhD from *ETH Zurich* and worked as a design engineer for major offices in London and Zurich. He taught at the architecture department at *ETH Zurich*, the *Lucerne University of Applied Sciences* and the *Tor Vergata University Rome*. In several design and build workshops, he explored material-based design and craftsmanship. He is a cofounder of the *International Association of Structures and Architecture (IASA)*.

Anne Romme
Anne Romme is Associate Professor and the head of program at *Finder Sted / Taking Place* at the *Royal Danish Academy, School of Architecture*. She also runs an independent architecture practice invested in critical, experimental

projects. Her work ranges from theoretical inquiries into the commons in architecture to digital fabrication and the design of a building system based on pure plates shell structures.

Victoria Schweyer

Victoria Schweyer studied architecture at the *Technical University of Munich* and at the *École d'Architecture de la Ville et des Territoires Paris-Est*. She worked in several architecture offices in Munich and Berlin. Victoria worked as Teaching Assistant at the *Chair of Architectural Design and Conception* at the *Technical University of Munich*. In 2018 Victoria Schweyer and Jana Wunderlich founded the architectural practice *pflücken*, where they research and build livable housing in old age. In 2021, they started teaching at the *Technical University of Munich* and the *Katholische Stiftungshochschule* at the *Faculty of Health and Nursing* in Munich. Since 2022 Victoria Schweyer works as a Teaching and Research Associate at the *Professorship of Architecture and Design* at the TUM School of Engineering and Design. In 2023 she was a *Goethe Institute* resident fellow at the *Villa Kamogawa* in Kyoto, Japan.

Asli Serbest

Asli Serbest studied architecture in Istanbul and Stuttgart, where she graduated in 2004. She completed her doctorate at the *University of Stuttgart* in 2009, where she continued to work as a scientific associate until 2017. During this time, she held several teaching assignments in Stuttgart and a professorship at *Rhode Island School of Design*. Since 2017, she is a professor for temporary spaces at the *University of the Arts* in Bremen and a member of the *CRC 1244 Adaptive Skins and Structures*. As a collective, she and Mona Mahall work at the intersection between art and spatial practices.

Tim Simon-Meyer

Tim Simon-Meyer studied architecture at the *UdK Berlin* and the *UAL Lisboa* and gained practical experience in the architectural offices of *Pezo von Ellrichshausen* in Concepción, Chile, among others. He was a teaching assistant with Uta Graff at the *Technical University of Munich* and with Matthias Ballestrem at the *HafenCity University* Hamburg. From 2022 to 2023 he led the design studio *Studio SM/S* at the HCU together with Daniel Springer. Since 2023 he is professor at *Bauhaus-Universität Weimar*.

Alessandro Tellini

Alessandro Tellini is since 2014 head of the *Rapid Architectural Prototyping Laboratory (Raplab)* and a lecturer at the *Department of Architecture ETH Zurich*. He runs his own Zurich-based design and craft practice, *Faber Atelier*, with his partner. Trained as both a graphic and product designer, he developed a strong interest in pedagogy, fabrication, and construction throughout his career. He applied his practical knowledge in various settings, including architectural modelmaking, product development, the fabrication of large-scale architectural prototypes, and in international workshops and conferences. Teaching, researching, and investigating projects at the intersection of craft knowledge and design thinking is always at his activities core.

Tina Vestermann Olsen

Tina Vestermann Olsen is an assistant professor at the *Faculty of Architecture, Design and Media Technology* at the *University of Aalborg* affiliated with the urban design research group within transformation and mobilities. Tina has multiple years of practical experience as an urban designer committed to the design of public spaces and how user driven temporary installations can test future design scenarios on site. Tina obtained her PhD from *Aalborg University within Urban Design* with a focus on the strategic utilisation of temporary use projects in transformation processes. Today she teaches and conducts research into the potentials and processes related to the design of public spaces and on-site transformations.

Jana Wunderlich

Graduated from the *Technical University of Munich* in 2018 with her master in architecture having been an exchange student at the *École Spéciale d'Architecture* in Paris. After her studies she worked in several architecture offices in Munich. In 2018 Jana Wunderlich and Victoria Schweyer founded the architectural practice *pflücken*, where they research and build livable housing in old age. In 2021, they started teaching at *Technical University of Munich* and the *Katholische Stiftungshochschule in Munich* at the *Faculty of Health and Nursing* in Munich. Since 2022 Jana Wunderlich works as a Teaching and Research Associate at the *Professorship of Architecture and Design* at the *TUM School of Engineering and Design*. In 2023 she was a *Goethe Institute* resident fellow at the *Villa Kamogawa* in Kyoto, Japan.